Curriculum Materials Collections and Centers: Legacies from the Past, Visions of the Future

Edited
by Rita Kohrman

Association of College and Research Libraries
A division of the American Library Association
Chicago, Illinois 2012

The paper used in this publication meets the minimum requirements of American National Standard for Information Sciences–Permanence of Paper for Printed Library Materials, ANSI Z39.48-1992.
∞

Library of Congress Cataloging-in-Publication Data

Curriculum materials collections and centers : legacies from the past, visions of the future/ edited by Rita Kohrman.
   pages cm
 Includes bibliographical references and index.
  ISBN 978-0-8389-8602-8 (pbk. : alk. paper) -- ISBN 978-0-8389-9398-9 (kindle) ISBN 978-0-8389-9399-6 (epub) 1. Education libraries--United States. 2. Instructional materials centers--United States. 3. Education libraries--Collection development--United States. 4. Instructional materials centers--Collection development--United States. 5. Teachers--Training of--United States--History. I. Kohrman, Rita, editor of compilation.
  Z675.P3C88 2011
   027.7--dc23   2012

                              2011045087

Table of Contents

Introduction
Voices and Visions from CMCs: Importance and Theoretical Basis for Curriculum Materials Collections and Centers

Penny Beile, University of Central Florida

Curriculum materials centers share three traits that make them distinct from general academic libraries. First, while they all have highly specialized and unique collections that support PK–12 teacher education curriculum, their administrative structures can vary widely. For example, curriculum materials centers are generally part of either a college of education or a library, and some may report to both entities. Second, curriculum materials centers can range from a collection housed in the main library separate from the general collection to a full-service branch library. These variations in reporting structure and organization illustrate the administrative variation found across curriculum materials centers, and having stakeholders who are divided between the college and the library can make it challenging to explain decisions that support the college to library stakeholders, and vice versa.

A third shared characteristic of curriculum materials centers is the effect of technological innovations on their services, collections, and staffing. Certainly new technologies have dramatically impacted operations of all libraries, but curriculum materials centers must also contend with technological implications for pedagogy and curriculum and must integrate these technologies into their operations accordingly. It is widely recognized that acquiring, organizing, and housing curriculum materials, when compared to general academic materials, is more time-consuming and labor-intensive. Now curriculum materials centers are adding e-books and links to online textbook materials to their catalogs, which often requires mediation by acquisitions and cataloging staff, and are providing access to educational software and new learning technologies, which involves additional support from systems departments. As curriculum materials centers have shifted from simply providing access to curriculum materials to assisting patrons with creating curriculum, the center's staff is also affected, in terms of both time and skills.

Finally, curriculum materials centers support a distinct but relatively small population of users compared to the general academic library. This specialization requires that the curriculum materials librarian be aware of and be able to align services and collections to curriculum reform movements, governmental policies and accreditation standards, and educational programs offered by the college. The role of the curriculum materials center often falls outside the understanding of many library administrators, and given the expense of maintaining separate collections or branch libraries, it is not surprising that centers are often scrutinized at times when administrative budgets are flat or decreasing. The differences between curriculum materials centers and general academic libraries support the idea that curriculum materials collections and services are distinct enough to warrant their own centers or libraries, but these differences also highlight what puts the centers at risk when tight budgets call every library service and collection into question.

Without doubt, managing curriculum materials centers has become more complex. In the face of fiscal cuts and technological change, the curriculum materials librarian is challenged to demonstrate worth and show that funds put into curriculum materials centers relate to increased student learning and better prepared teachers. The astute curriculum materials librarian continually seeks to market the center's services and collections to its constituents, actively supports the library's and college of education's mission and goals, aligns the center's resources with educational programs offered by the college, plans for and integrates new technologies and pedagogical changes, and develops a strong base of support from its stakeholders, which might include library administrators, education faculty, teacher candidates and other students, and local teachers.

It is in response to this environment that editor Rita Kohrman conceived of and developed *Curriculum Materials Collections and Centers: Legacies from the Past, Visions for the Future*. For this book, Kohrman has selected chapters from some of the most pre-eminent curriculum materials librarians in the country and organized them into a handbook that describes how to successfully manage the curriculum materials center of today and position it for the future. The chapters are arranged chronologically and fall into three main parts; Past, Present, and Future.

The first section, Past, describes the history and development of curriculum materials collections and services in the United States and the way their development has influenced centers at the beginning of the twenty-first century.

Opening this section in chapter 1, Rita Kohrman reviews the development of curriculum materials centers through 1940 and describes how their function and purpose have adapted over time to external forces. She goes on to present a compelling case for the importance and connection of curriculum materials centers to teacher education and offers suggestions on how to advocate for the continuation of curriculum materials collections and services. Suzan Alteri's chapter picks up where Kohrman's ends, in the mid-twentieth century, and traces the development of curriculum materials centers to the present. Justifying the need for curriculum materials centers to library and campus administration relies on a variety of factors, and Alteri connects this fact to the idea that increased teacher professionalism relates to increased competence in the classroom. In turn, this relationship has created a need for teacher candidates to practice their craft prior to entering the classroom, and curriculum materials centers have evolved into places where teacher candidates can find out what is being used as well as how to use it most effectively.

While Kohrman and Alteri explore the evolution of the curriculum materials center, the next set of chapters serves as an operating manual for responding to current changes and challenges. The Present section is introduced by Ann Brownson's essay, chapter 3, which explores the role of children's literature in the curriculum materials center. Brownson argues that access to these collections provides the opportunity for teacher candidates to read "widely and deeply" and to explore how to integrate literature into their teaching while also questioning their own assumptions about diversity, culture, and values. Brownson concludes by noting the importance of CMC staff in preparing topical booklists and bibliographies and making suggestions based on personal knowledge and finding aids.

In chapter 5, Nadean Meyer continues the discussion about curriculum collections and elaborates on how high-quality, "learner-centered" collections are an essential part of teacher education. Meyer describes various collections that can be found in a center, advocates for funding models that are comparable to those used for academic programs, and presents options for supplementing the collection budget.

Meyer notes that 35 percent of curriculum materials centers listed in the sixth edition of the *Directory of Curriculum Materials Centers* serve as textbook review centers, which sets the stage for Nancy O'Brien and Judy Walker's study of American textbooks in chapter 8. O'Brien and Walker review historical trends in textbook development and suggest that the addition of learning objects and supplements, such as workbooks, filmstrips, and sound recordings, helped to create the need for a place to acquire and maintain materials in various formats. By extension, curriculum materials centers are expected to purchase and organize electronic supplements and e-books, and O'Brien and Walker note that open source electronic textbooks are on the horizon, which will allow for customized content and a variety of multimedia formats to accommodate varying learning styles. As school districts move from print to digital formats, O'Brien and Walker acknowledge that incorporating these new formats will require additional staff time, adding another layer of complexity to managing textbook collections.

Similarly, Linda Teel argues in chapter 6 that as services change, so does staffing. Technology-driven changes place a demand on staff members that they must constantly learn and adapt to new software and applications. Curriculum materials centers have staffing structures that rely heavily on paraprofessional and student assistant support, and educational technologies like Smart Boards and editing software are often staff-mediated. With education, innovation, and outreach as key components of successful curriculum materials centers, staffing is one of the center's most critical investments. Highly specialized services and collections require highly competent and engaged staff, and Teel provides guidelines on how to identify needed skill levels as well as how to determine the number of staff members needed to effectively operate a curriculum materials center.

Dealing with increasing complexity is one broad theme in this book, and another is garnering strong support for curriculum materials centers from various stakeholders. In chapter 4, Pat Farthing and Margaret Gregor explore the role of library instruction in curriculum materials centers and build the case for its importance as a vehicle for forging relationships with college faculty and students. Farthing and Gregor stress that, in addition to maximizing students' use and understanding of curriculum materials, library instruction can create faculty/librarian working relationships, which can lead to additional opportunities for collaboration. The often-unacknowledged outcome of these interactions is the potential for support in the event of financial threats. Hazel Walker, in chapter 7, likewise acknowledges the importance of garnering external support and describes an outreach program that goes beyond the institution to area schools and educators. Walker suggests that strategic alliances such as the extension program described in her chapter are mutually beneficial; practicing teachers benefit from the center's collections and services, and the curriculum materials center has increased circulation and use and strong community support.

Social media, online learning models, electronic collections, and other digital innovations will continue to impact curriculum and consequently the collections and services of the curriculum materials center. In the final section of the book, Future, an array of essays describes the role and evolution of curriculum materials centers in the digital age and presents practical advice on how to cogently and coherently respond to the changing nature of teaching and learning. In the first chapter of the section, Julie Miller and Nadean Meyer revisit the basics for their perspective on building successful curriculum materials centers for the twenty-first century. Miller and Meyer remind us of the purpose and usefulness of mission statements and propose that librarians move beyond describing what curriculum materials centers do and capture the dynamism of today's centers and their relation to preparing new teachers. Again tying into the theme of building support from stakeholders, Miller and Meyer advocate mission statements as a way to demonstrate relevance to users in a rapidly changing environment.

Curriculum materials librarians are well aware of the importance of providing curriculum materials to support and improve teaching and learning, but in their quest to stay abreast of changes in curriculum and pedagogy, they may forget to build a strong base of support from stakeholders. This omission can in turn make curriculum materials centers susceptible to budget cuts, reorganization, or even closing during times of decreased funding to libraries. Shonda Brisco's chapter, "Staying Relevant: Re-engineering for the Future," presents a cautionary tale, arguing that curriculum materials librarians should transcend their emphasis on collections and learn to collaborate with a variety of stakeholders and constituents to provide essential services. Brisco contends that curriculum materials librarians must be open to opportunities that arise from "the implementation of new technology, new services, and new methods in providing for the instructional needs of CMC patrons," and that by embracing a collaborative model, librarians can demonstrate the value of their centers in teacher preparation.

Jo Ann Carr and Anna Lewis, concurring with Brisco's perspective, state, "To successfully respond to these changes and challenges, CMCs must adopt a new vision of their role." Carr and Lewis analyze formats and services provided by curriculum materials centers across time and conclude that the addition of certain hardware and equipment reflects the move from providing access to curriculum materials to allowing for the creation of curriculum. Based on new skills expected of teachers by accreditation agencies, Carr and Lewis challenge us to move from a model of the curriculum materials center that simply provides computers to a model where mobile units, such as iPads, are offered, allowing the centers to change from learning environments that support individual learning to environments that support collaboration through Web 2.0 technologies. Similarly, they challenge us to move from providing traditional word processing and presentation software to adding personal Web technologies that support organizing and creating curriculum. No longer do curriculum materials librarians simply need to be conversant about education standards; they must actively incorporate and market programs that help faculty and students meet those standards.

To close the section and the book, Kathy Yoder and Linda Scott provide an upbeat case study that shows how outreach, collections, and services can coalesce into comprehensive and innovative programming. This culminating chapter also emphasizes the importance of embracing new technologies, supporting the goals of the institution, marketing services and collections, and actively striving to be a center of excellence. In doing so, Yoder and Scott tell the story of how Scott planned and opened a well-respected and vibrant curriculum materials center and include an array of ideas that any center can easily adopt.

Reading *Curriculum Materials Collections and Centers: Legacies from the Past, Visions for the Future* is like sitting at a table having a conversation with some of the most knowledgeable curriculum materials librarians in the country. The chapters present a range of perspectives from librarians who come from a variety of academic environments and institutional settings, perspectives that identify issues pertinent to managing curriculum materials centers. Common themes emerge, however: curriculum materials centers must continue to meet—or surpass—the expectations of their stakeholders or risk diminished support; they changed very slowly over a long period of time, but they are now in a state of flux due to the impact of new technologies; these conditions can be catalysts for positive change that provide opportunities for curriculum materials centers to become more innovative and vital.

Chapter authors have presented a number viable strategies that include revisiting the basics of staffing, mission statements, collections, services, and outreach; integrating new technologies and programming into the day-to-day working of the curriculum materials center; and increasing and marketing the center's worth to its constituents. The essays collected here offer ideas that can be adapted for use at your curriculum materials center, and each relates those ideas to the significance and worth of the center to the institution. This text is an indispensable addition to every curriculum materials librarian's professional collection. It builds on and complements Gary Lare's *Acquiring and Organizing Curriculum Materials: A Guide and Directory of Resources* and Jo Ann Carr's *A Guide to the Management of Curriculum Materials Centers for the 21st Century: The Promise and the Challenge* and should be within arm's reach on the bookshelf, ready to be referred to over and over again.

Penny Beile
University of Central Florida

Part I: Past

From Collections to Laboratories to Centers: Development of the Curriculum Materials Collections or Centers to 1940

Rita Kohrman, Grand Valley State University

The need for curriculum materials collections/centers is evident with a study of the development of education practices in the United States. 'Keeping-school' was viewed with such disdain that anyone without training was believed to be able to teach—"Any farmer can teach" (Bowen, 1887, p. 14). As education became more important to the growth of the nation and its citizens, teacher preparation changed from mimicking how one was taught to be being viewed as a science and requiring its own laboratories similar to science and medical laboratories.

Western Michigan University's Education Library is recognized as the first continuously used curriculum materials center in institutions of higher education in the United States (Leary, 1938; Mac Vean, 1958). Originally called Western State Normal School, the school opened in 1903 and started a curriculum bureau in 1922. It was a research based center containing textbooks intended for faculty use (Knauss, 1953). But where did the idea arise for such a facility or collection? Many studies and dissertations (Drag, 1947; Ellis, 1969; James, 1963; Syropoulos, 1971) on curriculum materials centers report that the idea for such facilities arose in the early 1920s, but a careful reading of autobiographies and memoirs written in the 1700s and articles and books written in the 1800s reveal the existence of curriculum collections, laboratories, or libraries well before 1920. Curriculum centers were intended to allow preservice teachers to experiment with lesson planning and learn the tools of the trade, textbooks and teaching aids, hence the appropriated use of the term laboratories. These interesting avenues and back roads that trace the beginning of curriculum materials centers are linked to teacher preparation and curriculum reform in the United States.

In the 1700s, community leaders seeking to acquire a school teacher would often greet incoming ships from Europe. The ships' manifests would list such commodities as "various Irish products ...including school masters, beef, pork, and potatoes" (Hofstadter, 1962, p. 313). The listing of "healthy" indentured apprentices or school masters ready for disposal would result in a rush to the arriving ships by town officials to "buy a school master" or apprentice (Sedlak, 1989, p. 259; Knight & Hall, 1951, p. 15). Knight and Hall cite the publication of a legal notice of the apprenticeship of John Campbell to a New York City schoolmaster, George Brownell. The obligations and responsibilities of Campbell and Brownell clearly stated that Campbell was to be "taught and instructed in the art trade of calling of a schoolmaster," in exchange for his meals, clothing, lodging and washing for ten years and three months (pp. 13–14).

Gazettes from across the colonies often carried advertisements for masters or apprentices. It was not uncommon for literate men to advertise themselves as school masters, hoping to obtain a teaching position until a more promising career, such as ministers, doctors, or lawyers, could be obtained (Elsbree, 1939; Fraser, 2007). John Adams, after graduating from Harvard in 1755, kept school for a year until he was able to apprentice himself to a lawyer by means of a two year contract (McCullough, 2008). A study of Harvard and Yale graduates during the colonial period revealed that 40 percent of Harvard graduates and 20 percent of Yale graduates held positions as teachers until they obtained positions as ministers or other professions (Rury, 1989).

Many early Americans viewed teaching apprenticeships as a waste of time. Teaching was a matter of mimicking how one was taught. It was considered a "by-product of learning" (Miller, 1922, p. 131). Standard teaching methods included recitations and simultaneous chanting choirs (Johnson, 1994; Rice, 1892). Apprentices and ushers, the next level above apprentices, would assist school masters by listening to the recitations of small groups of students, often referred to as scholars in period writings. The recitations were frequently limited to just two or three math problems or six or more lines of reading (Fowle, 2005). Copies of the master's copy book or lessons were handed down to apprentices or ushers. If a scholar questioned the answer to a mathematical problem, for example, the teacher would refer to the master's copy. What was written, even if incorrect, was the final answer. Inquiring scholars would often be reprimanded for questioning the teacher (Fowle, 2005). Preparing for the next day's lessons included apprentices and ushers handwriting copy slips from their masters' books (Elsbree, 1939) and preparing the quill tips two hours a night (Fowle, 2005).

Master teachers could also be self taught. John Jenkins advertised his book *The Art of Writing* (1791) as a means of self study that would aid "an ambitious American youth ...and set himself up as a teacher of others without any regular apprenticeship" (cited in Nash, 1969, pp. 4–5). If a person could not obtain proper training as a teacher, then reading Jenkins' book or Samuel R. Hall's *Lectures on School-Keeping* (1829) would suffice, and potential teachers would "be made acquainted with the science of teaching" (Hall, 1829, p. iv). James Guild wrote in his autobiography, *From Tunbridge, Vermont to London, England: The Journal of James Guild, Peddler, Tinker, Schoolmaster, Portrait Painter, from 1818–1824*, that he had only 30 hours of instruction, but opened a school and obtained students without "any recommendation or specimen of penmanship ...but I told them I was a writer... and in the first day I had 11 scholars.... I thought that if I did not say but little and be careful how I spoke, they would not mistrust that I was nothing but a plowboy" (cited in Nash, 1969, p. 6).

Unfortunately, these inconsistent methods of training resulted in an unfavorable reputation for many teachers. Since many were hired as indentured servants, apprentices or school masters were often associated with "convicted felons, rogues, rascals, villains, and others of low degree ... [including] political prisoners, captives of war, debtors and adventurers" (Elsbree, 1939, p. 27). The low regard for school keeping was reflected in a statement made by Benjamin Franklin in 1750. He recommended teacher training for the "poorer sort... to act as schoolmasters" (Ogren, 2006, p. 13). Catharine Beecher in 1846 described male teachers as "coarse, hard, unfeeling men, too lazy or too stupid to follow the appropriate duties of their sex" (Beecher, 1981, p. 40). Jewell (1865) stated that "the business of public school teaching is a subject to such a depression as prevents it from taking rank among the learned professions.... [Regarded by the masses] with little or no respect... and even teachers themselves evince little or none of that reverence of love" (p. 530). Teachers were viewed as "little better than a dog" (p. 582). Bowen (1887) described the education system as having "degenerated into routine... starved by parsimony by the late 1880s. Any hovel would answer for a school-house, any primer would do for a text-book, any farmer's apprentice was competent to teach school" (p. 14). Rice's authoritative and ground breaking 1892 studies of teaching in 36 urban settings revealed that professionally trained teachers were still held in low esteem, even by teachers and administrators who felt that teacher training was not necessary or desirable (Rice, 1892).

Carl Kaestle (1973) researched New York City teachers from 1750 to 1850 and found that the teaching was viewed as "more a trade than a profession" (p. 5) and teachers were viewed as a lower status occupation than educated men such as a lawyers, ministers, or doctors, often holding part time positions as grocers, choristers, and grog shop owners (p. 40). Jewel (1865) stated that teaching was not considered "true professional labor" (p. 579) ...[and] "a position degrading to the calling and to be the death of all its professional aspirations" (p. 583).

Soon though, the need for teacher preparation was recognized by citizens and state governments, resulting in the beginning of normal schools. Many were originally established as vocational training schools with admission vocational aptitude tests (Harper, 1939). College was intended for those planning to be ministers, lawyers, or doctors. School keeping was viewed as vocational training separate and lower than a college education, subject to annual examinations to verify the students' suitability to teach, and to be recommended for a position or certification (p. 13). Borrowman (1865) cites a study sponsored by the Carnegie

Foundation for the Advancement of Teaching on the history and function of normal schools in Missouri. It reported that the normal school system in Missouri was to provide "intensive professional training, exclusively for teachers" (p. 185) and was not a college, but "a vocational institution of college rank" (p. 189).

Since the colonial times, a variety of books were used in teaching. It is an often held misconception that early schools in the United States used only hornbooks, or titles like McGuffey's Reader, or Webster's spelling books. Reality is that teachers often had to contend with textbooks passed down among family members (Venezky, 1986). A study in 1839 revealed 141 different schoolbooks used in the Connecticut schools in five different subject areas. The Wisconsin state superintendent of schools complained in 1854 that there were fifteen different spelling books, eighteen readers, ten geographies, fifteen arithmetics, and twenty grammar textbooks in use in schools statewide (Elsbree, 1939). As a way to bring consistency into teaching practices, textbooks published in the United States became a means for curriculum reform (Cuban, 1993; Manzo, 1999).

Textbooks were believed to be the best means for mental discipline and exercise for the mind (Elsbree, 1939; Kliebard, 1986). Harris (1880), a textbook advocate, believed that textbooks were an instrument "... to preserve and teach a valuable and substantial human experience (p. 6)... as the most direct and effective method of initiating the individual man into spiritual participation in the activity of his race" (p. 9). According to a Yale faculty study in 1828, the recitation of passages and standardized questions and answers found in the back of textbooks provided the content necessary for learning (cited in Kliebard, 1986). California even prohibited the use of any other texts than the state approved and published textbooks in the 1800s (Manzo, 1999). It was felt that children to lose their ability to use and navigate books, and teachers could not properly discipline the mind without the use of textbooks (Rice, 1895).

Various teaching techniques did find their way into the school rooms, often through the textbooks themselves. Many textbooks contained "To the Teachers" sections where one could find essay questions, arithmetic problems, maps, graphs, charts or detailed teaching suggestions for art, music or penmanship (Nietz, 1961, p. 5). Samuel Temple's *An Arithmetical Primer* (1809) provided space for the students to write answers (cited in Nietz, 1962, p. 153).

As with any vocational training/apprenticeship, preservice teachers were expected to purchase their own tools, such as textbooks, manuals, and instructional devices or apparatus. Henry Barnard (1846), the Commissioner of Public Schools for Rhode Island, stated that "much of the inefficiency of school education of every grade is mainly owing to the want of such cheap and simple aids for visible illustration... which every teacher of ordinary intelligence can acquire and practice" (p. 150). Teachers could find listings for teaching materials at end of journals or books (Book department, 1893; Dwight, 1835; Hall, 1829). It was not unusual for employed teachers to bring in their globes or maps into classrooms if the schools did not have such items (Fuller, 1989). School masters in Boston were even allowed to use newspapers at their discretion as early as the 1790s (Fowle, 2005).

Starting in the 1800s curriculum reform advocates felt that dominance of textbooks was "outmoded as a central instructional device" (Goodlad, 1967, p. 281). Theodore Dwight, Jr., encouraged the use of apparatus or handmade teaching aids, such as a pumpkin for a world or a celestial globe (Dwight, 1835). Dwight also listed pages of apparatus or other teaching aids in his book, *The School-Master's Friend*. One teaching aid was advertised as containing "valuable articles... to aid in the instruction of the young. Cards and maps are put on binders' boards, etc., and may be washed, and will last for years. They are fitted to hang in schools as literary ornaments" (pp. 207–210).

Meanwhile, educators in Europe saw the value of using aids and devices years, even centuries before. McGuinness (1969) cited the 1578 Ashton's Ordinance in Shrewsbury, England which required school buildings' libraries and "gallerie... [be] furnished with all manner of books, mappes, spheres, instruments of astronomye and all things apperteyninge to learning" (p.154). Tracing tablets to assist children in trace letters were unearthed in volcano buried Pompeii. Flash cards were used as far back as the fourteenth century (Dale, 1953).

With the introduction of Swiss educational reformer Johann Pestalozzi's object learning theory in the early 1800s, teachers in Europe and the United States found they could enhance student learning through the use of physical objects, and moved away from the tyranny of the textbook, memorization, and recitations. Between 1809 and 1813, a school in Philadelphia based its lessons on the Pestalozzi method of using objects or object learning. Unfortunately, the school did not continue its use after the teacher left (Elsbree, 1939).

James Carter, a politician from Massachusetts, and Thomas Gallaudet, a minister from Hartford, Connecticut, proposed in 1826 that teaching schools allow observation, practice schools, and provide a library and teaching apparatus (Harper, 1939; Ogren, 2006). Upon learning this, the enterprising Josiah Holbrook started the Holbrook School Apparatus Manufacturing Company in the same year to meet a new market demand. Holbrook offered a large variety of devices, along with teacher's manuals. By the 1860s, he had established stores across the United States (Ogren, 2006, p. 225).

Horace Mann shared his observations of his 1846 tour of European schools and reinforced the use of objects or manipulatives to stimulate a student's engagement. Mann observed European teachers using various objects including cards, animal and plant specimens, portraits, weights and measures, reading boards, library books, blackboards, models and musical instruments (Mann, 1846, pp. 51–55). Cyrus Peirce, after his 1849 European tour, wrote to Henry Barnard in 1851, stating that such modern devices as maps and globes in the classroom were of little value in the learning process without prior knowledge on how to use them by the preservice teachers (cited in Borrowman, 1965, p. 70).

Slowly, and with little financial support, state and county boards of education made provisions for the purchase of school apparatus including maps, globes, learning charts, and books for libraries (Dwight, 1835; Fuller, 1989; *List of library books*, 1888; Miller, 1922). The blackboard was unknown until 1809 and did not become a standard device in classrooms until after 1820, but was rarely used (Elsbree, 1939, pp. 222–223). School board members, superintendents and principals would purchase instructional aids and library books. Unfortunately, the purchased of useless or inappropriate apparatus, books and other devices became common, resulting in numerous complaints by teachers and the public (Held, 1959).

New York ranks as one of the earliest examples of a state legislature supporting the purchase of books and apparatus for their schools and teaching institutions (Held, 1959; Miller, 1922). The annual reports (1835–1851) of the New York Regents of Education revealed how the state financed schools districts and academies for teacher preparation. The reports were expected to describe the methods used by teachers to instruct and drill the pupils. Visual materials and mechanical devices were used during astronomy, geography, geology, and similar subjects. Cabinets containing minerals and plant and animal specimens were purchased (Miller, 1922, p. 124). Blackboards were listed as devices, as were the "rod and ferule" for disciplinary purposes (p. 128). New York Regents in 1823 and the Legislature in 1827 advocated and provided financial support for the training of the teachers by providing "well-equipped laboratories and libraries" for them to be deemed competent (p. 136). A total of $309 was designated for each of the teaching academies. Adjusted for inflation, $309 would be equal to $6,860 in 2009. The money was to cover such devices as

> orrery ("an apparatus for representing the motions and phases of the planets, satellites, etc., in the solar system" (Orrery, 1968)), numerical frame and geometrical solids, globes, movable planisphere, tide dial, optical apparatus, mechanical powers, hydrostatic apparatus, pneumatic apparatus, chemical apparatus, 100 specimens of mineralogy, electrical machine, instruments to teach surveying, map of the United States, map of the State of New York, atlas, telescope, [and] quadrant (p. 138).

California, following New York's example, enacted a law in 1866 requiring the purchase of books for libraries; in 1874 the law was modified to include apparatus. Unfortunately, teachers were viewed as not trustworthy to purchase useful materials. Instead, administrators, principals and trustees were swindled into buying useless books and apparatus from traveling salesmen. Complaints were often made regarding the wasteful spending on "unsuitable books or on books that never reached the libraries" or the purchasing of apparatus would "destroy the inclination for study" (Held, 1959, p. 87).

True to the vocational nature of normal schools, many normal schools offered manual training as a part of teacher preparation. Calvin Woodruff, an early promoter, saw manual training as "essential to the right and full development of the human mind... [and] a means of a complete and efficacious educated brain" (Woodruff, 1885). Hampton Normal and Agricultural Institute and Tuskegee Normal and Industrial Institute may have been models of manual training for many normal schools. Hampton opened in 1868 and Tuskegee in 1881 to provide training for freed slaves to teach in African American schools. Booker T. Washington used Tuskegee's manual training laboratory as a way to put Pestalozzi's theory into practice and to stimulate intelligence and critical thinking for preservice teachers (Washington, 1904). Both Hampton and Tuskegee built manual training facilities on their campuses, but their main emphases continued to be the training of teachers. Manual training facilities were a means to teach object lessons or the hands-on approach to teaching (Anderson, 1988; Washington, 1904). It was not until 1916 that Dewey would advocate manual training for children and adolescents. (Dewey, 1916; Generals, 2000).

By the late 1880s the United States Bureau of Education, local school districts, education faculty and theorists called for the establishment of libraries and laboratories in normal schools to assist student teachers in learning how to make a simple apparatus and to learn other practical teaching skills needed as teachers. Preservice teachers would learn their trade much the same as apprentices learned their trade by participating in the work under the supervision of a master (Kliebard, 1999). In 1907, educators campaigned for the establishment of laboratories within the normal schools so preservice teachers could experience lesson planning, teaching, and classroom management of students. Only through exposure to content and expectations would the preservice teachers know how to utilize teaching materials (Bolton, 1907).

It was recognized that those teaching the sciences needed to train in a science laboratory (Howe, 1892); biology teachers needed animal laboratories (Sudduth, 1893). A chemistry laboratory at the Normal School Bridgewater, MA, in 1872, and a physics laboratory at the Normal School at Emporia, KA, in 1888, was built for preservice teachers where they could learn the foundations of science experiments in order to teach their future students. In 1894 a botany laboratory was provided for the student teachers at the normal school at Westfield, MA, to enable student teachers to "observe, draw, describe, experiment and teach" (Fraser, 2007, p. 122). Why not a general teaching laboratory?

The Colorado State Normal School experimented with such a concept. They opened a Pedagogical Museum in 1898 whose purpose was to provide older and newer textbooks, pictures, apparatus (charts, thermometers, anemometer, etc.), games, toys and school furniture to assist in teacher training (Roberts, 1990). Unfortunately, it is believed that many of the non-print items were scattered throughout the school's departments after 1908 and were not centrally located into one room again until sometime in 1950s in the Education Resource Center of the library.

Teachers College's Bureau of Elementary Curriculum Research opened in 1924 and was later called the Curriculum Construction Laboratory. The faculty believed textbooks and other materials should be included a library or laboratory facilities for the preservice teachers' and students' use. This would end the needless duplication of materials by individual faculty members and make items available to anyone at the institution (Stratemeyer, 1925).

The Louisiana Rural Normal School at Grambling started its Curriculum Laboratory in 1936 and was seen as "integral part of the Normal School" (McAllister, 1938, p.137). The laboratory was deemed a unique feature for a teacher-education program. School administrators recognized that lesson plans should include the use of textbooks, manuals, and teaching aids, and therefore needed to be provided in adequate library facilities such as the Curriculum Laboratory. It was the goal of the teachers at Louisiana Rural to provide their students with "experiences which would prepare her to assume successfully the responsibilities of the job… and to contribute to the all-around development of the ideal rural teacher" (pp. 135–136).

Curriculum laboratories, as a distinct term or phrase, first appeared in an article written by Henry Harap (1932). He was describing the curriculum laboratory at Western Reserve University which started in 1929. Harap stated that the word laboratory did not necessary mean a science laboratory and the term was misleading since the etymology was of a more general nature. He viewed curriculum laboratories as a work place for the preparation of curricula. Harap described "the curriculum laboratory is to classroom practice what the architectural office is to the finished structure" (p. 634). The term 'curriculum laboratory' was confusing or easily misunderstood because of the use of the word laboratory. Drag states that the term was often used to designate curriculum planning or curriculum committees (Drag, 1947). Leary made a similar claim of the confusion of the term (Leary, 1938). It has since come to be defined as

a department within a library or a separate unit within a school or college, organized to provide teaching aids for students such elementary and/or secondary students textbooks, courses of study, tests, sample units, pamphlet materials, a picture file, filmstrips, slides, and other materials which may be helpful to the teacher in preparation of a unit of work. Synonymous [with] curriculum materials center, curriculum laboratory, curriculum library, instructional materials center, textbook library (Good, 1959, p. 309).

The changing nature of curriculum reform, the need for curriculum centers or laboratories, and the use of the term is found in the history of Western Michigan University's Education Library. The Curriculum Bureau, at the then called Western State Normal School (later Western Michigan University), was identified in both Leary's and Drag's studies as one the earliest curriculum center. Started in 1922, the Curriculum Bureau was in an office of a faculty member located in the training school building. It provided textbooks and other books related to curricula improvement for the faculty. Its purpose as a research center was to "appraise the training school curriculum and to recommend changes that would improve the work of the school" (Knauss, 1953, 105). Mac Vean (1958) noted the purpose of the Curriculum Bureau was as an education library first and never a curriculum material center. Leary's study indicated that they collected and assembled curriculum materials, produced curriculum materials, advised and directed, and loaned materials (Leary, 1938, p. 32). Renamed the Text-book Library in 1939, the library modified its purpose from faculty focus to one of teacher-training and student research. A requirement for research work by the preservice teachers changed the collection focus to include the purchase of research and resource materials, journals and magazines. Curricula resource materials included teaching aids, files of pictures, and workbooks, but also research materials to meet the preservice teacher needs. In 1943, the facility was again renamed to Educational Service Library, and moved to the old administrative building and continued to provide teacher-training support (Knauss, 1953).

Colson reported that in 1931 the Virginia State Board of Education began a three year program of curriculum revision that required the organization of curriculum centers in the state's teacher training institutions. These facilities offered courses in curriculum development to meet the needs of "Negro children" and to provide "materials for use in curriculum construction" (Colson, 1934, pp. 312). Virginia State College for Negroes was already addressing the above issues with its 1931–1932 "The Needs of the Negro in America" (p. 312). The group developed specified curriculum materials which concentrated on the needs of African American children. The development of 103 units of work (or curriculum units) resulted in the group's work dissemination of the materials to African American teachers and over 300 white teachers in Virginia (p. 313).

George Walter Rosenlof's 1929 study is an early study of library facilities found in teacher training institutions, including seminar and textbook collections. He defined seminar libraries as temporary collections found in laboratories or seminar rooms, usually found in departments rather than central libraries. Rosenlof also highlighted what he referred to as the Textbook Exhibit Libraries, noting they were a recent phenomenon. These special libraries had well-defined purposes including the displaying of publishers' textbooks, supplemental materials, and children's literature books to assist "in organizing curricula by student teachers" (p. 69). Rosenlof found 16 such libraries but did not identify them. He encouraged teachers colleges to "provide for the establishment of a distinct and separate collection of books to known as the 'Textbook Exhibit Library' (p. 152).

Beatrice Leary (1938) followed Rosenlof with her 1936–1937 study of state, districts, or academic curriculum laboratories for the U.S. Bureau of Education. She reported on 107 such agencies: 11 state agencies, 61 city agencies, and 35 higher education agencies. Leary reported that the Detroit City School system was connected with the College of Education at Wayne State University, then called Detroit Normal School, since approximately 1918 and its main activity was the producing of curriculum materials. Detroit Normal School was founded in 1881, renamed Detroit Teachers College in 1920, then Wayne State University in 1933 and was under the direction of the Detroit Superintendent of Schools (Engle & Borgman, 1984). The Division of Instructions, as it was referred to at that time, was housed separately (at Wayne State) and included a reference library and workrooms (Leary, 1938).

Leary's examination of 35 curriculum laboratories in colleges, universities, teachers colleges, and normal schools provided a clearer picture as to the function and purposes of these facilities. While Western Michigan State Teachers College was listed as the earliest such facility (1922), Leary did not provide a detailed explanation of Western in her narrative, as with such institutions as Teachers College, George Peabody College of Teachers, and Northwestern University (Leary, 1938). Resources at the latter facilities included textbooks, professional books and periodicals, but also maps, posters, charts, standardized tests, and "enrichment materials" such as airplanes, flowers to supplement and enrich the curriculum (p. 11).

Frances Drag (1947) provided an extensive study of curriculum laboratories in the United States. His study revealed an explosion of curriculum laboratories or curriculum research bureaus after the Leary report of 1938: 353, Drag; 107, Leary. Of the 842 inquiries sent to institutions of higher education, 145 (17.2%) responded in the affirmative as to having curriculum laboratories; Leary reported 35 in higher education. Drag noted 3 unidentified institutions of higher education between 1887 and 1900, and reported departments or divisions in these institutions whose primary function was curriculum building or study. Between 1901 and 1920, he reported 7 unidentified curriculum laboratories in colleges or universities; between the years 1921 and 1930, 18 curriculum laboratories were identified. From 1931 to 1940, 52 such facilities in higher education institutions were in existence. By 1945, Drag reported on 145 institutions of higher education as having a curriculum laboratory (Drag, 1947).

James (1963) provided a succinct overview on curriculum development and the curriculum laboratory as a place for pre-service teacher instruction. She stated that the reorganization of curriculum in the 1890s had its distinct beginnings with the Committee of Ten. The Committee made no mention of curriculum laboratories, but by the 1930s, education leaders, such as Henry Harap, were including the term in their public writings. As mentioned previously, Western Michigan State's Curriculum Bureau in 1922 was a research based facility and only changed to a pre-service emphasis in 1939. Teachers College's Bureau of Elementary Curriculum Research at Columbia University, opened in 1924, but, as with Western Michigan, changed its emphasis and name to a Curriculum Construction Laboratory in 1928. Both illustrate the importance of a shifting understanding of teacher education and the students' and teachers' participation and responsibility for curriculum development for their students. It was not an overnight happening but a gradual change in how teachers were best able to develop the pedagogical needs for their students.

Conclusion

A variety of materials were used when preparing to instruct students throughout history, as evidenced with the tactile tablets found in Pompeii, which was buried by the volcanic ash in 79 AD. This journey from Pompeii to the current vision of Curriculum Materials Centers has traveled on many avenues, arriving in the twentieth century with 145 curriculum center by the 1940s. Teachers and faculty have continued to acknowledge the need for hands-on materials and the need to preview other materials in the classroom. The purchasing or making their own devices so to have these tools of their trade was one avenue. But traveling private collections were cumbersome, expensive, and, at times, duplicated by other teachers.

Gradually, school administrators, board members, and faculty in teacher preparation programs realized the importance of resources beyond textbooks and provided financial support for the purchase of these materials. This trend toward using materials in the classroom parallels the increased awareness and views held by educators and the public for quality pre-service education. As educators, community leaders, and national leaders realized the need for well trained and certified teachers, they called for laboratories, centers, or libraries at teacher training institutes where pre-service teachers could gain the necessary skills to develop their own materials and incorporate a variety of media to motivate student engagement.

References

Anderson, J. D. (1988). *The education of blacks in the south, 1860–1935*. Chapel Hill: University of North Carolina Press.

Barnard, H. (1846). *Report of the condition and improvement of the public schools of Rhode Island*. Providence, RI: B. Cranston.

Beecher, C. (1981). Remedy for wrongs to women. In N. Hoffman (Ed.), *Woman's "true" profession: Voices from the history of teaching*. New York, NY: The Feminist

Press.

Borrowman, M. L. (Ed.) (1965). *Teacher education in America: A documentary history.* New York, NY: Teachers College Press.

Bolton, F. E. (1907). The preparation of high-school teacher: What they do secure and what they should secure. *The School Review, 15*(2), 97–122.

Book department [Review section]. (1893). *School Review, 1*(1), 48–66.

Bowen, F. (1887). Memoir of Edmund Dwight. *American Journal of Education, 4*(10), 5–22.

Colson, E. M. (1934). Program of curriculum revision in Virginia. [Special section of Current events of importance in Negro education]. *Journal of Negro Education, 3*(2), 311–313.

Cuban, L. (1993). *How teachers taught: Constancy and change in American classrooms, 1980–1990* (2nd ed.). New York, NY: Teachers College Press.

Dale, E. (1953). Improved teaching materials contribute to better learning. In H.G. Shane (Ed.), *The American elementary school* (pp. 233–251). New York, NY: Harper and Brothers.

Dewey, J. (1916). *Democracy and education.* New York: Macmillan.

Drag, F. L. (1947). *Curriculum laboratories in the United States: A research study: San Diego County Schools.* San Diego, CA: Office of the Superintendent of Schools.

Dwight, T., Jr. (1835). *The school-master's friend, with the committee-man's guide: Containing suggestions on common education modes of teaching and governing.* Retrieved from http://books.google.com/books?id=brFMAAAAMAAJ&pg=PA200&dq =apparatus+pump#

Elsbree, W. E. (1939). *The American teacher: Evolution of a profession in a democracy.* New York, NY: American Book.

Ellis, E. V. (1969). *The role of curriculum laboratory in the preparation of quality teachers.* Retrieved from ERIC database. (ED031457)

Engle, C.B., & Borgman, B.C. (1984). Profile of the Kresge (Education) Library, Wayne State University, Detroit, Michigan. *Education Libraries, 9*(1–2), 21–25.

Fowle, W. (2005). Memoir of Caleb Bingham. In H. Barnard (Ed.), *Educational biography: Part 1. Teachers and educators. Vol. 1. United States: Memoirs of teachers, educators, and promoters and benefactors of education, literature, and science* (2nd ed.) [Sabin Americana version]. Retrieved from http://galenet.galegroup.com

Fraser, J. W. (2007). *Preparing America's teachers: A history.* New York, NY: Teachers College Press.

Fuller, W. E. (1994). *One-room schools of the middle west.* Lawrence: University Press of Kansas.

Generals, D. (2000). Booker T. Washington and progressive education: An experimentalist approach to curriculum development and reform. *Journal of Negro Education, 69*(3), 215–234.

Good, C. V. (1959). *Dictionary of education* (2nd ed.). New York, NY: McGraw-Hill.

Goodlad, J. L. (1967, March). Innovations in education. *Educational Forum, 31,*

280–284. doi:10.1080/00131726709338055

Hall, S. R. (1829). *Lectures on school-keeping.* Boston, MA: Richardson, Lord and Holbrook.

Harap, H. (1932, April). The curriculum laboratory. *New York Education, 19,* 634.

Harper, C. A. (1939). *A century of public teacher education: The story of the state teachers colleges as they evolved from the normal schools.* Washington, DC: American Association of Teachers Colleges.

Harris, W.T. (1880, September). Text-books and their uses. *Education, 1,* 1–9.

Held, R. E. (1959). The early school-district library in California. *The Library Quarterly, 29*(2), 79–93.

Hofstadter, Richard. (1962). *Anti-intellectualism in American life.* New York, NY: Knopf.

Howe, J.L. (1892). The teaching of science. *Science, 19*(481), 233–235.

James, M. L. (1963). *The curriculum laboratory in teacher education institutions: Its essential characteristics.* (Unpublished doctoral dissertation). University of Connecticut, Storrs, CT.

Jewell, F. S. (1865, December). Public school teaching: Can it become a profession? *American Journal of Education,* (41), 579–591.

Johnson, W. R. (1994)."Chanting choristers": Simultaneous recitation in Baltimore's nineteenth-century primary schools. *History of Education, 34*(1), 1–23.

Kaestle, C.F. (1973). *The evolution of an urban school system: New York City, 1750–1859.* Cambridge, MA: Harvard University Press.

Kliebard, H. M. (1986). *The struggle for the American curriculum, 1893–1958.* (2nd ed.). New York, NY: Routledge.

Kliebard, H. M. (1999). *Schooled to work.* New York, NY: Teachers College Press.

Knauss, J.O. (1953). *The first fifty years: A history of Western Michigan College of Education, 1903–1953.* Kalamazoo, MI: Western Michigan College of Education.

Knight, E. W., & Hall, C. L. (1951). *Readings in American educational history.* New York, NY: Appleton-Century-Crofts.

Leary, B. E. (1938). *Curriculum laboratories and divisions: Their organizations and functions in state departments of education, city school systems, and institutions of higher education* (Bulletin #7). Washington, DC: United States Department of the Interior, Office of Education.

List of library books recommended by the state board of education state of California. (1888). Retrieved from http://www.archive.org/stream/oflibraryboolist00calirich/oflibraryboolist

Mac Vean, D. S. (1958). *A study of curriculum laboratories in midwestern teacher-training institutions.* (Unpublished doctoral dissertation). University of Michigan, Ann Arbor.

Mann, H. (1846). *Report of an educational tour in Germany, and parts of Great Britain and Ireland.* [Sabin Americana version]. Retrieved from http://galenet.galegroup.com

Manzo, K. (1999). The state of curriculum. *Education week, 18*(36), 21–27.

McCullough, D. (2008). *John Adams*. New York, NY: Simon and Schuster.

McAllister, J. E. (1938). A venture in rural-teacher education among Negroes in Louisiana. *Journal of Negro Education, 7*(2), 132–143.

McGuinness, D. A. (1969). Developing learning resources in secondary schools. In N. P. Pearson & L. Butler (Eds.), *Instructional materials centers: Selected readings* (pp. 154–156). Minneapolis, MN: Burgess.

Miller, G.F. (1922). *The academy system of the state of New York*. Albany, NY: J.B. Lyon.

Nash, R. (1969). *American penmanship, 1800–1850: A history of writing and a bibliography of copybooks from Jenkins to Spencer*. Worchester, CN: American Antiquarian Society.

Nevil, L. (1975). *A survey of curriculum laboratories in selected colleges in Pennsylvania*. (Unpublished thesis). Wilkes College, Wilkes-Barre, PA.

Nietz, John A. (1961). *Old textbooks: Spelling, grammar, reading, arithmetic, geography, American history, civil government, physiology, penmanship, art, music—as taught in the common schools from colonial days to 1900*. Pittsburgh, PA: University of Pittsburgh Press.

Ogren, C.A. (2006). *The American state normal school: "An instrument of great good"*. New York, NY: Palgrave Macmillan.

Orrery. (1968). *The Random House Dictionary of the English Language* (College ed.). New York, NY: Random House.

Rice, J. M. (1892, October). Our public school system: Evils in Baltimore. *Forum*, 145+. Retrieved from American Periodicals Series Online database.

Rice, J. M. (1895, August). Substitution of teacher for text-book. *Forum*, 681+. Retrieved from American Periodicals Series Online database.

Roberts, F.X. (1990). An early example of a curriculum materials collection in an institution of teacher education. *Behavioral & Social Sciences Librarian, 9*(1), 21–28. doi:10.1300/J103v09n01_03

Rosenlof, G.W. (1929). *Library facilities of teacher-training institutions*. New York, NY: Bureau of Publications, Teachers College, Columbia University.

Rury, J.L. (1989). Who became teachers? The social characteristics of teachers in American history. In D. Warren (Ed.), *American teachers: Histories of a profession at work* (pp. 9–48). New York, NY: Macmillian.

Sedlak, M. W. (1989). Let's go and buy a school master. In D. Warren (Ed.), *American teachers: Histories of a profession at work* (pp. 259–262). New York, NY: MacMillan.

Stratemeyer, F. (1925, May). Teachers College Bureau of Elementary Curriculum Research. *Teachers College Record, 26*, 782–785.

Sudduth, W.X. (1893). Animal biology in high schools and colleges. *Science, 22*(561), 242.

Syropoulos, M. (1971). Analysis of the Detroit Public Schools curriculum laboratories including the possible need for expansion and changes in their structure (Unpublished doctoral dissertation). Wayne State University, Detroit, MI.

Venezky, R.L. (1986). Steps toward a modern history of American reading instruction. *Review of Research in Education, 13*, 129–167.

Washington, B. T. (1904). *Working with the Hands.* New York, NY: Doubleday, Park and Company.

Woodruff, C. M. (1885, July). Manual training in general education. *Education, 5*, 614–626.

Wright, F. W. (1930). The evolution of the normal schools. *The Elementary School Journal, 30*(5), 363–371. doi:10.1086/456419

2 Curriculum Materials Laboratories: Blast from the Past or Institutionally Relevant?

Suzan A. Alteri, Wayne State University

This chapter explores what has happened to curriculum materials centers (CMCs) in the last ninety years at large academic libraries. Several trends, including cultural and educational change, curriculum wars, professionalization versus academia, and the growth of technology have all had an enormous impact on CMCs. The chapter examines these changes and how libraries, departments of education, and CMCs coped with rapid change. Many CMCs were closed by academic libraries, others were moved to departments of education, and some remain open today, albeit in changed form. The chapter concludes with a case study of Wayne State University—its history with curriculum materials and how it dealt with the rapid societal changes that altered the educational landscape.

Change in curriculum and education have never occurred in a vacuum. Pressures from the general public, the teaching profession, governments, and competing educational philosophies have had a direct impact on teacher preparation and the educational landscape. The previous chapter illustrated the vocational aspects of curriculum materials centers (CMCs), initially called curriculum laboratories, and how they have changed since the eighteenth century. For almost one hundred years, education and teacher preparation changed very little. It wasn't until the beginning of the twentieth century that education and teacher preparation saw rapid change that would forever alter the environment in which teachers were prepared and taught. The swiftness of change that occurred between the 1920s and today threw teacher preparation and education itself into an almost constant state of uncertainty. This chapter will illustrate why the changes occurred so quickly and the effects these changes had on CMCs.

"As early as the 1920s, collections of textbooks and samples of curriculum guides, research and teaching units, and lesson plans were set aside in what were called 'curriculum laboratories'" (Clark, 1982, p. 1). What caused this initial change in teacher preparation? The answer lies in the movement from normal schools to teachers colleges, as teaching and preparation of teachers became more professional, particularly as school districts and state governments began to require more competence of new teachers. "There has been a growing pressure toward greater professionalization of the teacher. Recently, this has been taking the form of a demand for higher competence on the part of the newly certified teacher" (Andrews, 1950, p. 260). Andrews goes on to argue that the introduction of a functional laboratory experience was crucial in the movement towards a more professional course. After all, "where are teachers going to get the chance to practice these [teaching] behaviors in a safe environment for them, and in an environment where they cannot harm children while teachers are learning their pedagogical craft" (ACRL, 1984, p. 4). Indeed, practicing the actual art of teaching was viewed as essential before teachers were sent out to perform their duties in a school. These laboratories were more than a mere collection of materials for teachers-to-be to peruse. They were places were trainee teacher could not only find out what was being used, but also concentrate on how materials can be most effectively used. In addition, laboratories, which were used in courses under the guidance of professors or professionally trained teachers, also taught preservice teachers the importance of providing the right material in the right hands at the right time (Estvan, 1956, p. 113). These curriculum laboratories rarely changed in form and content (textbooks, manipulative games, courses of study, lesson plans, research, and teaching units) until after the Second World War largely because the educational philosophy of the time supported active learning with such resources by trainee teachers. As normal schools became teachers colleges and finally combined with other institutions of higher learning, however, curriculum laboratories were likely to come under serious, often undermining attacks from universities, faculty, and educational philosophers. Curriculum laboratories continued to grow throughout the period between the World Wars, especially at institutions of higher learning. But even though the surge of interest in instructional materials continued during the Second World War (Estvan, 1956, p. 113), a change in teacher preparation had already begun. It was a change that threatened the very existence of curriculum laboratories, although at the time, no one had an idea of the impact these changes would have on preparing America's teachers. Beginning in the 1930s, the word *normal*, for *normal school*, had a large black stamp across it. "It was essential to blot out the word normal and replace it with the university's new and more respectable name" (Fraser, 2007, p. 174). Normal schools, the training ground for teachers during the nineteenth and early twentieth centuries, began to seek college status. In effect, they renamed themselves "teachers colleges," and as a result, standards rose. Applications to teachers colleges required a high school diploma, and the colleges offered a four-year baccalaureate program. Normal schools were seen as "ladies schools" (Fraser, 2007, p. 175), and the teaching profession wished to encourage a more male clientele. This was a major shift in the training of teachers, one that introduced a course of study that was the first step away from the older style of teacher preparation.

But state and city teachers colleges were a rather short-lived experiment in the development of curriculum and teacher preparation as another sweeping change was amidst. Teachers colleges, whether state or city, were becoming a burden on the sometimes strained finances of municipal and state governments. As a result, these governments encouraged the merging of teachers colleges with regular universities. The movement employed by these governments was one in which the teachers colleges merged with regular universities. "Something quite different took place in the 1940s and 1950s. The move from teachers college to college was not just a logical extension of long-term developments. It was, on the contrary, a radical break with the past, and a turn in a quite different direction" (Fraser, 2007, p. 185). This turn was a shift from institutions whose sole focus was to prepare teachers to multipurpose institutions that served a wide range of students from many different backgrounds. Thus, teacher education became just one part of a college's or university's mission, one that was often marginalized in favor of more academic programs. "After 1965, virtually no future teachers received such an education [one dedicated solely to teacher preparation]. For better or worse, future teachers were now prepared in schools, colleges, or departments of education in large multipurpose colleges and universities. After 1965, virtually nowhere was teacher education the prime mission of the schools that prepared the nation's teachers" (Fraser, 2007, p. 187). As we will see, this change in teacher preparation would have subsequent influences on curriculum laboratories and later CMCs.

It would seem, on the surface, that the move from teachers college to merger with general colleges and universities would be beneficial to teacher preparation. In fact, the situation was just the opposite, as a clash of cultures arose between professional teachers and academics, many of whom had never set foot in a school classroom. Thus the appearance of uniformity, with every teacher required to have a college degree from a multipurpose university, was in reality superficial. "[There was] a deep divide within these institutions of higher education between the teacher education faculty who had dominated the normal schools, and the now dominant faculty from more traditional university disciplines, especially in the arts and sciences" (Fraser, 2007, p. 197). Teacher educators often complained that the number of courses offered in actual teacher preparation were not enough to prepare teachers-to-be, and on the other side, academic professors complained that the large number of courses devoted to teacher preparation, "emasculated the liberal arts program" (Fraser, 2007, p. 187). This clash, which was eventually won by the academic professors as more teacher education faculty were pushed out of departments of education, had a disastrous effect not only on the preparation of teachers, but also on curriculum laboratories. The academics focused less on teacher education and more on research and educational philosophy. In this arena, curriculum laboratories, which served only teaching education faculty and students, were unnecessary in their eyes.

But the move from vocational training to professionalization and academia was not the only significant change that affected curriculum laboratories and materials centers. There were far more dangerous criticisms of teacher education that threatened the active learning approach to teacher education. These criticisms, often referred to as the "curriculum wars," created an environment where curriculum, teacher preparation, and therefore curriculum materials were in a constant state of flux.

In the 1930s, the dominant educational philosophy regarding the teaching of children was based on John Dewey and life adjustment education. This type of education was "associated with the principles of social efficiency and with certain brands of child-centered education, particularly the activity curriculum" (Franklin & Johnson, 2008, p. 461). Later, this movement would be called the Progressive movement, and its main goal was that school curriculum should be derived from the needs and abilities of students, and not necessarily solely from academic disciplines. However, beginning in the 1950s, an alternate viewpoint on education and curriculum, namely that of a discipline-centered curriculum, would take hold over academia and eventually lead to demise of the Progressive movement in education. This new group of players focused on intellectual development, and the attack was framed as a national security issue centered on technological and economic supremacy over the Soviet Union. But who were these new players, and why were they such a threat to teacher education?

The key players in this new shift in educational philosophy largely came from outside the world of teacher education. They were foundations (National Science Foundation, the Ford Foundation, the Carnegie Foundation), university faculty from the general liberal arts and sciences, and to a greater extent than before, the United States government. From their viewpoint, "The academic disciplines were the best sources for a curriculum that would both prepare articulate and thoughtful citizens and would produce the scientists and engineers who would enable the nation to compete militarily with the Soviet Union" (Franklin & Johnson, 2008, p. 462). Their goal was to create a curriculum that would teach students the content and methods of traditional academic disciplines in ways that were similar to the ways the disciplines were employed in the real world. This type of education, they argued, was key to the nation's survival so that it could maintain superiority over not just the Soviet Union, but also any economic or technological rival. In the eyes of these new players, life adjustment education "[n]eglected the teaching of the academic disciplines, particularly science, mathematics, and foreign languages, and it promoted instead the teaching of routine and virtually self-evident life skills that lack intellectual content" (Franklin & Johnson, 2008, p. 463). Even though it appeared that mining the field of curriculum materials was difficult due to constant changes in educational philosophy, most children in the 1970s were studying the same way they had for most the twentieth century—namely by textbooks, seatwork, student recitations, and teacher direction. But the discipline-centered movement didn't last long either. During the late 1960s and early 1970s, drastic changes were occurring in society. These changes forced educators and academics to once again re-evaluate what was being taught in America's schools.

Issues such as social dislocation, popular protests, race relations, poverty, sexism, and militarism due to the Vietnam War were all missing from discipline-centered curriculum. It became apparent to many young Americans that this discipline-centered curriculum had nothing to do with the world outside, or indeed with their personal programs. "It was a change that saw the schools beginning in the late 1960s, attempting to provide for every possible student interest and concern, often to the detriment of the place of academic disciplines within the curriculum" (Franklin & Johnson, 2008, p. 467). Thus a new era of curriculum change was ushered in—a curriculum of diversity that mirrored society at large. "The impetus for this curricular diversity was the presence of a multitude of competing rationales for organizing the curriculum. The academic disciplines represented one such possibility. There were, however, other organizational schemes that reformers invoked including self-esteem, personal growth, career preparation, student interest, and political transformation" (Franklin & Johnson, 2008, p. 467). However, these competing rationales had a negative effect on curriculum materials and on education in general. As Franklin and Johnson (2008) argue, these theories "created a chasm between the research interests of curriculum scholars in the university and the concerns of teachers and administrators with selecting, organizing, and delivering the curriculum" (p. 468). By the late 1970s, the curriculum in schools was split due to declining SAT scores. There was a more rigorous curriculum for more able students and another curriculum for remedial and special education students and students with learning and behavior problems.

During this time of rapid change in curriculum and educational theory as well as infighting in schools, colleges, and departments of education, there arose another problem. Since curriculum materials were still being collected, whose responsibility was it to house these materials—the university library or the department of education? One will see that the answer has never been entirely clear. In her doctoral dissertation, Elinor Ellis reported that in 1969, 56 percent of responding institutions of higher learning located their CMC in colleges of education while 37 percent located it in the library (cited in Clark, 1982, p. 15). Another study, conducted by Donald MacVean in 1958 found that curriculum centers were located in either the library or the college of education. Those that were located in the library were occasionally criticized by education faculty for their distance from the college of education faculty members and students (Mac Vean, 1960, p. 343). There was also argument over who should have ultimate control over selection of curriculum materials. In Harlan Johnson's study of curriculum centers, 52 percent of respondents stated that wherever the CMC was located, it should be directed and controlled by the education department (Johnson, 1973, p. 30). Those with a stake in developing curriculum materials believed that whoever chose these items must have appropriate qualifications. "Many reports indicate that the primary researcher did not see librarians as experts in materials evaluation and information retrieval, elements which are a large part of curriculum development" (Clark, 1982, p. 5). Without support from the education department, most scholars felt that CMCs would not flourish and would eventually close. Thus, it is apparent that not only was there fighting within education departments over whether these materials were necessary, but also fighting within the university between the library and the education department over location and control over materials.

If infighting, curriculum wars, curriculum diversity, and the ever-shifting landscape of education were not enough for teachers-to-be to deal with during their education, they also had to cope with one of the most significant cultural changes of this century—technology. Computer-assisted instruction (CAI) began to become a reality in the 1970s. "Computer technology as a resource for education is fast becoming a disseminated reality" (Hansen & Harvey, 1970, p. 46). CAI had the potential for significant impact on the roles of teachers in classrooms since it could perform information presentation and correctional functions (i.e., grading). This would allow teachers to spend more time designing specific instructional strategies and to have greater involvement in guiding individual students. As Hansen and Harvey argued, "The requirement for new teaching competencies will center around computers, and would necessitate the training of teachers in the knowledge and behaviors necessary to operate many of the functions of the computer" (Hansen & Harvey, 1970, p. 47). Technological changes allowed teachers to perform tutorial instruction and allowed students to focus more on independent learning. Therefore, teaching and curriculum were not defined solely by textbooks or printed courses of study (VanderMeer, 1970, p. 56).

The communications revolution that was rapidly increasing in influence changed almost everything about education. No longer did education have to occur in a classroom or even during school hours. Also, "learners need to know more than mere information—they need to know how information is gathered, identified, and transformed; in short, they need to know how information is used" (Burns & Brooks, 1970, p. 8). These technological changes would also have a strong impact on curriculum materials since "they will need updating or replacing much more rapidly in response to the speed with which information is discovered and to the degree that our knowledge of what is true is altered" (Burns & Brooks, 1970, p. 9).

But technological change has had an impact not only on teacher preparation, but also on how teachers-to-be and current teachers find curriculum materials. Today, there exist an uncountable number of websites dedicated to providing teachers with different curriculum materials, activities, exercises, etc. There are businesses devoted to providing teachers with curriculum materials. Many publishers provide free curriculum materials and readers guides for the books they publish for school use. Even textbook publishers provide additional information on websites for use with one of their particular textbooks. Has this situation undermined the CMC? At first glance, it would appear so. Why would students or teachers go to a CMC when they can just plug in a computer and download what they need? But just because teachers and teachers-to-be have curriculum materials literally at their fingertips doesn't mean they don't need the expertise in the CMC to tell them which materials they should use or how best to use these materials in classrooms. In fact, technological change has made CMCs even more important for schools, colleges, and departments of education. Not only do teachers need to learn how to use computers and computer-assisted instruction, but they also need guidance in choosing materials because there is such a glut of curriculum aids on the Internet.

Today, there are fewer than 300 CMCs in the entire nation (ACRL, 2009). During the 1970s, many universities closed their CMCs for good due to economic strains on budgets, the need for space, the constant upkeep required by CMCs, and a severe decline in enrollment in schools, colleges, and departments of education. This was a mistake—not only because of technological change, but also due to the rise of another curriculum movement—one of accountability and standards. This new movement, still occurring today, requires teachers-to-be to have an increasing awareness of standards and curriculum materials *before* they enter the classroom if they are to succeed.

In 1983, President Ronald Reagan's National Commission on Excellence in Education published one of the most important reports on education in the United States, *A Nation at Risk*. Like previous Cold War research and reports, it echoed many criticisms lobbed at teachers during that period. "The Commission noted a largely economic challenge by other industrialized countries, particularly Germany and Japan. They argued that the nation's system of education, which they deemed to be inadequate, undercut the United States' ability to create the skilled and knowledgeable workforce necessary to maintain its industrial and technological superiority" (Franklin & Johnson, 2008, p. 470). The commission based this assessment on declining test scores, adult illiteracy, and the business community's complaints about the lack of skilled graduates. In the commission's eyes, the nation's curriculum had been weakened by curriculum diversity, creating an education of unnecessary electives, nonacademic tracks, and student unwillingness to enroll in difficult courses. "Their solution was the introduction of an academic, discipline-centered curriculum that they labeled the New Basics" (Franklin & Johnson, 2008, p. 470). The new basics, as defined by the commission, included four years of English, three years of mathematics, three years of science, three years of social studies, a half year of computer science, and two years of foreign language at the high school level (Franklin & Johnson, 2008, p. 471.

A Nation at Risk was not without its detractors, however. Critics, largely academics from schools of education and practicing teachers, argued that the claims made by the commission were a distortion of facts. There was not a decline in educational standards or a decline in the quality of teaching students. What had happened, instead, was that curriculum diversity had created a chasm in which focus was placed almost solely on high-achieving students rather than all students. High-achieving students continued to do well on standardized tests, but they represented the minority of children in schools. It was the so-called "average" students that were neglected and disserved by state standards and minimum requirements on test scores. However, their complaints fell on deaf ears as the media glommed onto the report and sent the general public into a panic about standards of education in this country. This was the first time in which the media dictated reactions to the American educational system, and it would have disastrous consequences for teachers and teacher preparation because it served as the impetus for the No Child Left Behind Act of 2002, which would embed standards and accountability into the nation's education system.

In early 2000, arguments again arose over the state of the nation's so-called declining education system that was failing students, parents, and the country. While many outside the education system felt that *A Nation at Risk* had identified the problems of American schools, others felt it didn't go far enough. They thought that "A Nation at Risk had done nothing to improve the schools. American schools continued to remain at the bottom in international comparisons of educational achievement. If there was hope of improvement, it lay in the movement to create national standards of academic achievement" (Franklin & Johnson, 2008, p. 472). The then-president, George W. Bush, couldn't have agreed more. He set six national educational goals, which were then recommended to states as the basis for standards for local school districts. But that wasn't enough, since *A Nation at Risk* had put forth the same basis for standards. Now, the 2001 NCLB Act "has instituted such mechanisms as mandatory student testing [throughout the student's career] and penalties for low performance to ensure that such teaching actually takes place" (Franklin & Johnson, 2008, p. 473). No longer was curriculum about the best way to convey information and education to students, but about standards and outcomes.

With local, state, and national standards in firmly in place, it has become even more important that teachers-to-be be able not only to work with and analyze curriculum materials before they enter the classroom, but also to understand how these curriculum materials can aid them in meeting national standards. If there ever was a time for CMCs to be prevalent among departments, colleges, and schools of education, it is now. Without proper preparation before entering the classroom, teachers cannot be expected to produce the results required by the state and federal governments, and yet they are held accountable. "It is surely hollow for students to be told in education methods or curriculum planning courses how and why to use materials in a wide range of formats if the use of such media is never demonstrated in on-campus teaching"

(Gallinger, 1974, p. 3). Paul Witt echoed the same sentiments in an article: "[T]eachers will not be properly trained if they do not have actual experience with materials. Education students need to study materials by actually examining them, judging them and then using those they select," (cited in Clark, 1982, p. 4).

And yet today, most teachers-to-be do not have any type of access to these materials. In a study of newly hired teachers, Grossman and Thompson (2008) interviewed three teachers in different schools and concluded that beginning teachers had a hard time finding resources to support their instruction. One teacher "had not yet learned what types of curricular materials are available to her, materials that could in fact help her develop knowledge about the teaching of English" (p. 2014). They argued that with the increasing reliance on prescribed curriculum programs and materials (due to the standards movement), "the significance of curriculum materials in shaping both teachers' practice and learning has heightened" (p. 2016). New teachers are hungry for curriculum materials and the guidance these materials can provide in their teaching, and yet they aren't exposed to these materials until they are already on the job. This combination has made it almost impossible for new teachers to achieve the standards necessary for their students to succeed in mandatory testing.

Still today, teacher educators believe that a CMC is the only way to prepare well-trained teachers. The role played by CMCs enables teachers-to-be to prepare and present curriculums in a safe environment where they can evaluate materials and receive feedback from other students and professors. As Osa and Musser argued in a 2004 paper on creating posters and bulletin boards, "The competence of teachers is contingent to a large extent on the quality of the teacher education program that has prepared them. The quality of resources that support the teacher education program has been recognized as a crucial determinant of the quality of the knowledge and skills which the prospective teachers store in their repertoire" (p. 16). Today, however, there are fewer CMCs than at any time since teacher preparation became formalized in American education.

There were many reasons that institutions of higher learning gave for closing even more CMCs in the last ten to fifteen years. Most were closed due to declining university budgets, lack of state funding, lack of support from the university administration, lack of space, and mergers of library materials, which curriculum materials often fell under. At Wayne State University, the closure of the curriculum laboratory included all of these factors, plus infighting between the library and the College of Education regarding control over the materials. Once the Education Library was merged into the general library, the curriculum materials laboratory and center vanished. Most materials were discarded, although there remain some older curriculum materials kept for historical research. When looking at the history of Wayne State University's curriculum laboratory and the politics of this university, it becomes clear why, for better or worse, the laboratory ceased to exist.

Wayne State University is a large, urban research university located in the cultural center of Detroit, Michigan. It was formed from several educational institutions: the Detroit Medical College, the Detroit Teachers College, and the Detroit Junior College. The merger of these institutions created a multipurpose university, initially called Wayne University in 1930, in which education and teacher preparation were just small parts of the larger mission. Indeed, as Wayne University struggled to find its identity, it came to focus primarily on research and less on professional vocations, as teacher education was viewed at the time. But that didn't stop Dr. Gertha Williams (educational psychology), Lois Place (library science), and Eloise Ramsey (English education) from creating a curriculum laboratory from the materials they inherited from the Detroit Teachers College and from their own collections of materials. These three instructors held their classes in this laboratory room and shared responsibility for care and circulation of books. This was probably the first reason why the curriculum laboratory (later Education Library) would eventually come under siege. The laboratory was not established by the College of Education, although it certainly benefited from usage of these materials, but by three women with a committed vision towards providing the best in teacher preparation. It wasn't until G. Flint Purdy, the new library director, was hired in 1953 that the curriculum laboratory had any university support. When he arrived, he viewed the curriculum laboratory as

> a tremendously significant and highly successful pedagogical experiment. The "Laboratory" was a joint project of English Education, Educational Psychology, and Library Science. Physically it consisted of an embryonic but astutely selected collection of children's literature, educational psychology books and library science tools, housed in and adjacent to a classroom in which relevant courses were taught (Purdy, 1956).

Because of this "successful pedagogical experiment," Ramsey was able to secure a spot for the curriculum laboratory in the general library, as well as library funds to support the laboratory. Thus, the Education Library was formed and continued to thrive until the 1980s, when budgetary constraints on the library and infighting between the library and the College of Education caused a major shift in curriculum materials control. "Decline in the enrollment of Wayne State's College of Education was paralleled by a similar decline across the university. Because of this, the library system suffered a budgetary crisis that led to the unification of the separate divisional libraries housed in the Purdy/Kresge Library [formerly known as the general library]. The Education Library as a separate entity ceased to exist" (Corby, Jefferies, & Nichols, 1998, p. 17).

But even prior to the demise of the Education Library, the university libraries and the College of Education were already fighting about who should have control over these materials. The education faculty was against the initial talks of a merger in 1973 and sent many testimonials along with a letter to the Director of Libraries, Vern Pings. At this time, they felt that the service the Education Library provided was essential for the success of the College of Education. But in essence, the writing was on the wall. After 1973, the relationship shifted between the College of Education and the university libraries. After all, it was imperative to the College of Education to keep these materials.

In 1974, the College of Education wrote to Vern Pings stating its intent to develop a curriculum laboratory within the College of Education (Pings, 1974). To fuel its argument for a change in location, the College of Education cited comments made in the National Council for Accreditation of Teacher Education (NCATE) report. In a letter dated June 27, 1974, John W. Childs, Acting Dean of the College of Education wrote Pings. The letter began, "I am sorry to inform you that our discussions of a Curriculum Services Center located on the second floor of the Education Library are not viewed as being satisfactory to the Division Heads and faculty, (Childs, 1974). He then goes on to propose that the College of Education begin development of its own curriculum laboratory, which would in no way be competitive with the curriculum materials already located in the library. In his closure, and probably impetus for the sudden change in tone, he mentioned the NCATE report, "which comments upon the inadequacy of the professional educational collections in terms of copy depth for major titles and journals" (Childs, 1974). The library requested a copy of the report, but there is no record that it was ever sent.

A jurisdictional dispute had begun, and it was one in which the general library administration did not want to involve themselves. As far as they were concerned, the curriculum materials could be housed anywhere, and if it didn't affect the university budget, they were determined to stay out of the dispute. There is evidence that a series of meetings took place between the university libraries and the College of Education, but no real decision was reached except that it was clear the College of Education was going to embark on the endeavor to create its own curriculum laboratory. However, the College of Education's representative, Chris Howey, who was responsible for the college's Curriculum Services Center, stated in a meeting that the college's laboratory was gathered from education departments and faculty offices. Already it had collected kits, learning packages, textbooks, video and audio, films, records, and other teaching aids. More important, however, was that Howey told the library committee that, "it was not feasible for the Center to absorb our [the library's] textbook and curriculum guide collection, but all felt that our [the library's] filmstrip and record collection could be integrated" (College of Education, Minutes of Staff Meeting, N.D., 1974). Therefore, it was decided that print materials would remain in the library, while other materials and teaching aids would go to the Curriculum Services Center in the College of Education.

In 1982, the Director of Libraries, Peter Spyers-Duran, put forth a project for the merger of all divisional libraries in Purdy/Kresge, including the Education Library. The College of Education's response was to hold an emergency executive committee meeting regarding the proposal. In 1984, after the merger was well underway, the College of Education sent a letter to Pings that this merger "may have resulted in a serious deterioration of reference services and accessibility to materials for students and faculty" (College of Education, Official memo, December 11, 1984). The College of Education undertook a survey of its students to see if the merger had any ill effects on their work. The survey was largely inconclusive; some students liked the merger of materials, and others found the library difficult to use. Therefore, the College of Education had no concrete evidence to use to have the Education Library reinstated. Unfortunately, they had no idea at the time of the survey that the merger meant that the library, as a cost-cutting and space-saving measure, would discard most curriculum guides and materials, including textbooks. The only aspect of the Education Library that was spared was the juvenile collections, which still remain one of the nation's largest holdings of juvenile literature in an academic library, and the education periodicals required by students to perform research.

Today, the library houses its juvenile collections on the fourth floor of Purdy Library. Alongside it, for historical research, remains a small collection of textbooks and curriculum guides. It has been the complaint of many education students that the textbook collection in particular is not robust or up-to-date, and therefore does not allow them to complete their assignments. The College of Education, however, does have a Reading Resource Laboratory, a reading and writing tutoring program, a state-of-the-art instructional technology center, and a functioning laboratory school, the Early Childhood Center, for students entering early childhood education. Whether it still maintains its Curriculum Services Center remains unclear.

Due to declining budgets, technological change, professional infighting, and constant curriculum changes, many CMCs were forced to close at institutions of higher learning. However, the current climate of education—one of standards and accountability—makes CMCs vitally important in the preparation of today's teachers. If teachers-to-be cannot have access to curriculum materials used in local school districts and both evaluate and learn to use these materials in a practice setting, they are seriously disadvantaged upon entering a classroom. It is a disservice to teachers-to-be and to teacher preparation for schools of education not to provide the proper tools for learning to become a teacher. While declines in enrollment and a serious economic downturn across the nation in the 1970s and 1980s appeared to force the closure of CMCs, in reality it was the lack of support from university administrations and, occasionally, large segments of faculty from schools of education. It is clear, however, that CMCs must be revived at institutions of higher learning if the nation wants competent, well-educated teachers.

References

American Library Association. 1984. *Curriculum Materials Center Collection Development Policy*. Chicago: Education and Behavioral Sciences Section, Association of College and Research Libraries.

Andrews, Leonard O. 1950. "Experimental Programs of Laboratory Experiences in Teacher Education." *Journal of Teacher Education* 1 (4): 259–267. doi:10.1177/002248715000100402.

Association of College and Research Libraries. 2009. *Directory of Curriculum Materials Centers*, sixth edition. Chicago: American Library Association.

Burns, Richard W., and Gary D. Brooks. 1970. "The Need for Curriculum Reform." *Educational Technology* 10 (2): 8–12.

Childs, John W. 1974, June 27. [Letter to Dr. Vernon M. Pings]. Walter P. Reuther Library (Libraries, Education Vertical File), Detroit, MI.

Clark, Alice S. 1982. *Managing Curriculum Materials in the Academic Library*. Metuchen, NJ: Scarecrow Press.

College of Education, Wayne State University. 1984, December 11. [Letter to Mr. Peter Spyers-Duran]. Walter P. Reuther Library (Libraries, Education, Vertical File). Detroit, MI.

College of Education, Wayne State University. 1974. [Minutes of Staff Meeting]. Walter P. Reuther Library (Libraries, Education, Vertical File). Detroit, MI

Corby, Katherine, Shellie Jefferies, and Darlene P. Nichols. 1998. "Cooperation, Collaboration and Coordination: Education Librarians in Michigan." *Education Libraries* 22 (3): 13–18.

Estvan, Frank J. 1956. "Introduction." *Review of Educational Research* 26 (2): 113–114. Retrieved December 24, 2009, from http://www.jstor.org/stable/1168834.

Franklin, Barry M., and Carla C. Johnson. 2008. "What the Schools Teach: A Social History of the American Curriculum since 1950." In *The Sage Handbook of Curriculum and Instruction*, edited by F. Michael Connelly, 460–477. Thousand Oaks, CA: Sage.

Fraser, James W. 2007. *Preparing America's Teachers: A History*. New York: Teachers College Press.

Gallinger, Janice. 1974, July. "Educational Media Selection Centers and Academic Libraries." Paper presented at the Annual Meeting of the American Library Association, New York, NY. Retrieved from ERIC database. (ED095838).

Gendernalik, M. 1982, January 25. "Minutes of Last Two Committee Meetings" [memorandum]. Libraries, Education Vertical File. Walter P. Reuther Library, Detroit, MI.

Grossman, Pam, and Clarissa Thompson. 2008. "Learning from Curriculum Materials: Scaffolds for New Teachers?" *Teaching and Teacher Education* 24 (8): 2014–2026. doi:10.1016/j.tate.2008.05.002.

Hansen, Duncan N., and William L. Harvey. 1970. "Impact of CAI on Classroom Teachers." *Educational Technology* 10 (2): 46–48.

Johnson, Harlan R. 1973. "The Curriculum Materials Center: A Study of Policies and Practices in Selected Centers." Retrieved from ERIC database (ED081449).

Mac Vean, Donald S. 1958. "A Study of Curriculum Laboratories in Midwestern Teacher-Training Institutions." PhD diss., University of Michigan–Ann Arbor.

———. 1960. "Report of an Evaluation of Curriculum Laboratory Services in a Teachers College." *Journal of Educational Research* 53 (9): 341–344. Retrieved January 5, 2011, from http://www.jstor.org/stable/27530359.

National Commission on Excellence in Education. 1983. *A Nation at Risk: The Imperative for Educational Reform*. Washington, DC: Government Printing Office.

Osa, Justina O., and Linda R Musser. 2004. "The Role of Posters in Teacher Education Programs." *Education Libraries* 27 (1): 16–21.

Pings, Vern M. 1974, July 25. "Curriculum Services Center" [memorandum]. Education Library (Box 4). Walter P. Reuther Library, Detroit, MI.

Purdy, G. Flint. 1956, March 7. [Letter to Dean Magee]. Walter P. Reuther Library (Eloise Ramsey Collection, Box 1, Folder 1.4). Detroit, MI.

Roney, C. 1984, April 16. "College Library Committee Meeting, April 9, 1984" [memorandum]. Libraries, Education Vertical File. Walter P. Reuther Library, Detroit, MI.

———. (1985, Winter). "College of Education Library Survey." Copy in possession of Lothar Spang.

Spang, Lothar. 1984, October 30. "Proposals for Merging Purdy and Kresge Collections." Copy in possession of Lothar Spang.

VanderMeer, Abram W. 1970. "The Impact of New Materials and Media on Curricular Design." *Educational Technology* 10 (4): 53–57.

Part II: Present

3 The Role of Children's Literature in the Curriculum Materials Center

Ann E. Brownson, Eastern Illinois University

Most curriculum materials centers have children's literature in their collections. Some of these collections include historical trade books; others attempt to collect the newest offerings in a variety of formats. In this chapter, the history, current practices, and future of the children's literature collection in curriculum materials centers and its use by preservice teachers and teacher educators are discussed.

Historical Background

While libraries or colleges of education have housed curriculum materials centers (CMCs) since the late nineteenth century, it is unclear whether children's literature was included in those early centers. Clark (1982, p. 70) states that many CMCs inherited children's literature collections when they were transferred from the campus laboratory school, with many of those transfers occurring in the 1950s and 60s. The National Council for Accreditation of Teacher Education (NCATE), in its *Standards for Accreditation of Teacher Education* from 1960 regarding the importance and purpose of curriculum materials, stated that "this laboratory should include a wide array of books commonly used in elementary and secondary schools"(McGiverin, 1988, p. 120).

Sixty-six CMCs were surveyed in 1973 by Harlan Johnson, and of those surveyed, fifty-two responded that they had collections of children's literature. McGiverin's study from 1988 included responses from twenty-nine CMCs, with twenty-two indicating that they held collections of children's literature.

In 1984, the American Library Association published the *Curriculum Materials Center Collection Development Policy*. One of the types of materials to be collected is juvenile literature:

> Books appropriate for the preschool child through young adult are located in the collection. Award winners, honor books, and the young adult notable books should be collected comprehensively. Other examples of literature located in the collection include children's classics, beginning-to-read books, picture books, wordless picture books, folk literature, mythology, modern fantasy, poetry, realistic fiction, historical fiction, informational books, biography, and autobiography (ALA, 1984, p. 8).

Guidelines for Curriculum Materials Centers was published by the Education and Behavioral Sciences Section of the Association of College and Research Libraries in 2003. These guidelines also recommended the collection of children's and young adult literature:

> This collection should include fiction, nonfiction, picture books, folk and fairy tales, plays, and poetry appropriate for preschool through grade 12. The collection should be consistent with the recommendations of standard reviewing tools and include annual acquisition of award books (EBSS, 2003, p. 472).

Use of Children's Literature to Teach Pedagogy

For in-service teachers to be well versed in the use of children's literature, preservice teachers should have access to children's literature and the opportunity to read both widely and deeply. The CMC provides this access, and teacher educators provide opportunities through a variety of children's literature reading assignments. Teacher educators may assign children's novels that explore some of the themes and theories they are teaching. For example, preservice teachers are asked to examine their values and assumptions about culture and diversity; reading a young adult novel like *Monster* by Walter Dean Myers (1999) may encourage discussion about those values and assumptions. *Joey Pigza Swallowed the Key* (Gantos, 1998) provides beginning preservice teachers an accessible way to explore classrooms and students (Brenner, 2003) and also gives preservice teachers an introduction to learning styles and students with disabilities.

Many preservice teachers have read the Harry Potter series. The setting of this series, at Hogwarts school, can provide the opportunity to discuss many aspects of schooling: teaching styles, discipline, who decides what should be taught, how learning experiences should be organized, and what the role of the teacher should be (Kornfeld & Prothro, 2005, p. 217).

The young adult novel *Speak* by Laurie Halse Anderson (1999) can be used to illustrate the power of teachers in the classroom. The young protagonist's history teacher says, "I decide who talks in here" (p. 56), thus thrusting his students into silence. Reading such a book can lead to extensive conversation on classroom behavior of students and also of teachers.

History of the Use of Children's Literature in the Teaching of Reading

Children's literature has long been used to teach reading to children. Nila Banton Smith (1986) has identified several broad periods of reading education. In many of these periods, books were written for the express purpose of teaching reading, but they also had other uses, including religious education, moral education, education for citizenship, and around the turn of the twentieth century, education as a cultural asset. Louis Wilson, in a *Library Journal* article from 1912, talked about setting up school libraries and said that

> provision should be made for the training of teachers in the use
> of books and children's literature. It is not sufficient to set the

bookcase beside the teacher's desk or place it in a corner and let it stand there. It must be properly used. It is the clear duty of the departments of pedagogy of the various state universities, of the special normal schools, and of the conductors of summer schools and teachers institutes to give this instruction. (p. 183)

Smith (1986) wrote that during this period teachers used supplemental reading materials, with older students having access to classic works of literature, while younger students had readers that typically contained traditional fairy tales, nursery rhymes, and fables.

In the early part of the twentieth century, in the period Smith (1986) calls the "Initial Period of Emphasis upon Scientific Investigation in Reading" (p. 157), the use of children's literature in the teaching of reading faded, not to reappear for the better part of a century. During this period, two separate groups formed, each with its own professional organization. One was focused on the teaching of reading, and the other emphasized children's literature. Reading educators criticized the literary diet of previous periods and called for the teaching of factual materials that would be encountered later in "practical life reading" (Martinez & McGee, 2000, p. 157).

During the 1950s, reading was taught through basal selections that typically featured white, suburban, middle-class families, although readers gradually expanded to include more diverse lifestyles and roles. Readers were primarily written in house, and children did not read outside of those prescribed, formulaic basals. If children's literature was included in textbooks, it was generally adapted by the publisher, to "fit standards of acceptability for content, language, and values" (Goodman et al., 1988, p. 60). Goodman and his colleagues also argued that the original authors would likely not have recognized their own work.

Relatively few books for children were published during the late nineteenth and early twentieth centuries. Even as increasing numbers were published in the mid-twentieth century, teachers did not have access to many of them. It was not until the passage of the Elementary and Secondary Education Act in 1965 that school libraries became a reality in many schools (Huck, 1996). With this increased access came an increased interest in and use of children's literature in the teaching of reading. The individualized reading movement first emerged in the 1920s through the Winnetka plan and was reintroduced by Veatch in the 1960s (Huck, 1996). However, because of the dominance of basal reading programs throughout most of the century, authentic children's literature was not central to reading instruction, even when availability was no longer an issue. Rather, children's literature played a supporting role, with children reading these books after their other, "real" work was completed (Martinez & McGee, 2000).

From the 1970s and into the 1990s, three movements led by practicing teachers put literature at the center of reading and writing instruction. Those were the reading workshop approach, the shared reading approach, and the whole language approach, which included the other two within it. Whole language had an "emphasis on an extensive use of children's literature, student choice and ownership, language across the curriculum, integration through the use of thematic units, and integration of reading and writing" (Martinez & McGee, 2000, p. 161).

Since the 1990s, reading instruction has shown a major shift, from the use of basals as the main form of reading instruction to a more balanced approach that combines skills and literature. Baumann et al. (1998) replicated a survey originally done by Austin and Morrison in 1963. The results showed that trade books played a much greater role in the teaching of reading than they did previously. Among the key findings:

- Of all teachers, 94 percent had a goal of developing independent readers who could choose, appreciate, and enjoy literature.
- Most first grade teachers used Big Books and picture trade books extensively, and 72 percent of fifth grade teachers reported moderate or greater use of chapter books.
- Of pre-K–2 teachers, 97 percent regularly read aloud to their classes from trade books.
- Of grade 3–5 teachers, 67 percent used trade books instructionally.

+ Only 2 percent of teachers said they relied on basals exclusively. Teachers typically reported using basals supplemented by trade books (56 percent) or trade books supplemented by basals (27 percent); 16 percent used trade books exclusively (Baumann et al., 1988, p. 643).

In 2006, Mesmer conducted a survey about the types of materials being used to teach reading by K–2 teachers throughout the United States. She reported that children's literature was used more than three times per week by 77 percent of respondents; in contrast, basals were reported to be used by 70 percent of teachers two or fewer times per week (p. 398). She described the archetypical in-service primary school teacher from her survey results:

> The primary grade teacher has the power to select many of the texts used in his or her classroom. This teacher embraces a balanced literacy philosophy. He or she uses literature and leveled text on a daily basis. This teacher relies on literature mostly for comprehension purposes but uses leveled text for many different purposes including teaching decoding, sight words, concepts of print, fluency, and comprehension. Materials like predictable text and decodable text receive moderate use for very specific instructional purposes. This teacher might use a basal once or twice per week but rarely uses workbooks. He or she values leveled text, predictable text, and literature a great deal. In essence, this primary grade teacher is selecting materials and using them in ways that are congruent with his or her beliefs. (p. 407).

Reading Instruction

Because children's literature is used mostly for comprehension purposes, it is employed throughout the school day, not just in direct reading instruction, but across the curriculum. One of the ways both reading comprehension and fluency are developed is through scaffolding: that is, providing fiction and nonfiction texts that build on vocabulary and ideas. If you have ever seen a second grader who is obsessed with dinosaurs, you have seen scaffolding in action. That second grader is able to read and understand books well beyond his or her tested reading level. "Gradually and seamlessly, students will find themselves ready for texts of increasingly greater depth and complexity" (Adams, 2010, p. 10).

Another way that students are encouraged to become independent readers is through the use of reading programs such as Scholastic's Reading Counts or Renaissance Learning's Accelerated Reader. Because they are used in many school districts as part of sustained silent reading (SSR) activities, it is important for preservice teachers to become knowledgeable about how they operate. CMCs can provide access to children's literature listed in these programs as well as the assessment materials associated with them.

Many reading textbook series now include, among their many components, libraries of children's literature that are used in conjunction with the reading textbook. These libraries are cost-prohibitive for purchase by most CMCs, but fortunately CMCs already own many of the trade books in those libraries. Preservice teachers can still have access to the trade books from the series, even though they are not in the packaging provided by the textbook publishers.

Literature circles provide yet another opportunity for preservice teachers to become familiar with children's trade books. These circles may be made up of either small groups of preservice teachers led by a teacher educator or a single preservice teacher, possibly in a practicum situation, leading several children discussing a book that all have read. According to Daniels (2002), the key ingredients of literature circles are that students choose their reading materials; small groups are determined based on those choices, topics for discussion come from the students, and evaluation is by both teacher observation and student self-evaluation (pp. 18–25). Through literature circles, preservice teachers can learn how to encourage higher-order thinking by their students.

Current practice in teacher education is that preservice teachers are taught to develop thematic units about topics that their future students need to learn. These units include a variety of materials and activities that will support the teaching of that topic. Children's literature is almost always included in the development and teaching of those units. For example, a unit on weather for second grade could include read-aloud fiction like *Cloudy with a Chance of Meatballs* (Barrett, 1978) and nonfiction such as *I Face the Wind* (Cobb, 2003), a Sibert honor book that includes experiments young children can perform.

Martinez and McGee (2000) have identified five trends in children's literature that have met critical needs in literacy instruction:

- books to move children into beginning reading
- books to sustain and expand beginning readers
- books to make the transition from easy-to-read picture books to longer and more complex chapter books
- books to nourish children's interest in the historical and natural world
- books that reflect the diversity of children and their experiences (p. 161)

All of these types of books should be available for examination by preservice teachers in the children's literature collection of the CMC. Teacher educators and CMC staff can assist preservice teachers in selecting literature appropriate to each of these critical needs.

Crosscurricular Instruction and Integrated Learning with the Children's Literature Collection

As in the weather example above, children's literature is being used daily by in-service teachers to teach reading, but also to teach science, mathematics, and social studies. Both fiction and nonfiction trade books can draw children's attention, increase vocabulary acquisition, encourage higher-order thinking, and address learning standards.

One of the most common ways preservice teachers learn about crosscurricular instruction and integrated learning is through the development of the above-mentioned thematic units, courses of study about broad topics that reach across subjects. The trick, of course, is to pick a topic that will build reading, mathematical, and critical-thinking skills and that will provide content in all subject areas.

For example, a preservice teacher might come into the CMC looking for books on mammals for a thematic unit. The initial foray into children's literature will probably take her to the Dewey 599s—mammals. As she delves into the topic, she may find that she can teach about what characteristics make these animals mammals (biology); where mammals are found (geography); why some mammals becoming endangered (social studies and science); and the percentage of students in her class who are dog owners versus cat owners (mathematics). The children's literature collection is there to provide books related to each of these subtopics. In a well-developed thematic unit, the preservice teacher will also find fiction that is related to the topic. For example, *Julie of the Wolves* by Jean Craighead George (1972), a Newbery Award–winning book of literary merit, can teach about animal behavior.

In a well-managed CMC, where attention is paid not only to providing books on various topics but also to providing literature at many reading levels, the preservice teacher can also find literature that will meet the needs of all learners, from those who struggle to read to those who read well above their grade level. Thus, the preservice teacher can become more aware of the needs of all students.

Beyond thematic units, children's literature can be used effectively in any subject area. If preservice teachers in physical education, for example, are asked to read sports fiction as part of their methods courses, they may develop a greater understanding of the mind-muscle unity embodied in this assignment, see connections between school learning and real life, and learn a valuable crossdisciplinary lesson about encouraging literacy among their future students (Tixier & Edwards, 2002, p. 53).

Promotion of the Children's Literature Collection

Even an extensive children's literature collection will not be used appropriately without the knowledge and skills of the CMC staff. Staff can provide added value to the collection by putting curriculum-related subject headings in bibliographic records in the catalog. By developing bibliographies of children's literature on different subjects and themes that are popular, staff provides easy access to quality children's books on selected topics.

For example, at Eastern Illinois University, the CMC staff has developed booklists on articulation that are used by special education and communication disorders majors; lists of books for children about disabilities; books about various ethnic cultures; and a bibliography of children's books that address specific concept skills such as counting, colors, shapes, and sizes. A booklist that contains picture books that meet the requirement for a yearly assignment in an American Sign Language class was developed when numerous students asked for help in locating such books.

A major way the CMC librarian promotes the children's literature collection is through contact with all of those faculty members who are preparing preservice teachers. When articles are published related to the use of children's and young adult literature in the curriculum, the librarian can provide links to those articles. Lists of new books, perhaps with ideas for curricular use, can also be sent. Occasional attendance at departmental meetings of education faculty can serve as an opportunity to promote the collection as well.

The CMC librarian may also help students in accessing the children's literature collection by purchasing finding aids. One finding aid that is used daily in Eastern Illinois University's teachers' center is *A to Zoo: Subject Access to Children's Picture Books* (Lima & Lima, 2006). If, for example, preservice teachers are looking for picture books about friendship, they can look up that subject in *A to Zoo* and find a list of children's picture books that is several pages long. An online finding aid such as *Children's Literature Comprehensive Database* (CLCD Company, n.d.) can assist preservice teachers, especially those looking for children's literature at a particular reading level.

The CMC librarian also serves as collection development specialist, purchasing children's literature that meets the curricular needs of preservice teachers. By noting topics that reappear as requests each semester, the librarian can purchase children's literature about those topics in a variety of levels, both simple and complex, and also fiction and informational books.

A CMC staff member serves as a cheerleader advocating the use of children's literature in the classroom. By modeling the behavior of a school library media specialist and by promoting the value of the school library, the CMC staff member can show preservice teachers the way school library media specialists can help them find children's literature as they develop units in the curriculum. A well-read staff member can also model ways that a teacher can "hook" a student's interest with a spur-of-the-moment book talk or positive review of a particular book.

The Future of Children's Literature in the Curriculum Materials Center

The age of the e-book and audiobook has arrived. According to Publishers Weekly, the Association of American Publishers reported sales of e-books during 2009 increased 176.6 percent, reaching $313 million (*Publisher's Weekly*, 2010). While sales of audiobooks decreased slightly in 2009, their growth rate over the past seven years is still a healthy 4.3 percent. In the meantime, hardbound books for children and young adults fell 5 percent, though paperbound books for children and young adults grew 2.2 percent. Meanwhile, it was estimated that six million e-readers would be sold in 2010, with a projection that the market will grow to $2.5 billion in 2013 (Molchanov, 2010). NookColor, one of the dedicated e-readers, was heavily advertised during the 2010 holiday season as a good choice for those interested in purchasing picture books, some of which now offer interactive features. Many of the heaviest users of dedicated e-readers and tablet computers like the iPad will be digital natives—those born since the beginnings of the World Wide Web. Many e-book readers have also developed applications that allow e-books and audiobooks to be downloaded to smartphones. One major question yet to be answered is whether CMCs will purchase these electronic reading devices for checkout or will expect preservice teachers to supply them.

In addition, subscription services like BookFlix, Tumblebooks, and Big Universe and the Web presence of the donation-supported International Children's Digital Library are being used more and more with emerging and developing readers. BookFlix, for example, pairs fiction and nonfiction books for grades K–3 and offers options such as turning the readalong on and off while watching a video of the fiction title (Collier & Berg, 2010, p. 23).

Many public and school libraries already subscribe to services like NetLibrary, EBrary, and MyMediaMall (from OverDrive Digital Library Reserve). Eastern Illinois University, as part of a consortium of libraries, has purchased access to both adult and children's literature in MyMediaMall, including both e-books and audiobooks that can be downloaded for a limited time period to a variety of electronic devices.

In addition to subscription services, there are also many popular e-book collections that are available freely online. Some of these include the IPL2 ForKids (http://www.ipl.org/kidspace), Children's Books Online (http://www.childrensbooksonline.org), and Project Gutenberg (http://www.gutenberg.org).

So how will this paradigm shift in the way we view—and read—children's literature affect CMCs? Some of the subscription services listed in the paragraphs above are very expensive. If e-books are purchased at a consortium level, this will affect the ability of CMC staff to acquire children's and young adult literature that meet the specific needs of their preservice teachers. On the other hand, preservice teachers will have access to e-books 24/7. They will not need to come to the bricks-and-mortar CMC to check out items for their use as they develop teaching units and prepare for practicums and other preservice opportunities. As copyright issues are worked out (as they must be), there will be many more opportunities for preservice teachers to share digital content with their classmates and later with their students. We will need to come up with new ways to catalog, showcase, and otherwise market e-books to preservice teachers so that they are aware of the extent and variety of children's and young adult literature available to them.

Portable digital content, such as audio, video, and interactive material, is the foreseeable future of children's literature. The next step beyond that can only be imagined.

References

Adams, Marilyn Jager. 2010. "Advancing Our Students' Language and Literacy: The Challenge of Complex Texts." *American Educator* 34 (4): 3–11+.

ALA (American Library Association). 1984. *Curriculum Materials Center Collection Development Policy*. Chicago: Educational and Behavioral Sciences Section, Association of College & Research Libraries. Retrieved from ERIC database (ED256360).

Anderson, Laurie Halse. 1999. *Speak*. New York: Farrar Straus Giroux.

Austin, Mary C., and Coleman Morrison. 1963. *The First R: The Harvard Report on Reading in Elementary School*. New York: Macmillan.

Barrett, Judi. 1978. *Cloudy with a Chance of Meatballs*. New York: Simon & Schuster.

Baumann, James F., James V. Hoffman, Jennifer Moon, and Ann M. Duffy-Hester. 1998. "Where Are Teachers' Voices in the Phonics/Whole Language Debate? Results from a Survey of US Elementary Classroom Teachers." *The Reading Teacher* 51: 636–650.

Brenner, Devon. 2003. "Bridges to Understanding: Reading and Talking about Children's Literature in Teacher Education." *Action in Teacher Education* 24 (4): 79–86.

Clark, Alice S. 1982. *Managing Curriculum Materials in the Academic Library*. Metuchen, NJ: Scarecrow Press.

CLCD Company. N.d. Children's Literature Comprehensive Database. http://www.childrenslit.com.

Cobb, Vicki. 2003. *I Face the Wind*. New York: HarperCollins.

Collier, Jackie, and Susan Berg. 2010. "Student Learning and E-books." In *No Shelf Required: E-books in Libraries*, edited by Sue Polanka, 19–36. Chicago: American Library Association.

Daniels, Harvey. 2002. *Literature Circles: Voice and Choice in Book Clubs and Reading Groups*. Portland, ME: Stenhouse.

"E-Book Sales Jump 176% in Flat Trade Year." (2010). *Publisher's Weekly*. Retrieved July 20, 2011 from http://www.publishersweekly.com/pw/by-topic/digital/content-and-e-books/article/42173-e-book-sales-jump-176-in-flat-trade-year.html.

EBSS (Education and Behavioral Sciences Section). 2003. "Guidelines for Curriculum Materials Centers." *College & Research Libraries News* 64 (7): 469–474.

Gantos, Jack. 1998. *Joey Pigza Swallowed the Key*. New York: HarperCollins.

George, Jean Craighead. 1972. *Julie of the Wolves*. New York: Harper & Row.

Goodman, Kenneth S., P. Shannon, Y. Freeman, and S. Murphy. 1988. *Report Card on Basal Readers*. Katonah, NY: Richard C. Owen.

Huck, Charlotte. 1996. "Literature Based Reading Programs: A Retrospective." *The New Advocate* 9:23–33.

Johnson, Harlan. 1973. "The Curriculum Materials Center: A Study of Policies and Practices in Selected Centers." Retrieved from ERIC database (ED081449).

Kornfeld, John, and Laurie Prothro. 2005. "Envisioning Possibility: Schooling and Student Agency in Children's and Young Adult Literature." *Children's Literature in Education* 36 (3): 217–239.

Lima, Carolyn W., and John A. Lima. 2006. *A to Zoo: Subject Access to Children's Picture Books*, 7th ed. Westport, CT: Libraries Unlimited.

Martinez, Miriam G., and Lea M. McGee. 2000. "Children's Literature and Reading Instruction: Past, Present, and Future." *Reading Research Quarterly* 35 (1): 154–169.

McGiverin, Rolland. 1988. "Curriculum Materials Centers: A Descriptive Study." *Behavioral and Social Sciences Librarian* 6 (3–4):119–28.

Mesmer, Heidi Anne E. 2006. "Beginning Reading Materials: A National Survey of Primary Teachers." *Journal of Literacy Research* 38 (4): 389–425.

Molchanov, Dmitriy. 2010, January 20. "Yankee Group's US E-book Reader Forecast: Kindling a Fire." Yankee Group website. Retrieved December 30, 2010, from http://www.yankeegroup.com/ResearchDocument.do?id=52910.

Myers, Walter Dean. 1999. *Monster*. New York: HarperCollins.

Smith, Nila Banton. 1986. *American Reading Instruction*. Newark, DE: International Reading Association.

Tixier y Vigil, Yvonne, and Sarah Edwards. 2002. "Using Sports Fiction in Physical Education." *JOPERD: The Journal of Physical Education Recreation & Dance* 73 (9): 53–57.

Wilson, Louis R. 1912. "A Constructive Library Platform for Southern Schools." *Library Journal* 37: 179–185.

4

Promoting Library Instruction for Education Students: A Model for CMC/Faculty Collaboration

Pat Farthing and Margaret N. Gregor, Appalachian State University

Many curriculum materials center (CMC) librarians believe that collaboration with education faculty members creates opportunities to teach information literacy skills and maximize students' use and understanding of CMC resources. The collaborative ideas highlighted in this chapter may serve as a blueprint to foster partnerships between librarians and teaching faculty. They are based on the experiences of librarians in the Justice-Query Instructional Materials Center at Appalachian State University, whose forty-year partnership with faculty members in the Reich College of Education has resulted in a strong instructional program. Correspondence with librarians who are members of the North Carolina Curriculum Materials Center Association and CMC librarians in various parts of the country provides other examples of collaborative efforts.

Introduction

Curriculum materials centers (CMCs) support the teacher preparation programs offered by colleges and schools of education. Their missions, as stated in the Association of College and Research Libraries *Guidelines for Curriculum Materials Centers*, are to provide materials and access to digital resources that enhance the education of preservice teachers and to provide instruction in the identification, evaluation, and use of these resources for PK–12 instruction (ACRL, 2009). As information sources become more diverse and technologies for instructional delivery expand, it also becomes critical for preservice teachers to acquire information literacy skills so that they can identify and evaluate resources throughout their teaching careers and teach information literacy skills to their students (EBSS Instruction for Educators Committee, 2010; NCATE, 2009). This emphasis on information literacy skills is reiterated in the American Association of School Librarians *Standards for the 21st-Century Learner*. These standards state that students and, by implication, teachers, must acquire digital, visual, textual, and technological literacies to select, evaluate, and use information effectively (AASL, 2007). Thus, each of the four standards cited in this paragraph emphasizes the need for preservice teachers to acquire information literacy skills and a familiarity with the types of resources available to enhance classroom teaching.

CMCs are housed in the colleges of education, the university library, or another facility. They are administered and budgeted under various management models and differ in name, collection size, and staffing patterns (Hagenbruch, 2001, p. 137). Regardless of location, administration, or unit title, CMCs contain materials and access to digital resources that may be used to create lesson plans, enhance classroom teaching, and research issues in education. Librarians working in these units understand that students who learn to use CMC resources as undergraduates and graduate students are more likely to use their school media centers and collaborate with school media specialists throughout their careers as teachers and administrators than those who do not access CMC resources. These preservice teachers are also more likely to possess the ability to teach information literacy skills to their own students.

Two of the biggest challenges CMC librarians face are familiarizing faculty and students with CMC materials and services and finding opportunities to teach information literacy skills. Some librarians have concluded that collaboration with education faculty members is the key to maximizing students' use and understanding of these resources and often provides opportunities to teach information literacy skills. To this end, CMC librarians design library and information literacy instruction opportunities by identifying courses where CMC resources may be used. They work with instructors to create course assignments that require CMC materials and teach students the research and information literacy skills needed to locate those resources. In some instances they are embedded in education courses as co-instructors and model collaboration between teachers and media specialists. This emphasis on teaching and the goal of becoming embedded instructors in specific courses require that these librarians develop strong professional relationships with education faculty members (Heider, 2010; Kesselman & Watstein, 2009; Manus, 2009; Shumaker, 2009; Siess, 2010).

Establishing these collaborative partnerships is an ongoing process that takes many forms. CMC librarians have identified a variety of strategies that enhance working relationships with college of education faculty members. The collaborative ideas contained in this chapter are based on the forty-year partnership between the Justice-Query Instructional Materials Center (IMC) librarians at Appalachian State University (ASU) and faculty members in the Reich College of Education, as well as the experiences of members of the North Carolina Curriculum Materials Center Association. Correspondence with CMC librarians in various parts of the country has provided other examples of collaboration. Throughout our discussion we have retained Harriet Hagenbruch's definition of collaboration "as forming partnerships with a variety of constituencies on campus such as College of Education faculty" (Hagenbruch, 2001, p. 138). These collaborations facilitate the implementation of the teaching mission of CMCs and enhance preservice teachers' understanding of the use of CMC resources and of information literacy skills.

Collaboration with Faculty Members in Colleges of Education

Strategies for Engaging Faculty Members

Collaborations between librarians and education faculty members take many forms and involve many types of partnerships. Establishing personalized working relationships is the first step in developing collaborative opportunities between the CMC and the college of education. This is an ongoing process because new faculty members arrive each semester as programs expand or as individuals retire or move to positions elsewhere. It is helpful to obtain a list of new faculty members and to make an initial contact by e-mail, letter, phone or in person to introduce the CMC librarians and services. Subsequent contacts may be made in person, via e-mail, and by providing information in e-newsletters, blogs, and wikis. At ASU, the IMC librarians concentrate on developing relationships with new faculty as well as with veteran faculty who teach introductory courses, subject methods courses, research courses, and the children's and adolescent literature courses, all of which rely heavily on IMC resources.

The IMC librarians find that it is useful to visit education faculty members in their offices to establish relationships and to ask how classes and research projects are progressing. These conversations, both formal and informal, allow librarians to offer assistance with library research, discuss assignments requiring library resources, and encourage faculty members to schedule instructional sessions for their students. In almost every conversation the ASU IMC librarians affirm the multicultural nature of the IMC collection and state that the IMC is a model PK–12 school media center. They often show faculty members features of the IMC website (www.library.appstate.edu/imc/index.html) and encourage them to use this resource in their teaching. These conversations help librarians to understand what faculty members are researching, how they are teaching, and how they use information offered to them.

Another example of collaboration exists at East Carolina University. Their Teaching Resource Center (TRC) librarians begin their association with new faculty members by participating actively in the university's weeklong new faculty orientation. The first day of this orientation is held in the university library. TRC librarians meet new education faculty members at this event, offer tours of the TRC, and discuss the importance of faculty input in collection development. Additionally, TRC staff members provide an orientation to services such as Blackboard and Onestop. A collection development session is held, and faculty members are encouraged to submit purchase requests. TRC faculty members send their new colleagues follow-up e-mails encouraging them to use TRC services and resources. They also work to find opportunities for face-to-face interactions and ongoing communication (Linda Teel, personal communication, October 29, 2010).

Offering faculty consultations as an ongoing CMC service and scheduling professional development sessions in areas of interest to faculty members also enhance librarian/faculty associations. A one-on-one consultation showing a faculty member how to search library databases or a professional development session on the use of Smart Boards or other technologies shows faculty members that CMC librarians understand the needs of faculty members as researchers and teachers. Additionally, involving faculty members in collection development and expressing interest in their areas of research helps to enhance librarian/faculty relationships.

Strategies for Engaging Administrators

Communication with administrators in schools or colleges of education is critical to the accomplishment of any CMC's teaching mission. At ASU, IMC librarians have worked for a number of years to establish positive formal and informal relationships with the dean of the Reich College of Education and with the associate deans. Periodic face-to-face conversations and e-mails inform the deans of IMC services, resources, projects, and instructional efforts, as well as of IMC needs. This communication also keeps the IMC librarians apprised of new initiatives in the College and serves as a good starting point for developing collaborative efforts. It often influences the work that is done with teaching faculty members. For example, the College of Education recently designed a new core of five courses for undergraduate education majors. The IMC librarians were made aware of these changes via e-mail communication from the dean and were invited to presentations outlining new course content. Receiving information about these changes early in the development process provided opportunities for timely collection development and for informal input in the course selection and decision-making process. Early knowledge of curriculum changes afforded the opportunity to redesign the IMC orientation module and to lobby faculty successfully for the inclusion of this module in one of the new courses. In another instance, a chance meeting between the IMC coordinator and the dean resulted in initial funding for the Idea Factory, a facility for the creation of educational materials that is housed in the IMC and used by education students and practicing teachers in the service region. Such innovations would not be possible without ongoing contact and overtures on the part of the IMC librarians.

The librarian in the Mary L. Williams Curriculum Materials Library (CML) at Oklahoma State University contacts the College of Education administrative offices every semester to request a copy of each professor's syllabus and the course schedule. This practice allows her to learn what types of projects will be assigned, what materials will be needed to complete these assignments, and what changes have been made to the instructional content of each course. If she discovers collaborative instructional opportunities, she contacts the individual professor to discuss resources and options for instruction. She also sends out e-mails each semester reminding administrators and faculty of the instructional materials and services provided in the CML, provides an RSS feed through the library's website so that faculty can access bibliographies of new materials in their areas of interest, and uses the CML's Delicious account to bookmark special resources such as Outstanding Science Trade Books for Students 2009. Additionally, she posts resources for class assignments and provides links to resources that are useful to school librarians and classroom teachers on the CML Wiki. A chat box is available on the CML homepage for reference queries (S. Brisco, personal communication, November 9, 2010).

Establishing Joint Committees

Creating a college of education library advisory committee whose membership includes one faculty member from each of the college's departments is valuable. In this forum collection development, service provision to on- and off-campus students, services to faculty members teaching face-to-face and online courses, and CMC instruction can be discussed. Work with this committee often results in invitations to attend departmental meetings where services, collection development, and library instruction may be discussed in depth. Regardless of whether an advisory committee can be created, CMC librarians may wish to request invitations to attend departmental faculty meetings periodically. This may require some diplomacy, as faculty members may be unsure why a librarian wants to attend their meetings. Once the purpose of meeting attendance is explained, librarians are usually welcomed. These meetings provide opportunities to discuss new services and resources, to invite faculty members to attend special programs, and to discuss the need for library instruction that meets specific student needs.

In some instances CMC librarians must work with established college of education committees. At Western Carolina University, the Education Reference Librarian recognized that some education majors were not aware of CMC resources or, in some instances, of the existence of the CMC. She presented a CMC orientation proposal to the Professional Leadership Council, an advisory group for the teacher education program. The council recognized the need for this orientation and recommended that it be incorporated into the Foundation of Education course, a beginning course required of all majors. Although the proposal was approved on paper and supported by the council, it took significant outreach on the part of the Education Reference Librarian to overcome faculty resistance and to make the orientation a reality. After seeing that the information gained in this session improved student coursework, the faculty embraced the orientation class as a valuable part of their course (Beth McDonough, personal communication, October 30, 2010).

Working Collaboratively on Conferences, Research, and Special Events

Positive relationships are facilitated when CMC librarians attend conferences, lectures, and presentations sponsored by the college of education. Volunteering to work on planning committees for these events can establish strong ties between librarians and teaching faculty. Participating in research projects and grants, writing articles with education faculty members, and co-presenting at conferences also strengthen these associations. Additionally, sponsoring or co-sponsoring events such as children's or young adult author and illustrator visits for the benefit of preservice and practicing teachers, schoolchildren, and the community is an asset to both the college of education and the CMC. CMC displays highlighting these authors and illustrators advertise these presentations and encourage interest in literature.

Sample Collaborative Efforts

In the mid-1990s, a library science professor and the IMC librarian at ASU collaborated to develop an international service-learning project with the Bolivian teachers who founded Biblioteca Th'urachapitas, the only children's library in that country. The project was designed to provide multicultural and service-learning experiences for ASU graduate students and PK–12 schoolchildren in the ASU School Partnership Program while also building the collection of the Biblioteca Th'urachapitas. The Bolivian teachers purchased artifacts, crafts, toys, music, and books representative of their culture for inclusion in instructional kits with funding provided by the Richard T. Barker Friends of the ASU library. Students at ASU and ASU School Partnership public school teachers incorporated these kits into instructional units on Bolivia and its children's library. This project was so successful that the IMC and the Biblioteca Th'urachapitas were awarded "Sister Library" status in 2000 by the White House Centennial Commission. Today public school and ASU students participate in fund-raising events to purchase Spanish language books and materials for the Biblioteca Th'urachapitas. Library science graduate students travel to Bolivia to deliver the books to the library and engage in research on libraries in developing countries.

The Educational Resources Laboratory (ERL) at Oakland University's School of Education and Human Services in Rochester, Michigan, hosts an annual cultural celebration for the university community. Each year the culture of one country or cultural group is highlighted. Education faculty work with ERL staff to plan activities, speakers, and displays of artifacts, traditional costumes, and children's books in an attempt to promote understanding between cultures and to help preservice teachers gain a more diverse worldview. While the entire university community is invited to this event, education students and faculty are encouraged to attend, and some faculty members offer students extra credit as an incentive to stimulate attendance (A. Phelps, personal communication, November 9, 2010).

The head of the Education and Social Science Library and faculty and staff members from the College of Education and the Graduate School of Library and Information Science at the University of Illinois at Urbana-Champaign work with graduate students, local teachers, school media specialists, and public librarians to host a biennial Youth Literature Festival. This festival includes author presentations, storytelling, music, dance, puppetry, bookmaking, and other activities for children. University students, especially preservice teachers, are involved in many of the on-site events. Prior to the festival, authors visit local public and private schools and speak at public libraries in an attempt to reach as many children as possible (Nancy O'Brien, personal communication, December 7, 2010).

In 2009, the IMC at Appalachian State University sponsored a visit from Susan L. Roth, the illustrator and co-author of *Listen to the Wind: The Story of Dr. Greg and Three Cups of Tea*. Children's literature faculty members were involved in the planning for this visit and engaged their students in multiple activities related to Ms. Roth's presentation. She demonstrated the technique of collage and introduced her Let's Hold Hands multicultural project to education students, classroom teachers, schoolchildren, and participants in a public library workshop. Students made an autobiographical paper doll and sent it to children in another country as an ambassador of peace and understanding. Ms. Roth taught education students and teachers how to create the dolls and offered curricular guidance for incorporating this art project into social studies classes. Many classroom teachers in the ASU service region adopted this project and used *Listen to the Wind* and Let's Hold Hands to teach their classes about other countries and cultures. This event illustrated the power of children's literature and provided our preservice elementary majors with an example of how to use picture books to teach across the curriculum and to engage schoolchildren in service-learning projects.

At East Carolina University, the TRC sponsors an annual Librarian to Librarian Networking Summit for school media personnel. The summit is designed to encourage media specialists to communicate with each other and the educational community and to promote the role that school media specialists play in student academic success. In 2011 the summit will be expanded to include preservice teachers with a special session titled Integrating Children's Literature into the Classroom. The session will feature Vaunda Nelson, author of *Bad News for Outlaws: The Remarkable Life of Bass Reeves, Deputy U.S. Marshal,* and winner of the 2010 Coretta Scott King Award (Linda Teel, personal communication, November 22, 2010).

These collaborative efforts are designed to illustrate the impact of children's literature and to connect authors and illustrators with preservice teachers, children, and teachers in a university's service region; a goal held in common by many CMC librarians and educators. By working together on this type of project, librarians and faculty develop positive working relationships that will transfer to other initiatives. Moreover, they gain a greater understanding of the roles that librarians and faculty play in the education of preservice teachers.

Once good communication channels and strong working relationships are established between CMC librarians and education faculty, opportunities for CMC instruction will follow. Faculty members are sometimes unaware of the services and resources that librarians can provide and may not understand how to teach information literacy skills. The outreach strategies mentioned above help to educate faculty about the value of the CMC and the role of CMC resources in preservice and graduate-level instruction. These strategies also promote the establishment of rapport and trust between librarians and teaching faculty that, in turn, encourages the development of teaching partnerships.

CMC Instruction for Students—Moving beyond the Library Orientation Tour

These outreach efforts result in a greater willingness on the part of education faculty members to request library instruction sessions. At

ASU the IMC librarians build upon their collegial relationships with education faculty members to become involved in collaborative instruction for both on- and off-campus students. They work continually to familiarize themselves with the teacher preparation curriculum, identify the courses that lend themselves to the inclusion of IMC resources and instruction, and identify technologies that will allow them to deliver this instruction effectively. They also work with faculty members to teach education majors information literacy skills and the use of IMC resources in lesson planning.

Professor Emeritus Pat Farthing began this work during her thirty-nine-year career as Instructional Materials Center Coordinator at ASU. She expanded a small curriculum center into a model PK–12 school library media center that is now a 52,000-volume special collection in the Belk Library and Information Commons. Today the IMC houses a multicultural and international birth-to-12th-grade collection of children's and young adult literature, teaching materials, North Carolina–adopted textbooks, and media. Education databases and other virtual resources expand the collection. These resources are described on the IMC's website (http://www.library.appstate.edu/imc/index.html). Print and nonprint materials are classified using the Dewey Decimal Classification System. The IMC also includes the Idea Factory, a production facility used by preservice teachers and teachers within the ASU service region to create visual aids for course assignments and classroom use. Librarians and staff members are available to assist students with the use of IMC resources. The IMC librarians believe that students need to learn to use this IMC collection and develop the information literacy skills needed to find course-related materials. For the past four decades, they have worked with education faculty to develop instructional opportunities.

One of the librarians' first instructional goals was to introduce the IMC and the IMC librarians to undergraduate education majors. Librarians identified a required introductory course—Curriculum and Instruction 2800: Teachers, Schools, and Learners—and designed a one-hour library session to complement its assignments. They contacted faculty members teaching that class to propose the inclusion of this library session in their course. Initially, several instructors responded positively to this proposal and scheduled a class in the IMC. In this instructional session students took a tour of the IMC and learned how to use the wide variety of materials housed there for lesson planning, textbook evaluation, and research in pedagogy. Students practiced searching the catalog for these resources and locating them on the shelves. Librarians discussed the use of those materials for teaching and introduced the resources included on the IMC website. Throughout the class, librarians stressed that the IMC collection was developed as a model PK–12 library and that they served as each student's "personal education librarian," available to assist with class assignments and research. They also emphasized that they were modeling the collaboration between school media specialists and teachers in a PK–12 setting. The course instructor who was present for the librarian's instructional session reiterated the need for this collaboration.

By the second year most faculty members teaching this introductory class scheduled IMC instructional sessions, and in the third year the IMC orientation was written into the syllabus for the course. At that time the IMC librarians began to participate in the instructors' annual course evaluation meeting. They were able to give the instructors feedback from a student research perspective, sharing the difficulties students had understanding assignments, terms, and research strategies. Over time these evaluation sessions were used to design or clarify assignments, add or revise course material, and expand library instruction content.

In 2009 core courses for the education major at ASU were restructured and CI 2800 was eliminated. When planning the new course sequence, education faculty members approached the IMC librarians and asked them to incorporate basic IMC instruction in an introductory course. Working in conjunction with teaching faculty, IMC librarians designed a research assignment and IMC lesson plan for a one-hour session taught to all students enrolled in Psychology 3010: Psychology Applied to Teaching. This one-hour session included a tour of the IMC, presented an overview of IMC resources, and taught students to locate materials for course assignments. This class was team-taught with education faculty members and was designed to model school media specialist/teacher collaboration in the preparation of a lesson plan. Again, IMC librarians emphasized that they were available to serve as each education major's "personal librarian." This class was taught for the first time in the fall of 2010. Student feedback indicated that they needed and wanted more extensive IMC instruction. Librarians and faculty members responded to this input in the Spring 2011 semester by extending the time allowed for this session and expanding the information literacy component of the lesson plan.

One of the most successful collaborative efforts between IMC librarians and faculty is in a required course for elementary education majors, Reading 3240: World Literature of Children. As IMC librarians worked with faculty members over time, they became embedded librarians in this course, working as co-instructors in the classroom and on the course Moodle site. During each semester they work with faculty members to design course goals and to create or revise reading and research assignments. Additionally, they ensure that the IMC has sufficient resources to support student research and share knowledge of those resources with faculty members. Librarians teach each course section three or four times during the semester to provide customized library instruction for an introductory assignment on the genres of children's literature, an author or illustrator research project, and a multicultural research project. Two Library Guides (LibGuides), RE 3240: Evaluating Literature for Children and RE 3240: World Literature for Children, and information on the IMC's webpage serve as resources for students as they work on these course assignments (Gregor, 2010). Students come to the IMC for scheduled library work sessions where librarians direct and monitor their research. Throughout the course librarians recommend reading selections that reflect the best works in the field of children's literature.

This close interaction with students provides the information that librarians need to give instructors feedback about material that should be reviewed in class and about challenges that students are having with assignments. Students recognize the IMC librarians as embedded instructors in these courses and often ask them questions about course content and assignments. They also feel comfortable requesting assistance with research projects. Since students become familiar with the IMC librarians in this world literature class, they feel comfortable coming to the IMC to study and complete research and assignments for other courses.

The collaborative effort that began with these introductory courses has established the groundwork for the inclusion of IMC instruction in a variety of undergraduate- and graduate-level courses. Early literacy courses, graduate-level children's and young adult literature courses, subject-specific methods courses, and research courses all contain subject matter and assignments that lend themselves to information literacy instruction and instruction in the use of specific IMC resources for classroom teaching. IMC librarians read course syllabi to identify assignments that require IMC support, ensure that adequate print and electronic resources are available for student use, design instructional strategies for teaching the use of those materials, and offer these instructional opportunities to education faculty members. They have found that most course instructors want students to move beyond Google and random Internet searches to locate information needed for class assignments and research. Faculty members respond positively to suggestions for library instruction and in some instances ask librarians to collaborate on course development and to be embedded instructors in their courses.

The excitement that a librarian can convey about including IMC materials in lesson plans and classroom activities is contagious and helps students understand the wide variety of resources available to expand their teaching. Once faculty members become familiar with the IMC librarians' instructional approaches, they are willing to make suggestions for change or to request the addition of information to lesson plan presentations. Likewise, librarians feel comfortable discussing the effectiveness of assignments and sometimes make suggestions for revision. If instructors are not satisfied with the work students submit as finished products, librarians can collaborate to determine how course assignments and the content of the library instruction sessions can be modified. In order to avoid duplication of instructional subject matter across courses, the IMC librarians tailor their presentations to the specific requirements of each course, to the course level, and to individual assignments.

Conclusion

Many CMC librarians realize that the most exemplary library collection cannot make a difference in the education of preservice teachers and graduate students if these students do not know it exists. Even if they realize the collection exists, students will not use it unless they are convinced that it has value. They must be encouraged or required to use these resources by education faculty, who must also come to understand the value and use of CMC resources and the knowledge that CMC librarians possess. In this chapter, we have described a number of efforts that CMC librarians have used successfully to engage education faculty in collaborative and teaching partnerships. These efforts have helped faculty understand how CMC resources and services enhance classroom teaching and contribute to the success of preservice teachers in their coursework and in their professional careers. These examples may be replicated, modified, or expanded within other CMCs to develop relationships between CMC librarians and education faculty, which, in turn, will increase instructional opportunities for education majors.

References

AASL (American Association of School Librarians). 2007. *Standards for the 21st-Century Learner*. Chicago: American Association of School Librarians. Retrieved November 10, 2010, from http://www.ala.org/aasl/guidelinesandstandards/learningstandards/standards.

ACRL (Association of College & Research Libraries). 2009. *Guidelines for Curriculum Materials Centers*. Chicago: Association of College & Research Libraries. Retrieved October 11, 2010, from http://www.ala.org/acrl/standards/guidelinescurriculum.

EBSS Instruction for Educators Committee. 2010, June. *Information Literacy Standards for PK–12 Pre-Service Teachers.* Chicago: Association of College & Research Libraries. Retrieved from http://connect.ala.org/files/39851/ebssstandardsrvsdjune0610_pdf_16275.pdf.

Gregor, Margaret. 2010. RE 3240: Evaluating literature for children. Retrieved from http://guides.library.appstate.edu/childrensliterature.

Gregor, Margaret. 2010. RE 3240: World literature for children. Retrieved from http://guides.library.appstate.edu/WorldLiteratureForChildren.

Hagenbruch, Harriet. 2001. "Outreach and Public Relations in CMCs." In *A Guide to the Management of Curriculum Materials Centers for the 21st Century*, edited by Jo Ann Carr, 137–147. Chicago: American Library Association.

Heider, Kelly L. 2010. "Ten Tips for Implementing a Successful Embedded Librarian Program." *Public Services Quarterly* 6: 110–121. doi:10.1080/15228959.2010.498765.

Kesselman, Martine A., and Sarah Barbara Watstein. 2009. "Creating Opportunities: Embedded Librarians." *Journal of Library Administration* 49 (4): 383–400. doi:10.1080/01930820902832538.

Manus, Sara J. Beutter. 2009. "Librarian in the Classroom: An Embedded Approach to Music Information Literacy for First-Year Undergraduates." *Notes* 66 (2): 249–261.

NCATE (National Council for Accreditation of Teacher Education). 2009. *Professional Standards for the Accreditation of Teacher Preparation Programs.* Washington, DC: National Council for Accreditation of Teacher Education. Retrieved October 11, 2010, from http://www.ncate.org/public/standards.asp (page now discontinued). Retrieved 7/27/2011, from http://www/ncate.org/LinkClick.aspx?filetick et=nX43fwKc4Ak%3d&tabid=474

Shumaker, David. 2009. "Who Let the Librarians Out? Embedded Librarianship and the Library Manager." *Reference & User Services Quarterly* 48 (3): 239–242.

Siess, Judith. 2010. "Embedded Librarianship: The Next Big Thing?" *Searcher* 18 (1): 38–45.

5 Collection Development and Budgets: Methods to Keep the Curriculum Center Current

Nadean Meyer, Eastern Washington University

This chapter explores collection development within allocated resources for the curriculum center. A viable curriculum center contains an assortment of resources for teacher candidates' use, including current versions of standard materials for each subject discipline area and a selection of children's literature in many age levels and genres. The increase in licensed and freely available digital resources creates changes in the resource allocation process and challenges past practices. Partnerships and consortial arrangements may contribute to the changing field of curriculum center collection development. Viewing the collection of resources through a learner-centered perspective is appropriate for the changing PK–12 educational environment and for prioritizing resource needs. While there are additional financial resources within academic libraries and universities, a targeted collaborative approach is essential to secure additional funds in order to meet the needs of the center's users.

Collection development in curriculum centers is a multidimensional process, and the curriculum center director or selector uses knowledge about educational resources and PK–12 practices as well as librarianship skills to effectively acquire quality resources at the best price available. Today's curriculum center continues to need a variety of resources in tangible formats while integrating many resources in digital format into the collection. In order to provide quality resources and services for education students and the faculty who teach those students, the curriculum center director must be flexible and creative in using the funds allocated to the center while seeking additional funds to achieve the primary goal of helping teacher candidates and the PK–12 students they encounter.

Collection development is a core skill in librarianship with many standard resources and methods (Bishop & Van Orden, 2007; Evans & Saponaro, 2005; Hoffman & Wood, 2005; Johnson, 2004). This chapter does not replicate core procedures explained in introductory books or the procedures provided a decade ago for curriculum center budgeting (Tillman, 2001). This chapter turns those core skills into a new framework, the "learner-centered collection" (Hughes-Hassell & Mancall, 2005), which focuses on the need of students learning about education to access a multitude of resources and formats. Because there are always competing demands for funds in the academic library and university, this chapter provides examples of how to make the allocated funds work harder by using techniques to "stretch the dollars." Additionally, seeking funds and support for resources beyond the allocated amount has traditionally occurred through grants and donations, but consortial and collaborative efforts provide resources as well. This chapter focuses on collection development for resource allocation in budget planning in light of current trends. It does not cover funding for personnel or facilities, and the suggestions contained in this chapter may not apply to all situations. Many of the ideas to consider are relevant for today's changing curriculum center environment and have been successful in collection development at the Curriculum Center at Eastern Washington University Libraries.

Mission/Guidelines/Practice

While each curriculum center has a unique mission to serve its particular users and circumstances, there are standards created by practitioners within the Education and Behavioral Sciences Section (EBSS) of the American Library Association (ALA) division of the Association of College and Research Libraries (ACRL). These guidelines provide a starting place for understanding basic fund allocations for curriculum centers. *Guidelines for Curriculum Materials Centers* (ACRL, 2009b) states, "The CMC [curriculum materials center] should have a budget that adequately addresses its needs." This broad statement works as an overarching goal, but today's curriculum center director must turn that goal into tangible actions and resources. Greater detail about the collection is included in the 2007 document *A Guide to Writing CMC Collection Development Policies* (Fabbi, Bressler, & Earp, 2007). This curriculum development policy document lists the typical types of resources and why those resources are important for users. That document states, "Funding level for collection materials should reflect the enrollment of education majors and pre-service teachers in comparison to other majors within the institution" (Fabbi, Bressler, & Earp, 2007, p. 14). This guideline treats the curriculum center users (primarily education majors and teacher candidates) as equal in weight to other students in formulas used to allocate resources for all departments across campus (Canepi, 2007). Whatever process a particular university uses to allocate resources for departments and users, the curriculum center should be part of the allocation beyond academic education materials. As the collection of teaching resources used in PK–12 schools, the center is vital for student learning, but these resources are not typically part of an academic education core collection. Since education philosophy and research are different from practical teaching materials, access to curriculum resources for coursework and field experiences should be unique in the formula or allocation within the academic library's budget in addition to the funds for the education department.

Some methods for allocating funds have been dependent upon peer institutions, number of faculty, number of students enrolled in a department, or history of circulation statistics (Canepi, 2007). These time-honored patterns are being challenged by new examination of the value of academic libraries (Oakleaf, 2010). Not many curriculum centers have calculated their statistics in terms of the whole academic library or have used circulation data as a means to justify additional funds, but this method can be an effective strategy (Canepi, 2007; Hazen, 2010). An inventory project at the Teaching Resources Center at East Carolina University resulted in massive weeding and a five-year plan of increased resource allocations. By the third year, the circulation figures showed that more than 40 percent of the library's total circulation was Teaching Resources Center materials (Teel, 2008, p. 99). After a request about circulation data in relation to funding was posted to the EBSS e-mail discussion group, only one respondent indicated knowledge of a connection between the two figures. The curriculum materials librarian at Chicago State University shared that 24 percent of the library's circulation statistics were for curriculum materials, while she estimated the curriculum center received approximately 1 percent of the total collection budget (B. Meyers, personal communication, April 29, 2010). While there should be connections between the use of library materials and funding, the current trend is to consider how use data such as circulation shows the impact of library resources on student learning and other university goals (Hazen, 2010). The curriculum center librarian needs to participate in discussion about the changes in funding and be knowledgeable about the current practices in the center's institution and others across the country.

Collection development in a curriculum center has always had distinct challenges. The collection development plan needs to guide creation and maintenance of a relevant and current collection. The resources need to be appropriate for the teacher candidates' class assignments or for field experiences in nearby schools. Teacher candidates need to see and use teaching materials found in today's schools (Dickerson, Cogdell & Gavigan, 2004). A curriculum center may resemble a school library media center by including items usually found in that setting. Consequently, the items purchased for teacher preparation for PK–12 schools may not fit typical academic purchase plans, vendors, or review journals such as *Choice*. The lack of conformity to the bulk of the academic library ordering causes more individual time in ordering and sometimes use of small vendors. On the other side, the vendors unique to the curriculum center are unaware of the ordering process of university purchasing; this may cause misunderstanding on either side of the ordering process. Collaboration with the acquisitions unit of the academic library is vital in order to understand the limitations and parameters of ordering, particularly when trying new sources and formats.

Learner-Centered Collection Development

Learner-centered collection development is an outgrowth of changing perspective in education to emphasize the learner. The philosophy as applied to school library media centers is summarized by Sandra Hughes-Hassell and Jacqueline C. Mancall in their book *Collection Management for Youth: Responding to the Needs of Learners* (2005). The philosophy, explanations, and tools for implementation evolved from the DeWitt Wallace-Reader's Digest Fund National Library Power Project of seven hundred schools (Hughes-Hassell & Mancall, 2005, p. xiii). The authors argue that school library media specialists (and in our case, curriculum center directors) "must re-imagine their collection management role, becoming *learner-centered managers* who act as change agents, leaders, learners, and resources guides.... We envision learner-centered collection managers working collaboratively and building on educational theory and practice to create policy, negotiate budgets, and select resources and access points that enable student learning" (p. xi). This framework of collection development and allocating resources fits within the larger goal of helping students learn. A learner-centered collection evaluates learner characteristics in terms of information storage and information dissemination. The selector or collector of resources in a learner-centered collection serves as a guide for the learner (in terms of curriculum centers, the teacher candidates) "to offer subject and learner-specific advice, expanding the potential utility of materials and information the learner encounters" (p. 8). The knowledgeable center selector knows how the materials purchased will be used for student learning. Research from the faculty viewpoint is rare about how teacher candidates are using curriculum resources. An intensive study about the use of science standards, pedagogy, and curriculum materials blends the analysis of all three factors for assessing student learning (Krajcik, McNeill, & Reiser, 2008). This is an area that needs further scholarship and action research by curriculum directors in collaboration with education faculty in order to truly provide a learner-centered collection.

Snapshot of Current Practices in Curriculum Centers' Allocations

The EBSS conducts surveys every few years to gather data about collections of current curriculum centers. In the latest survey, e-mail discussion lists, government statistics, and lists of previous curriculum centers identified nearly one thousand institutions with curriculum centers. Then voluntary surveys were dispersed in the spring of 2007, with directors and staff of 204 curriculum centers participating (ACRL, 2009a, p. 1). However, only 127, or 62 percent, of respondents gave detailed information requested, such as information on collection budget, collection development, collection statistics, and circulation data. These 127 centers provide a snapshot of curriculum centers in North America across public and private universities, from small to large institutions. From the survey responses, we can observe some current trends about budget and collection development. The questions range from number of databases to number of items in the collection by format. The budget questions are less precise but still provide valuable information. The

Figure 5.1. Number of curriculum centers: range of annual budget and in-kind value (ACRL, 2009a)

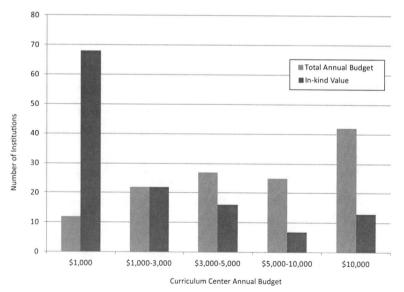

percentage of the budget received from the institutions (either academic library or department of education) ranges from 10 percent to 100 percent. The amount of the budget is more difficult to compare because of factors such as the size of the institution and the number of education students, but survey results spread from less than $100 to over $10,000. Figure 5.1 shows the broad budget ranges and number of institutions receiving certain amounts. One set of bars represents the budget amount received, and the second set is for the amount received in-kind.

While *in-kind* is not clearly defined, it presumably refers to books and other resources given to the center. According to this data, the prime source of funds for curriculum centers is the academic library budget, but four centers receive over 50 percent of their funding from donations, and many centers list gifts, library fines, or donations as significant sources of funding. These statistics reveal that most centers receive funding within the institution's budget, although a few are equally dependent upon in-kind contributions. Forty-five of the centers (35 percent) are textbook review centers for their state or region. As such, these curriculum centers receive recent textbooks from publishers to show to their students and faculty while also making them available to area schools. The data from across North America provides a benchmark when evaluating your own situation for resources and provides assistance in identifying peer institutions.

Countries beyond North America also have curriculum centers, and information from these centers may prove valuable as well. Rae-Anne Locke (2007) surveyed thirty curriculum collections in Australia, although respondents agreed that specific budget information would not be published, "Budgets varied significantly, ranging from $5000 to hundreds of thousands of dollars [Australian] per annum for serials and monographs" (p. 197). Information about weeding was also shared, with 60 percent (18 out of 30) weeding every three to five years. In comparison, the EBSS survey asked if the center had been weeded in the past ten years, and 89 percent indicated that the center had been weeded. While the number of years between deselections may vary, most centers need to deselect older materials on a regular basis. This has implications for the budget for replacements as well as for operations.

Collection Development within a Budget

The extent of information resources available for use in PK–12 education at times seems limitless, and libraries can be viewed as repositories with a constant wish list for more materials (Hazen, 2010). Developing processes for cost savings helps the curriculum center obtain more materials with its allocation. One of the first cost-saving methods is discounts. Vendors offer discounts, and the academic library acquisition department can assist the curriculum center director in providing access to the best vendors for the types of materials the center needs, often vendors for public and school libraries. Some vendors offer approval plans and clearance discounts of extra copies. Among these are Scholastic book fair warehouse sales or books sales by Junior Library Guild, Bound to Stay Bound, and other companies that purchase and often rebind publishers' copies of books. It is useful to know the sales' time of the year and to mark the calendar to fit within the academic purchasing cycle.

Streamlining procedures is a second cost-saving method. Four out of thirty, or 13 percent, of Australian curriculum collections use approval plans (Locke, 2007, p. 197). One example available to curriculum centers is Junior Library Guild (http://www.juniorlibraryguild.com). For an annual fee, this plan offers a broad spectrum of current children's and young adult literature delivered monthly in requested age ranges and genres. These plans streamline the acquisition process.

Review Books and Publisher's Copies

Many of the materials found in today's curriculum centers are part of a publishing cycle that uses review copies. Librarians who attend the annual ALA conventions, book trade conventions, or specialty conventions such as the Young Adult Library Services Association (YALSA) Literature Symposium or the workshop of the Assembly on Literature for Adolescents (ALAN—a membership group of the National Council of Teachers of English) know that they will bring home boxes of books from the publishers. The ALAN workshop, held in conjunction with NCTE's annual convention, features at least forty young adult authors, both new to the field and well established. Each workshop participant receives a box of the authors' books at registration. This is a windfall for the curriculum collection. Review copies are also sent to some children's literature professors as well as some larger public or school libraries. Some areas of the country share their copies in a reading council where books are given to particular libraries or to the library of the person who writes a review of the book. There are at least four councils in Washington State that share review copies. The Curriculum Center at EWU participates in the Eastern Washington Book Review Council by reviewing approximately 150 books annually; these titles are then added to the collection. The curriculum center staff may also cooperate with a children's literature professor so that review copies that he or she receives can be added to the curriculum center collection.

School textbook publishers have a quickly rotating stock, and area representatives try to maintain only the newest copies after each school year. Eastern Washington University has received generous donations of superseded textbooks by e-mailing our area representative and by collaborating with the university reading instructor, who contacts the representative for copies to add to the Curriculum Center. Faculty who attend their state and national conventions may bring back free samples or information on requesting sample copies. Arrangements with our nearest school districts result in the Curriculum Center receiving review copies sent for textbook adoptions after the school district's curriculum committee chooses the textbook series. The EWU Curriculum Center has received a large assortment of textbooks in this manner in order to provide a second published textbook series in a particular subject for comparison, as recommended in many assignments in education classes. While review copies cannot provide the entire textbook collection needed for a curriculum center, they can complement the core selections and provide different philosophies in teaching practice. Since free textbooks may be infrequently available unless a center is a textbook review center, a targeted approach and personal connections including e-mail requests may be necessary to obtain these valuable teaching resources.

Uniqueness of Resources: Children's and Young Adult Literature

Assembling a children's literature collection for infancy through high school requires a wide knowledge of choices in the literature. While classic titles are expected in an academic library, it is imperative to acquire current popular and distinguished books as well. It is this currency that affects the budget. While it usual for an academic collection to have annual Newbery and Caldecott winners, there is now a plethora of distinguished book awards, all worthy of inclusion in a modern curriculum collection. Some are age-specific (Michael L. Printz), some are cultural representations (Pura Belpré and Coretta Scott King), and some are format-specific (Odyssey and Theodor Seuss Geisel). The official announcements at ALA have grown to include nineteen award winners and multiple honor books or lists (ALA, 2010). Acquiring these titles on an annual basis means a certain amount, often over $600, of the allocation must be set aside for this purpose.

The emergence of awards determined by the votes of child readers adds the element of popularity and child interest to collecting titles. At the national level, the International Reading Association and Children's Book Council annually produce a list of approximately one hundred titles chosen by children as the best of each year (International, 2010). Most states (49 out of 50) have developed at least one award selected by various age groups (Smith, 2010). The importance of these awards for teacher candidates was reinforced when the National Council for Accreditation of Teacher Education (NCATE) site inspectors asked at the Eastern Washington University library interview if the curriculum center was purchasing the child-selected winners of the state's awards (a total of five winners per year). While NCATE's question indicates that including child-selected awards winners is important within teacher education, academic libraries tend to buy them less frequently. A title check in the Orbis Cascade Consortium shared catalog of thirty-four academic libraries one year after award announcements shows the disparity between child-selected and distinguished award winners in academic library collections. Comparing the academic library ownership of books winning three 2010 ALA primary-age awards (Caldecott: 76 percent; Newbery: 80 percent; Printz: 47 percent) with books winning the regional 2010 Pacific Northwest Children's Choice Award (junior: 38 percent; intermediate: 18 percent; high: 0 percent) offers the closest comparison for age levels and the children's-choice books that applies for the entire region. Figure 5.2 lists the 2010 awards and shows the number of academic libraries that owned the title winning each award one year after announcements of the distinguished awards and nine months after announcements of the child-selected awards.

Comparing ownership of the same titles by different institutions has implications for the cooperative use of resources as well as for decisions about which children's literature to purchase. Cooperative planning for the use of curriculum center resources across partner institu-

Figure 5.2. Number of academic libraries in Orbis Cascade Consortium that own books that won 2010 distinguished and child-selected awards

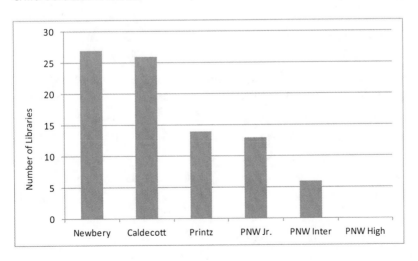

tions affects the type of resources considered (Atkinson, 2004; Kohl & Sanville, 2006).

Uniqueness of Resources: Textbooks and Teaching Materials

All teacher candidates need both textbooks and accompanying teacher's materials used in the PK–12 schools where education students will do their field placements. It is helpful to examine the student edition as well as the teacher's edition when planning and implementing sample lessons, although if cost savings must be made, most teacher editions have the student page within the teacher's edition. Today's textbooks also include supplemental material (often on CDs) of tests, transparencies, and posters. Additional materials offered to student of diverse backgrounds may include connections to home study, English as a second language (ESL), and other enrichment materials. These extra resources show an awareness of the need to customize materials for a range of students. The area of differentiating and adapting core materials to diverse learners is part of the teacher education program. It is imperative that teacher candidates see textbooks used in their areas of field placement and at least a couple of alternatives. If the subject discipline is in flux or presents contradictory theories of teaching, this is even more important. Students should be able to "read" a scope and sequence chart for a textbook series and compare the practice displayed in the textbooks with the theory they are learning in their education classes. Textbooks are updated annually, with major revisions every five to seven years. This publishing cycle has enormous budget implications for a curriculum center. In Washington State, the Office of Superintendent of Public Instructions (OSPI) adopted recommendations of three sets of math textbooks that meet the state standards in each of the grade spans K–3, 4–6, 7–8, and 9–10 (OSPI, 2010a). These textbooks and supplements are expensive. For example, the price of one grade level of one new mathematics series is $333 ($78 for each of the two volumes of the teacher's edition, $21 for the student edition, and $156 for the basic teacher package). If the supplemental materials were purchased (including CD-ROMs of tests, chapter worksheets, and more), the total would be $852. Few budgets can support a complete series for every grade, K–12, and then more than one textbook series as well. Financial concerns may mean that textbook series are not complete or that only the teacher's edition is purchased. Decisions must be made for acquiring reading, science, health, music, and other subject textbooks as well. Perhaps e-textbooks will offer a new model for access, but experiments both in K–12 and higher education with e-textbooks are just starting, and we need more trials and data about the results before committing resources.

Standards and Teacher Guides

Most national and state standards are available online (McREL, 2010; OSPI, 2010b). However, many library users expect shelf access to standards as well. Eastern Washington University licensed a commercial online source for many standards and other curriculum resources until we discovered our state did not allow inclusion of Washington State materials in the database since it is proprietary. We now manually add the Web source to our catalog and produce a research guide with current links to the state and national standards for all certification disciplines (http://research.ewu.edu/education, tab Standards). It is more time- and resource-consuming to make and maintain current paper copies, but to meet highest demand by our users, we print and paper bind some documents. The core curriculum initiative (Common Core State Standards Initiative, 2010) may reduce the number of standards on the national level, but in Washington State, local decisions of individual school boards are the cherished rule of practice, and it is necessary to keep local, state, and national standards for our students to have the materials they need in the classrooms.

Teaching materials come from many sources and publishers. One list shared on the EBSS e-mail discussion list presented 160 unique publishers (Lear, 2009). Each transaction takes time and money in the preparation of ordering. But these items enrich the collection with viewpoint and perspective. Using this list has resulted in acquisition of unique and valuable items about adoption, mental illness, cultural diversity, and other topics not always found in the mainstream textbooks and children's literature.

Funding within Academic Libraries and the University

Academic libraries have some flexibility within the allocation of funds, although flexibility is decreasing because licensing electronic products requires a large percentage of the collections budget (Hazen, 2010). Various approaches to collection budgeting are used, though most academic libraries try to determine value within the university's mission (Oakleaf, 2010). Different types of formulas have been applied over the years, and the curriculum center director must understand the resource allocation method of the particular institution before asking for additional resources. Many funding cycles have deadlines, and allocated funds that have not been expended for a variety of reasons (changes in departments, new licensing agreements, different discounts, and more) may be available for other purposes at the end of the fiscal year. The library at Saint Xavier University in Chicago shared its overall evaluation of collection development in a recent article. The approach was a holistic curriculum approach that produced an efficient and transparent budget aligned with the strategic planning process (Kusik & Vargas, 2009). The curriculum center can adapt many of its conclusions in its own collection planning. Within the academic library budget, a targeted approach for particular materials tied to the university's curriculum is often welcomed, and a list prepared ahead is often ordered near the end of the fiscal year. At the Curriculum Center at EWU, we have been able to start and expand collections in graphic novels and audiobooks through advance preparation in anticipation of end-of-year funds. The account containing collected library fines may be a source of funds for replacement of worn or lost copies. A selected list of core materials needing replacement can be prepared in advance to enable the curriculum center to participate in the replacement cycle of these titles.

Most universities have a procedure for adopting new classes and programs or for major revisions of classes. The library is frequently part of this process to show what resources are already available or to support requests for additional library funding to enhance collections for the program. At Eastern Washington University, when the provost provided one-time library funding for new programs, it was possible to explain that new teaching certificates and changes in education standards were equivalent to new programs, justifying use of these funds to support new purchases. This resulted in collaboration with the faculty of the new certificate programs and was very beneficial in terms of acquiring current materials on the topics of environmental sustainability and heritage language learning, along with materials to support a new integrated math and science teaching certificate.

Many universities have discretionary, competitive funding for particular programs in support of the university's mission. Cooperation in this type of grant may result in additional resources for the curriculum center. At Eastern Washington University, one such program provides summer research grants for faculty. A collaboration of the curriculum center librarian with an education faculty member in literacy resulted in additional books for a sixth grade classroom for the study of children's literature authors' memoirs. As an advisor to the grant, the curriculum center librarian created two bibliographies, one of all known children's authors' memoirs and one of appropriate and interesting examples of memoirs for sixth graders' use.

Diversity is an important foundation value for many universities, including Eastern. There are minigrants to increase cultural diversity in programs, teaching, events, and projects. The EWU Curriculum Center received a minigrant to preload youth audiobooks onto iPod Shuffles. The books were selected for three age levels: early elementary, older elementary, and young adult. The authors and content were selected from some of the best Asian American, American Indian, African American, and Latino or Latina authors. This grant allowed the center to try a new format (audiobook) and a new technology (preloaded iPod Shuffles) while still promoting the basic mission of the center and the university. This type of grant and internal funding allow for experimentation with fledging ideas. While grants take time to create and monitor, the information is valuable for creating connections across campus with faculty partners. In terms of larger grants, many universities have a formula for distributing grant overhead funds, with a small part of that percentage designated for the library. While this percentage may not be targeted to library resources, funds may be applied to library overhead. The idea of including teaching materials in successful teaching grants could extend beyond cooperating K–12 classrooms into the curriculum center for additional resources.

Web Materials and Electronic Resources

The field of Web and electronic resources is rapidly changing. While this chapter was being written, Google Books was announced, promising to add to the availability of e-books, particularly since Google Books is tied to the computing cloud rather than to a proprietary electronic book reader. Public domain copies of works of children's literature have been around for decades. The complete versions of classics such as Beatrix Potter's titles, Grimm's fairy tales, and others published prior to the 1930s are available. Free copies can be added to the library's catalog, or Web guides can point to Web portals such as Project Gutenberg, the University of Virginia's e-texts, or the Library of Congress. One of the most comprehensive additions to children's e-books is the International Children's Digital Library: A Library for the World's Children (http://en.childrenslibrary.org). This free electronic book collection brings together thousands of historical and contemporary children's books from around the world in multiple languages. It is the premier place to find samples of what children are reading in other countries and cultures. Since it was designed with children in mind and uses innovative technology, it is much more than a scanned copy of a book, allowing translations, book-like flipping of pages, and entire color copies of illustrated picture books. Even some copyrighted books have been added with permission. Though it may not be possible to individually add these titles to the standard library catalog, every education student using the curriculum center needs to be aware of this resource for children's literature, teaching, and global understanding. At EWU, demonstrations of this resource are included in many instruction sessions, large posters are displayed in the curriculum center, and brochures are distributed to share this important free resource. Other creators are experimenting with electronic versions of books. It is not uncommon for new graphic novel writers to offer their books as a free download, as Cory Doctorow did when he turned his futuristic tales into graphic novels (Doctorow, 2008). There are other projects that are also worthy of this time and attention. Curriculum centers need more sharing of innovative methods to integrate digital and standard physical resources.

Government organizations offer some children's books in downloadable form, and many departments offer downloadable teaching materials. An entire Web portal called FREE (Federal Resources for Educational Excellence, http://www.free.ed.gov) offers free government teaching materials that can be found by browsing or subject and keyword searching. Because of the sheer amount, valuable free material is hard to discover, so the challenge is how to incorporate examples of these rich resources into the curriculum center. Cooperation with the government documents librarian or electronic resources librarian can provide streamlined and standardized methods. More examples in the literature and at conferences would be beneficial to curriculum centers. In terms of children's literature, the Cooperative Children's Book Center at University of Wisconsin–Madison (http://www.education.wisc.edu/ccbc) provides, easily accessible on its website, innovative, useful, and current information pertinent to children's literature and its use with children and schools. Nonprofit groups are another source. A prime example is the Teaching Tolerance project (http://teachingtolerance.org) of the Southern Poverty Law Center (http://www.splcenter.org), which offers a complimentary monthly magazine, quality videos, curriculum (free to educational institutions and teachers), and Web resources concerning culturally responsive teaching and educational equity.

Many resources are available electronically, but must be licensed or purchased. One of the products we have experimented with at Eastern Washington University is TeachingBooks.net with many original author interviews. The links to the original author interviews are now catalogued in the library catalog, so when someone is searching for a children's literature author or illustrator, the video interview contained within TeachingBooks.net is in the search results. It is valuable to start connecting the databases with catalog access. WorldCat Local is our current method of displaying the collection; WorldCat's interfiling of all formats of content including articles from databases (OCLC, 2010) may promise increased standard access to all materials, digital or physical. Another recent addition for our academic library and curriculum center is downloadable audiobooks from NetLibrary. Again the youth collection and ten monthly new additions have complete records in the library catalog as well as within the NetLibrary database's search interface.

We have also tried converting some standard children's literature reference sources into e-reference books. Not only does this allow for off-campus access, but it also allows simultaneous users. The H. W. Wilson's Core Collection recently combined its reference works identifying standard collections for elementary, junior high, and high school into one electronic database. This type of digital access adds a feature that many librarians have wanted for years: the entries in the database are linked to the library's catalog, and the user can quickly check to see of the library owns a copy of the book. This connects the collection to the information in the reference database in ways that education students need. We have this feature linking database and library collection on two additional databases about children's literature: NoveList K–8 and Children's Literature Comprehensive Database. Demonstrating this feature during instruction sessions helps teacher candidates learn effective methods to find and physically retrieve the resources they need. Other standard children's literature references are available electronically, including Something about the Author Online and Children's Literature Review. In these two resources, each entry is available as a PDF document to be viewed, printed, or downloaded. The one-time fee for this product was substantial, so after the first conversion to electronic format, the cost is negligible with a similar annual update fee for either print or electronic version. The comprehensive search interface is more user-friendly than the multivolume printed versions, and the digital format allows for off-campus and simultaneous use. The conversion of standard print sources to digital should be learner-centered, with the electronic version offering features of better access and being evaluated for enhanced value.

There is an increase in online resources for classrooms with unique K–12 databases: ProQuest's CultureGrams, eLibrary, and World Conflicts Today; EBSCO's NoveList K–8, Searchasaurus, Primary Search, and Animals; World Book Online; Discovery Education streaming video; and many more. If our teacher candidates are to be prepared to use these resources in their class assignments, field experiences, and future classrooms, there needs to be licensed access for simultaneous users and the ability to use these sources on-site within their teaching experiences. Vendors currently market to the K–12 community or academic libraries with different pricing models and often different divisions within sales and promotion, making it more difficult for curriculum centers to select PK–12 databases. If an academic library wishes to provide access for its education students, the pricing may be based on the institution's total student enrollment or restrictive methods to prove the user is an education student imposed, making make access difficult. Licensing is an area of change as institutions develop new methods of gaining access. Some states already have database licensing agreements for all types of libraries (e.g., Ohio, Florida, and Maryland). In the *Directory of Curriculum Materials Centers* (ACRL, 2009a), only two centers (North Carolina and Connecticut) mentioned state consortia as their source of databases. In Washington State, the state-supported academic libraries have separate agreements from the Statewide Databases Licensing Project that serve the school and public library community. Individual discussion with vendors' representatives should start new models for all curriculum centers. The advantages of digital cooperation have been stated before, and they remain a good way to cooperate (Atkinson, 2004). At the Curriculum Center at EWU, we have been able to negotiate a reduced fee for World Book Online and Discovery Education streaming video without sacrificing easy access within our academic database listings. EBSCO provides a majority of our major academic databases, so we have been able to request and receive complimentary access to the

K–12 databases because of our licensing of so many other resources.

Since academic library resource acquisition in general is shifting to electronic resources, it is imperative that the curriculum center include databases designed for PK–12 students within this evolving environment in a cost-effective manner. The sixth edition of the *Directory of Curriculum Materials Centers* (ACRL, 2009a) lists reported databases, ranging from one to twenty databases, for 94 percent of the curriculum centers (119 out of 127 centers). A closer examination indicates all types of databases from general articles (ProQuest Research Library), to specific education databases (Education Research Complete), to specific tests (Mental Measurements Yearbook) that are useful for education students and faculty. There are also specific curriculum databases like Kraus Curriculum Development Library or children's literature value-added databases like Children's Literature Comprehensive Database.

Figure 5.3. Number of total databases and PK–12 databases for in curriculum centers (ACRL, 2009a)

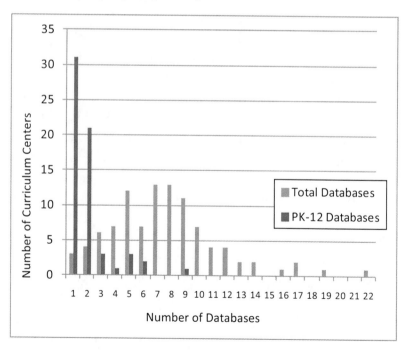

Only three electronic databases specifically designed for schools—Discovery Education streaming video (formerly Unitedstreaming), NoveList K–8, and LearningExpress Library—were listed on the original survey checklist; all other PK–12 databases were reported under the category Other and had to be named by the respondents (ACRL, 2009a, p. 143). Figure 5.3 shows the reported data in two categories: all databases listed (whether general or specific to education or children's literature) and PK–12 databases.

The difference between all databases and specific PK–12 databases indicates means to acquire those databases. Eastern Washington University, for example, has five specific PK–12 databases, ten interfaces to World Book Online (four age levels, three language levels, and three speciality encyclopedias), and NetLibrary with a section for children's literature and young adults books (http://research.ewu.edu/students). There are also four specific education databases beyond general databases that include articles of interest to education students. Frequently education databases are part of consortium agreements or larger licensing agreements, and some states have statewide agreements for all types of libraries. Acquiring PK–12 databases without a consortium may require negotiations and seeking resources, one at a time, for the curriculum center's users' access.

Integrating websites into the collection is a greater challenge. The 2007 survey of Australian curriculum collections showed that sixteen, or 53 percent, "did not include Web sites within the scope of their curriculum collections" (Locke, 2007, p. 196). Over a decade ago, Patricia O'Brien Libutti wrote a chapter about maintaining a curriculum center virtual collection (Libutti, 2001) for *A Guide to the Management of Curriculum Materials Center for the 21st Century* (Carr, 2001). This standard work has assisted many curriculum directors since its publication. Libutti noted the paradox of learning the technology and the resources simultaneously and the challenges of obtaining, promoting, and integrating Web resources with faculty's assignments: "The existence of such factors indicates that a cycle of planning for collection needs to be rapid with planning, actual practice, and review of practice being continuous (Libutti, 2001, p. 88). Increase in academic libraries' use of Springshare's LibGuides (Leeder & Cordova, 2010) has increased a common expectation for guides to digital resources with a template that offers individualization and emerging technologies. An additional benefit of this type of product is the readily available use statistics and link checker that provide easier management and analysis of use of the guides. Libutti listed four curriculum centers with exemplary virtual collection tools, and she suggested that, collaboratively within EBSS or through use of PK–12 portals, each curriculum center could provide quality, timely resources. One major educational portal is Thinkfinity (http://thinkfinity.org), provided by the Verizon Foundation, with ten content providers (including professional teaching organizations) and six affiliates (in education and technology). Rather than linking to each content area and organization, this model interface provides advanced searching ability and offers perspectives for students, parents, and educators. It is a vital free source for education students. While portals provide these added features, it has been difficult to offer multiple points of subject access to the content within the traditional library catalog or the new products such as LibGuides.

Keeping the Vision and Finding the Funds with Partnerships

Keeping a curriculum center relevant for teaching candidates and the faculty who teach them is a daunting task in an evolving educational climate. Forming partnerships provides background knowledge and more resources to achieve the goals of the curriculum center. The education faculty and faculty from other departments across campus who use the curriculum center resources are key people. The librarian should know their research interests, their contacts with area schools, and the service they perform for the PK–12 community. In this manner curriculum directors can leverage some funds. For example an elementary science faculty member recently proposed alternative energy science kits. He needs the best accurate elementary science books, kits, and teaching materials for his preparation of students, a grant proposal, and his K–12 partners.

The EWU Curriculum Center was able to purchase highly recommended sources for his students and partners to evaluate, and then when the same faculty member writes his next grant, he can augment the center's resources with funding written in the grant. The collection development and resources become a cycle of finding the best, telling others, and purchasing more quality resources as the topic expands.

Frequently state library personnel collaborate with all types of libraries, with an umbrella approach positioning curriculum centers as a bridge between PK–12 and academic libraries. The work of EWU's Curriculum Center with our state library has resulted in the Statewide Databases Licensing Project supporting the use of PK–12 databases for teacher candidates at academic institutions and suggesting the wording for the licensing agreement. The state youth librarian has provided resources and workshops for early childhood education, tribal sovereignty resources, and collaborative grants between public libraries and schools that feature new classroom research for students in social studies. These collaborative efforts share resources to assist teacher candidates. On the education side in Washington State, there are Education Service Districts that serve multiple school districts. Together these districts form a cooperative for technology purchasing that has been available to the university and thus the curriculum center. This cooperative agreement provided reduced rates for our purchase of presentation equipment (a Smart Board installed in a group study room and projector) with a moveable cart. The cooperative also provided reduced pricing for a digital microscope and sources for assistive technology devices.

Curriculum center directors as a network can collaboratively assist each other through the Education Librarian's Toolbox (ACRL, 2011) and the EBSS e-mail discussion list, where common collection questions and possible answers are shared. This community is valuable for new and practiced curriculum center directors, allowing sharing of information such as pertinent vendor lists (Lear, 2009).

Collection Development for Curriculum Centers

Curriculum center directors who re-evaluate the collection development process should consider the issues of resource allocation, consortium, collaboration, and streamlining procedures. The learner-centered approach is a valuable perspective for new ideas about the value of the curriculum collection in the academic library and university. The network of EBSS librarians provides a practical approach to how similar centers are approaching common problems, and cooperative agreements with consortial partners, local school districts, and state libraries are a method to expand resources.

Each center director should be informed about the center's resource allocation budget and its place within the academic library while practicing efficiencies and using discounts. The acquisitions unit of the library is a partner in this process. Other partners are education faculty and other faculty using the curriculum center resources. Action research and scholarship about how the physical and digital resources are used for teacher candidates' learning are important for acquiring the right materials and valuable to share with the entire field of education librarianship. The need to constantly acquire and weed materials makes the curriculum center a vital information location, and it should continue into the virtual world with the use of PK–12 databases, education content portals, and e-books in children's literature. These new challenges in the curriculum center collection development will provide current and future teacher candidates with resources for their teaching career.

References

ACRL (Association of College & Research Libraries). 2011. "Education Librarian's Toolbox." Retrieved from http://wikis.ala.org/acrl/index.php/Education_Librarian's_Toolbox.

———. 2009a. *Directory of Curriculum Materials Centers*, 6th ed. Chicago: American Library Association.

———. 2009b. *Guidelines for Curriculum Materials Centers*. Chicago: Association of College & Research Libraries. Retrieved from http://www.ala.org/acrl/standards/guidelinescurriculum.

ALA (American Library Association). 2010. "Youth Media Awards Fact Sheet." Retrieved from http://www.ala.org/ala/aboutala/offices/pio/mediarelationsa/factsheets/youthmediaawards.cfm.

Atkinson, Ross. 2004. "Uses and Abuses of Cooperation in a Digital Age." *Collection*

Management 28 (1): 3–20. doi:10.1300/J105v28n01_01.

Bishop, Kay, and Phyllis J. Van Orden. 2007. *The Collection Program in Schools: Concepts, Practices, and Information Sources*. Library and Information Science Text Series. Westport, CT: Libraries Unlimited.

Canepi, Kitti. 2007. "Fund Allocation Formula Analysis: Determining Elements for Best Practices in Libraries." *Library Collections, Acquisitions, and Technical Services* 31 (1): 12–24. doi:10.1016/j.lcats.2007.03.002.

Carr, Jo Ann, ed. 2001. *A Guide to the Management of Curriculum Materials Centers for the 21st Century: The Promise and the Challenge*. Chicago: American Library Association.

Common Core State Standards Initiative. 2010. "Common Core State Standards." Retrieved from http://www.corestandards.org.

Dickinson, Gail, E. A. Cogdell, and Karen W. Gavigan. 2004. "Transitioning from Curriculum Materials Center to School Library Media Center for Pre-service Teacher Education." *Education Libraries* 27 (1): 11–15.

Doctorow, Cory. 2008. *Futuristic Tales of the Here and Now*. Retrieved from http://www.archive.org/details/CoryDoctorowsFuturisticTalesOfTheHereAndNow.

Evans, G. Edward, and Margaret Zamosky Saponaro. 2005. *Developing Library and Information Center Collections*, 5th ed. Library and Information Science Text Series. Westport, CT: Libraries Unlimited.

Fabbi, Jennifer, Darla Bressler, and Vanessa Earp. 2007. *A Guide to Writing CMC Collection Development Policies*. Chicago: Association of College & Research Libraries. Retrieved from http://www.ala.org/ala/mgrps/divs/acrl/aboutacrl/directoryofleadership/sections/ebss/ebsswebsite/ebsscommittees/curriculummaterials/guidetowritingcmc.pdf.

Hazen, Dan C. 2010. "Rethinking Research Library Collections: A Policy Framework for Straitened Times and Beyond." *Library Resources & Technical Services* 54 (2): 115–121.

Hoffmann, Frank W., and Richard J. Wood. 2005. *Library Collection Development Policies: Academic, Public, and Special Libraries*. Good Policy, Good Practice, no. 1. Lanham, MD: Scarecrow Press.

Hughes-Hassell, Sandra, and Jacqueline C. Mancall. 2005. *Collection Management for Youth: Responding to the Needs of Learners*. Chicago: American Library Association.

International Reading Association. 2010. "Choices Reading Lists." Retrieved from http://www.reading.org/resources/booklists.aspx.

Johnson, Peggy. 2004. *Fundamentals of Collection Development and Management*. Chicago: American Library Association.

Kohl, David F., and Tom Sanville. 2006. "More Bang for the Buck: Increasing the Effectiveness of Library Expenditures through Cooperation." *Library Trends* 54 (3): 394–410.

Krajcik, Joseph, Katherine L. McNeill, and Brian J. Reiser. 2008. "Learning-Goals-Driven Design Model: Developing Curriculum Materials That Align with National Standards and Incorporate Project-Based Pedagogy." *Science Education* 92 (1): 1–31. doi:10.1002/sce.20240.

Kusik, James P., and Mark A. Vargas. 2009. "Implementing a 'Holistic' Approach to Collection Development." *Library Leadership & Management* 23 (4): 186–192.

Lear, Bernadette A. 2009, November 24. "Re: List of Education Publishers" [Msg. 000386]. Message posted to http://listserv.uncc.edu/archives/ebss-l.html.

Leeder, Kim, and Memo Cordova. 2010. "Digital Advocacy: Using Interactive Technologies to Reassert Library Value." In *Advocacy, Outreach, and the Nation's Academic Libraries: A Call for Action,* edited by William C. Welburn, Janice Welburn, and Beth McNeil, 124–144. Chicago: Association of College & Research Libraries.

Libutti, Patricia O'Brien. 2001. "Management Tools for Maintaining a CMC Virtual Collection." In *A Guide to the Management of Curriculum Materials Centers for the 21st Century: The Promise and the Challenge,* edited by Jo Ann Carr, 81–100. Chicago: American Library Association.

Locke, Rae-Anne. 2007. "More Than Puppets: Curriculum Collections in Australian Universities." *Australian Academic & Research Libraries* 38 (3): 192–215.

McREL (Mid-Continent Research for Education and Learning). 2010. *Content Knowledge: A Compendium of Content Standards and Benchmarks.* Retrieved from http://www.mcrel.org/standards-benchmarks.

Oakleaf, Megan. 2010. *The Value of Academic Libraries: A Comprehensive Research Review and Report.* Chicago: Association of College & Research Libraries. Retrieved from http://acrl.ala.org/value.

OCLC (Online Computer Library Center). 2010. "WorldCat Local: Lists of Content Included." Retrieved from http://www.oclc.org/worldcatlocal/overview/content.

OSPI (Office of Superintendent of Public Instruction). 2010a. "Teaching and Learning: Instructional Materials." Retrieved from http://k12.wa.us/CurriculumInstruct/InstructionalMaterialsReview.aspx.

———. 2010b. "Washington State Learning Standards." Retrieved from http://k12.wa.us/CurriculumInstruct/EALR_GLE.aspx.

Smith, Cynthia Leitich. 2010. "State Awards for Children's and Young Adult Books." Cynthia Leitich Smith website. Retrieved from http://www.cynthialeitichsmith.com/lit_resources/awards/stateawards.html.

Teel, Linda M. 2008. "Applying the Basics to Improve the Collection." *Collection Building* 27 (3): 96–103. doi:10.1108/01604950810885997.

Tillman, Mike. 2001. "Curriculum Materials Centers Budget." In *A Guide to the Management of Curriculum Materials Centers for the 21st Century: The Promise and the Challenge,* edited by Jo Ann Carr, 25–33. Chicago: American Library Association.

6 Staffing the CMC for Success

Linda M. Teel, East Carolina University

Librarians, paraprofessionals, and student workers employed in the curriculum materials center (CMC) require specialized skills to assist preservice and in-service teachers and faculty. As technology continues to drive changes in services, CMC staffing plays a vital role in delivering new technology-driven services while maintaining traditional ones. This chapter discusses the development of a CMC staff whose members possess unique skills necessary to deliver services successfully based upon the following factors: determining staffing needs, reviewing existing staffing patterns, creating new job descriptions and competencies for future services, developing a long-range staffing plan, hiring technology- and team-driven staff, retaining staff, utilizing performance evaluation as an effective staffing tool, and valuing the CMC staff.

Curriculum materials centers (CMCs) face a serious transition in the twenty-first century, a transition that involves examining staffing to assess roles, perspectives, competencies, and experiences in determining position needs today while planning to meet future challenges. The complex and expanded roles of libraries and librarians, the expansion of services, and the ubiquity of technology project that libraries, including CMCs, must anticipate the need to provide the most advanced technological access to a wide array of digital resources without losing sight of the basic commitment to print resources. When examining the history of CMC staffing, it is clear that over time duties have progressed from anticipating the needs of face-to-face users, all roughly the same age, for print resources to predicting the expectations of multigenerational users for socially networked digital or electronic resources in an information-rich society. (Jakubs, 2008).

From the first formally organized curriculum laboratory in 1922 (Nevil, 1975) to the 303 curriculum labs in institutions of higher learning by 1969 (Ellis, 1969) to thousands of CMCs in the twenty-first century (ACRL, 2009a), user needs and expectations have changed drastically, influencing the staffing necessary to meet present and future needs and expectations. CMCs have experienced numerous changes that have directly impacted services, impacting staffing in turn. Changes over time from print to electronic materials, from face-to-face communication to social networking, and from manual to digital technology have greatly influenced CMC services and resources, requiring significant changes in staffing roles to meet patron needs. Generational analysis of today's workforce and students, who include Traditionalists (born 1922–1945), Baby Boomers (born 1946–1964), Generation Xs (born 1965–1980) and Millennials (born 1981–2000), substantiates that learning styles, work ethic, and communication vary significantly among the generations based on ever-changing technologies and advancements of society (Dols, Landrum, & Wieck, 2010). With such differences and changes, staffing the CMC effectively becomes even more crucial to its success.

In order to staff the CMC with the future in mind, planners must anticipate users' needs and analyze the staff competencies required to meet those needs, developing new staffing models as necessary. The mission of providing excellent information service to patrons has not changed; however, technology has added new dimensions to the mission (Lipow, 1997). Flexibility is the key to successfully staffing the CMC, but unless staff members possess critical job competencies to perform the quality and type of services expected by patrons, high-quality services will be unavailable (Spiegleman, 1997). Realizing that technology is driving change across the entire range of library services, CMCs are faced with the need to rethink existing staffing patterns to develop staffing competencies and models that directly address current needs, yet are flexible enough to accommodate future needs (Youngman, 1999).

Analyzing job requirements and competencies, developing new staffing models, and hiring from outside of the profession are factors to consider in order to successfully prepare for the future. It is the responsibility of library and CMC administrators to review current position duties, considering competencies and skills needed in the CMC based on user needs and services. When applicable, core competencies for all levels of staff should be adjusted, recognizing that the CMC may need to employ types of staff other than just librarians and professionals. In cases where CMC staffing is limited to one position or a shared position, administrators must acknowledge that services for CMC patrons will be limited and interrupted. Therefore, it is extremely important to utilize the national support that is available while developing key partnerships with faculty and students in the educational institution's college or department of education. National support and partnerships can be effectively utilized to justify full-time CMC staffing. The recently approved *Guidelines for Curriculum Materials Centers* (ACRL, 2009b) and *A Guide to the Management of Curriculum Materials Centers for the 21st Century* (Carr, 2001) are resources that provide national support to document needs of the CMC. These two resources show that CMCs can influence faculty's delivery of information and students' learning experiences, which in turn critically impact future classroom teaching and learning processes. Partnerships enhance the voice of the CMC. Oral and written communication from faculty and staff are powerful in supporting the need for CMC staffing. While the CMC can offer enormous opportunity in supporting the education of our future teachers, such opportunity is not available without the support and direction of specialized staffing.

When justifying additional CMC staff, it is important to remember that in order to meet the challenges of an ever-changing profession, it is crucial that staff members have the flexibility and adaptability to acquire new skills. For this reason, it is vital to monitor position vacancies in order to remain abreast of trends in CMC services and structure

(ACRL, 2002). Administrators are faced with staffing challenges that include predictable and unpredictable staffing needs when planning for the future. According to the *Guidelines for Curriculum Materials Centers* (ACRL, 2009b), there are three key areas for which CMC staff is responsible:

+ Administration: mission/goals, budgeting, personnel, facilities, promotion
+ Services: reference, instruction, distance education, faculty liaison, outreach, production
+ Collections: development, access, assessment

Staffing to address these areas is mandatory if the CMC is to adhere to standard guidelines. Predicting staff needs is based upon the extent of services and collections as well as the number of users each CMC serves. Unpredictable staffing needs are based upon the continuously ever-changing, ever-more-complex technological environment demanding that staff constantly learn and adapt to new technologies (Metz, 2010).

Not only do CMC administrators face predicting future staffing needs, but they encounter staffing challenges resulting from economic downturns, budget collapses, retention issues, outsourcing of processes, and shortage of available professionals due to competition and the growing numbers of retirees. Even with the predictable and unpredictable staffing needs in conjunction with challenges, CMC staffing in the twenty-first century is a vital component of the overall success of the budgeting, services, and collections of the CMC and is accomplished by determining the number of needed positions, by reviewing and improving the hiring process, and by emphasizing retention and performance evaluation in order to project the value of the CMC staff.

Determining Needed Staff Positions

To initiate the process of determining needed staff positions of any given CMC, three factors must be analyzed:

+ the vision, mission, and strategic planning of the center
+ dynamic factors within and outside the center in comparison with other peer institutions

+   the physical location of the CMC in relation to the university

Analyzing the CMC vision, mission, and strategies provides direct insight into what the CMC projects for the future, what it currently does, whom it serves, and how it plans to accomplish the service now and in the future. The vision stretches the capabilities and enhances the image of the CMC, projecting what the CMC wishes to become in the future. The mission defines what the CMC is doing currently, why, and for whom it exists.

While the mission determines the resources and services needed based upon users, strategic planning encompasses written strategies that address achieving the mission with direct impact on the vision. Strategic planning includes setting goals, establishing criteria, and measuring actions. Consistently reviewing the vision and mission statements provides the ability to implement strategic planning that addresses the number (staffing level) and types (competencies and capabilities) of CMC staff members necessary to implement goals effectively now and in the future (Bechet, 2000). A simple example explains the importance of analyzing these statements. A given CMC serves a state university that produces the highest number of teachers in that state. The college of education within this university places preservice teachers for internships in thirty-eight public school systems in its region and enrolls the highest number of distance education students on the campus and in the state university system. The campus offers graduate programs through the doctoral level. The CMC serves a total of 3,000 education students and more than 40,000 in-service educators in the university regional community. In addition, the CMC serves an early childhood program that produces a high number of directors and teachers for preschools and early childhood education programs. The vision is to serve as a national model for other CMCs to emulate. The CMC mission statement says that the center facilitates teaching and learning initiatives by providing resources and services to educators at all levels within the university's regional community. Strategic goals include developing and maintaining an accessible, current birth-to-grade-12 collection; conducting reference and instruction services; providing outreach to the college of education, area schools, and educators; and supporting educators with technology and equipment for production purposes.

In addition to strategic goals that directly relate to the vision and mission, there are strategic goals that address other community and campus user needs and expectations that are not the primary functions of the centers, but nevertheless are services rendered due to the location and nature of the collection as well as partnerships formed by the university and center. These services include addressing the needs of homeschoolers, area PK–12 students, faculty members' children, and university preschool laboratories. In order to accomplish the strategic goals, competent and adequate staffing must be available to perform the quality and type of services determined through strategic planning based upon patron needs (ACRL, 2002). Seven full-time CMC staff and twelve student employees are necessary to accomplish the strategic goals and mission of this center. Commitment from library and campus administrators, dedicated support from the college of education faculty, and CMC goals addressing needs and expectations of preservice and in-service educators have played a major role in the justification for CMC staffing at this institution.

Establishing the direction of the CMC based on the vision, mission, and strategic plan provides the basis for analyzing the staffing needs by reviewing basic indicating factors that provide insight into determining the number and type of staff positions. Maintaining vital statistics of indicating academic and CMC factors can justify the need for additional staff for the center. Statistics in the form of readily available data are real and supporting evidence that can be used to reduce the disparity between actual staff and predicted needed staff; however, educating campus and library administration solidifies support for the CMC and helps justify the center's budget. The academic and CMC factors listed in figure 6.1 reflect indicating factors that correlate and support the number and types of staff positions (Burger, Clark, & Mischo, 1999). Statistics on the academic factors listed in figure 6.1 are maintained by the university and are readily available upon request. Analysis of numbers of programs, students, faculty, degrees, accreditations, and rankings provides standard factors that CMC administrators rely upon to determine and predict present and future needed services, collections, and resources. When these statistics are combined with indicating CMC factors, a wealth of data is available to validate and support the needs of CMC staffing. Centers located in the academic library setting will require staffing different from those housed outside of that environment. Hours of service for the center are not to be determined by the number of staff members available to cover the hours, but rather, within budgetary guidelines, by the needs and schedules of the patrons.

Figure 6.1. Academic and CMC factors

Academic Factors	CMC Factors
• Number of university programs and partnerships served • Number of faculty served by above-determined programs and partnerships • Number of students served in above-determined programs and partnerships • Level of university degrees offered (undergraduate degrees, certifications, master's degrees, doctoral degrees) • Recognition of university programs (national or state rankings) • Accreditation standards	• Location of center (Is it in academic library, branch library, or campus education department?) • Square footage of center • Circulation statistics • Cataloging needs/statistics • Size and type of collections • Service desk statistics • Hours of service • Collection development needs/statistics (weeding, volumes added per year, maintenance of the collection, etc.) • Services offered (instructional sessions, individual consultations, workshops, professional development for faculty, outreach services, production services, tours, distance education services, bibliographies, etc.) • Presence nationally, regionally, at state level, and locally • Equipment/technology services
(Adapted from Burger, Clark, & Mischo, 1999.)	

Indicating factors for determining the number and types of staff positions needed. Additionally, the type and number of patrons being served and the level of service offered at the center's reference desk are key to the types and number of positions needed to effectively operate the center. Circulation and cataloging statistics provide data regarding the use and access of materials and resources. Interlibrary loan services, reserve statistics, checkouts, renewals, and in-house statistics of CMC collection usage are all vital in substantiating needs of the center. Comparison of CMC circulation statistics with the overall academic library circulation statistics may prove helpful in supporting staffing. For example, if circulation statistics indicate that a CMC located within the academic library is circulating more than 40 percent of the entire academic library circulation, then such a statistic must be highlighted and accented, showing that the materials and resources within the center are needed, valued, and used by patrons. Staffing is needed to catalog materials for immediate access. If cataloging is centralized, then CMC cataloging staffing is not necessary.

CMC administrators must insist that knowledgeable professionals instruct and assist patrons in the use of the curriculum collection as well as developing, maintaining, and promoting the collection. Other factors of consideration in determining staffing are square footage of the center in conjunction with size and type of collections. It may be necessary in the vision of the center to include growth in staffing if expansion of the center is predicted. Also as important are future services needed based upon the increase in number of patrons and the ever-changing technology. CMC services range from basic reference desk services to instructional services for students, faculty, special groups, individuals, and community patrons with more specialized services that include technology, outreach, production, distance education services, and more. It is true that if you build a collection and promote it, patrons will come and investigate it. However, if knowledgeable staff members are available to assist patrons and instruct them in the use of the collection, then patrons will use it, embrace it, and tell others about it. As technology has impacted nearly every facet of librarianship, it is a definite indicating factor that directly affects staffing. As current and future technological services are advancing, technology is driving change across the entire range of library responsibilities, making staffing a key component to the support of technology-based services. Basic use of technology is normal in today's world; therefore, the job of the CMC staff to provide instruction in the integration of technology into the classroom and beyond is a standard expectation (Youngman, 1999).

Staffing has a major impact on the national, regional, state, and local presence and performance of the CMC. While it is possible to maintain a presence with minimal staff, the level of acceptable performance of the CMC in meeting patron needs will suffer when staff members are away participating in planning, conference presentations, and professional development unless there are sufficient staff members to maintain quality services. Once indicating factors (figure 6.1) are considered and analyzed, it is helpful to review peer institutions, examining staffing of CMCs in institutions with similar framework, enrollment profile, size, and settings as well as programs and degree offerings. In most cases, comparison of staffing in peer institutions strengthens and supports the case for staffing requested by the center.

The physical location of the CMC directly impacts the determination of staffing. Most CMCs are located within the academic library or within the academic education department or are a branch of the academic library. For CMCs located within the academic library, crosstraining and one-stop service desks are considered economic and consistent means by which regular library staff can cover the curriculum collection as well as the general collection. However, CMCs are specialized collections that demand knowledgeable professionals to meet the needs of users who expect assistance with subject-specific inquiries. Curriculum collections located in the academic library setting are most effective when the CMC provides a specialized service desk. Such presence emphasizes the validity and value of the collection and its users by library administration. The quality of services provided by knowledgeable professional staff determines the volume of usage and retention of users of the curriculum collection. Users requiring subject-specific resources and services quickly recognize whether professionals or staff members possess the necessary knowledge and experience to provide the desired and expected level of services, which determines continued usage. Assigning CMC staff to cover dual job roles within library collections other than the CMC must be avoided whenever possible. Such assignments, where responsibilities and focus encompass vast and varied collections, limit the effectiveness of the staff member in providing quality services for subject-specific patron needs. Additionally, the development and maintenance of the collection may suffer when staff is overloaded and overworked. In a study conducted by Teclehaimanot and Patterson (1992), the lack of qualified CMC staff (professional and support) was cited as one of the factors representing the greatest barrier to the future of CMCs. CMC administrators must obtain and retain the support of campus and library administrators to overcome this great barrier.

A major consideration when staffing a branch or a center housed separately from the academic library is security. The presence of security impacts the safety of the center, which determines hours of operation and usage. If the center is isolated from a main facility that provides security, then hours of operation are limited based on the high traffic patterns of building use and the ability to provide the acceptable level of security. Limitations placed on a CMC due to the lack of adequate staffing and security directly influence the access and services provided. Such limitations are directly linked to budgeting, which plays a primary role in the total staffing of the CMC. As academic library budgets decrease, the demands and competition for funds increase. For the CMC to be highly competitive in the budgeting process, it is essential to develop a staffing plan or time line to justify and forecast needs. This plan demonstrates to the administration the needs of the CMC and the direct relationship linking proper staffing to the achievement of strategic goals. A staffing plan is not a one-time request that is submitted or presented to administration in the hope that funding will be available, but rather a long-range plan developed based upon the implementation and consideration of the CMC's vision, mission, strategic planning, indicating factors, allocations, and funding. The plan strategically incorporates

current and future staffing needs, recognizing new positions and competencies that will be vital in accomplishing the vision, mission, and goals
of the center as traditional and technology-driven services change to
meet patron needs. Within the staffing plan, emphasis is placed on the
integration of new staff competencies into existing positions as needs
change. The plan must be concise, clear, and detailed, demonstrating the
need for new staffing and justifying the positions based upon strategic
planning and statistical and peer data as it relates to the level and quality
of services expected and needed by patrons (Burger, Clark, & Mischo,
1999). The long-range staffing plan serves as a tool for administration
to project and plan for timely changes in CMC staffing. The CMC administrator must be prepared to implement staffing changes based upon
the plan as they are considered and approved while realizing that adjustments may need to be made.

Determining Allocation and Funding for Needed Staff Positions

Once the necessary number and type of CMC positions have been determined by considering the indicating factors in figure 6.1, requesting
allocations is the next step. Based upon job responsibilities and competencies, requests are formulated for faculty (professional), staff (support), and student or volunteer positions. New positions requested may
be part-time staff members who become full-time as funding becomes
available, additional full- or part-time professional or support staff members, additional student employees, or approval of a volunteer policy to
allow competent professional or support volunteers to legally assist the
center. Positions may be filled through new hires, promotions, work
reassignments, use of contract staff, or other resources (Bechet, 2000).
Professional positions include and address competencies such as administration and supervision of the center; collection development; reference, research, and technology services; instruction; outreach services;
cataloging; and national, regional, and state presence. Support positions
involve circulation, copy cataloging and processing, limited reference services, stacks management, production services, tours, student employee

supervision, supply inventory, displays and exhibits, and gathering and compiling statistics. Student employee positions cover a range of competencies based upon student experiences. Graduate and undergraduate education students possess more experience in the field of education, enhancing their skills to serve in the CMC. These student positions will support duties including compiling and updating bibliographies, acquisition title searching, peer training, processing materials, reading shelves, pulling faculty-requested titles, and assisting generally with location of materials. Other student employee positions include such tasks as shelving materials, stamping new and discarded materials, recycling, shifting collections, reading shelves, simple catalog searching and locating materials, assisting with production services, and performing circulation duties.

While it is difficult to obtain funding for new staffing, a well-developed staffing plan enables the CMC administrator to communicate staffing needs for a given time period to the higher levels of administration. Once the staffing plan is presented, discussion can begin on its feasibility and implementation. Adjustments may be necessary, but openness and flexibility are instrumental in acquiring position allocations In order to provide the desired staff positions for the CMC, money must be available to fund them. Funding is a determining factor that affects full-time and part-time allocations. Budgeting may require that a position initially be temporary, changing to permanent part-time or full-time status when additional funding becomes available. Positions may be moved from other departments or areas to accommodate needs. In some cases, volunteer assistance can be considered as an option when funding is limited or not available. Even though university policy usually mandates that liability insurance be provided for volunteers, volunteers can be utilized at a minimal cost. The hiring of volunteers requires careful review of individual skills and experience in relation to the job competencies required by the CMC position. This will ensure a positive experience for the volunteer and the CMC. A volunteer position must be carefully considered before he or she is accepted for a volunteer position. "Free" assistance that is irrelevant to the CMC's mission and goals may not be needed or helpful.

Scheduling regular meetings between deans and CMC directors provides an avenue for continued discussion and updates of the direct relationship between CMC staffing and current and future services. During meetings, continued justification of needs must be supported by statistics, data, and strategic planning that is measured or evaluated based on the performance and accomplishment of the center's goals and objectives. Even with hard evidence to support CMC staffing needs, allocations for positions and adequate funding remain a major concern for CMC administrators (Teclehaimanot & Patterson, 1992). Key elements in implementing the staffing plan include remaining focused on the vision, mission, and goals of the center; understanding that staffing the CMC appropriately is a long-range goal; educating and informing administrators of CMC achievements and accomplishments; and continuously reviewing the plan.

The Hiring Process

When a new staffing position is allocated and funded, the hiring process begins by creating a job description based upon competencies needed to perform the responsibilities of the position. Once the approved job description is available for posting, advertising and recruiting for the position play an important role in determining the number of candidates available for interviewing. Upon the completion of the interview process, the appropriate candidate is chosen, which, at that point, the orienting of the new candidate begins. The hiring process is the means by which the staffing plan becomes a reality. Terrence Mech (1989, p. 63) states, "Personnel are the critical resource in any professional activity because the quality of work depends on the qualities of those hired." A deliberate process that creates efficient and effective models to identify, recruit, and hire top candidates is essential. Streamlining the inclusion of required and preferred qualities in the job description, with major emphasis on the development of competencies, is a key element in acquiring competent candidates for a position. Flexibility in job descriptions is essential in expediting the process. Responsibilities and qualifications remain an essential piece of the job description; they are just more broadly defined and more compatible with the reality of a technology-driven, changing environment. Hiring based on traits essential for the success of the CMC, in contrast with hiring based on a limited set of stated skills, allows the CMC administrator to consider attitude, values, cultural fit, and ability to adapt to change rather than just specific skills, which candidates can learn once they are hired. Experience is certainly a factor that should not be ignored; however, it is not a reliable indicator of an individual's ability to adapt, thrive, and make substantial contributions to the CMC (Raschke, 2003). The process of creating new job descriptions is an excellent opportunity to review and revamp the job descriptions of existing staff. A chance to rethink staffing patterns allows for analyzing current circumstances to determine the best arrangement for future staffing and services (Youngman, 1999). In advertisement and recruitment, the use of technology has proven effective in allowing organizations such as CMCs to overcome time, geography, space, and budget limitations in dissemination of job openings and information. The reduction in cost, quick distribution, and efficient management associated with electronic advertising and recruitment make them invaluable tools. Avoiding the traditional advertising and recruitment processes reduces the hiring process time, which could determine the difference between hiring a desirable candidate for the CMC position and losing the candidate to another job posting (Raschke, 2003).

Preparing for candidate interviews is a crucial stage in the hiring process. A considerable amount of time can be spent prior to and during the interviewing process. The length of time that libraries spend from the interview of the first candidate to the selection and contacting of the successful candidate averages forty-one days. This time does not include gathering initial applications, analyzing cover letters and resumes, or checking references, which must all be completed prior to interviewing; therefore, it is extremely important to improve the steps leading to interviews. CMC administrators must reduce the number of members on search committees, use technology to communicate with potential candidates, limit in-person search committee meetings by working independently to review and rank resumes, favor initial quick telephone and e-mail reference checks to formal written ones, and review applications as they arrive rather than waiting for an arbitrary deadline to begin the reviews. Streamlining the review process is essential because during this time candidates are anxious to hear from hiring institutions as they begin to develop their own list of possibilities (Raschke, 2003).

The job interview is a powerful component in the hiring process and must be carefully planned and implemented efficiently. Presentations, role-playing, responses to given CMC scenarios, solutions offered for specific CMC work situations, and answers to selected interview questions are all effective techniques used to assess candidate qualifications, trainability, adaptability to change, and speed of learning to perform job tasks (Guion, 1997). The inclusion of behaviorally based questions is of paramount importance in identifying specific characteristics and behavioral traits that the search committee feels are essential to the position and the CMC. Such questions allow candidates to accentuate specific experiences and examples demonstrating their ability to handle given situations. Employing such varied questions allows members of the search committee to gain insight into the behaviors that candidates utilized as they explain their reactions or solutions to the given situations. The interview provides an opportunity for the search committee and candidates to discover if their backgrounds, experiences, talents, skills, and interests are aligned to the position and the culture of the CMC. The search committee must realize that candidates are conducting their own interviews of the search committee and the CMC; therefore, the CMC culture, vision, mission, strategic planning, customer service model, and any other outstanding components must be presented to candidates clearly, concisely, and in a positive manner. Technical qualifications of the position must be explained, allowing candidates' responses, backgrounds, and experiences to be determining factors in the hiring process. Once the search committee has conducted all interviews and is satisfied that all elements of the interview process have been addressed and assessed, the committee reviews each candidate, noting all information collected during the hiring process to determine the best candidate for the position. A matrix listing required and preferred qualifications is a helpful tool in recording, reviewing, and assessing each candidate during and after the interview. Using such a tool allows the search committee to record fairly and consistently the traits of each candidate, providing information that can be retrieved and reviewed after each interview.

Once the search committee has selected the candidate for the CMC position and all hiring requirements have been addressed and approved based on institutional hiring policies and guidelines, the person should be contacted with the job offer. The length of time from the offer to acceptance of the job is determined by several variables including type of position, salary, negotiations, availability of the candidate to begin employment, and availability for funding the position.

As the logistics are finalized, the CMC administrator prepares for the arrival of the employee, devising an orientation that will address the needs of the employee and the employer. The orientation of employees to the CMC is the initial step in retention. The purpose of orientation is to reduce the anxieties of the new employee; to provide the employee with a deeper understanding of the CMC history, culture, vision, mission, and goals as well as the physical facilities and arrangements; to explain job expectations in relationship to overall operations of the CMC; to review the evaluation tools that will be used to assess the employee's performance; to discuss training and professional development opportunities; to establish personal goals in relationship to strategic planning; and to address day-to-day operations and policies of the center. Orientation processes vary in length from several days to several months. It is important to devise an orientation that is directly related to the position and the culture of the CMC. General topics are addressed with all new positions; however, each position will have specific areas in which new employees need specialized guidance. Well-developed orientations for new employees show the commitment and value placed on the new CMC position. The assignment of a mentor can further demonstrate commitment and value.

The investment made by the CMC in any position search and hiring decision is substantial; therefore, the hiring process must be flexible, thorough, and timely. The process leading to the identification and hiring of top candidates has challenges, but the ultimate goal is finding and retaining a candidate whose talents, trainability, adaptability, flexibility, and personality are compatible with the needs of the CMC (Raschke, 2003).

Retention of CMC Staff

Due to the time and effort required to secure funding for CMC staffing, retention of the employee and the position is indispensable. Quinn (2005) reported that meeting employee needs must be considered as a major factor in the retention of employees. According to the American Management Association's survey of best retention practices of organizations cited by Musser (2001), six factors are important to all employees:

+ mentoring
+ networking
+ career and learning opportunities
+ interesting work
+ good benefits
+ balance between work and home life

In most cases, mentoring is a mutual relationship involving the pairing of similar individuals. In the CMC, such a pairing may not be easy to set in place due to the limited size of staff; therefore, assistance from outside the CMC may be needed to develop a mentoring relationship. A mentor assists the new CMC employee in understanding the unwritten rules, organization, and culture of the CMC. Preferred CMC communication styles, the importance of socializing, in-house policies, acceptable norms, and creating the balance between work and home are all important factors in which a mentor assists a CMC employee. When developed and implemented properly, mentoring always produces a win-win situation. Networking provides the opportunity for the new CMC staff member to become acquainted with internal and external coworkers, faculty, students, and other patrons. One simple example of initiating the networking process is inviting the new CMC employee to lunch once a month. While lunch is a simple gesture, it is a powerful statement of inclusion in a team-driven environment. In today's workplace where continuous learning is essential, career and learning opportunities serve as retaining measures to increase performance, productivity, and satisfaction of employees. CMC administrators benefit from offering and allowing new training and continuous professional development, which not only increase performance, but enhance the value and confidence of each employee. Interesting and motivating work reminds employees that they are an integral part of the organization. When the new CMC staff member joins the team, interesting work is the catalyst for increased productivity. Metamorphosing ordinary tasks into challenging and enjoyable duties is vital in retaining the new CMC employee and adding meaning to work. While some employers consider good job benefits to be health insurance, retirement benefits, or other similar monetary gains, a good majority of employees have been known to stay with an organization just based on the fact that a flexible schedule allowed them to have a better balance between work and home life (Musser, 2001). If the CMC is truly committed to retaining the new employee, there must be continuous and sustained efforts to show that the employee is valued rather than periodic activity or set benefits (Musser, 2001).

Performance Evaluation of CMC Staff

Evidence of major contributions from CMC staff should be observed through job performance; therefore, a formal performance evaluation must be conducted at least once a year with an interim review mid-year for faculty, support staff, and student positions. While evaluation procedures and processes will vary among faculty, support staff, and students, evaluations are useful in achieving strategic goals and meeting the needs and expectations of patrons. Supervisors are responsible for performing evaluations for each CMC employee, both full- and part-time, in a regular and timely manner. The performance evaluation is viewed as a positive procedure with purposeful benefits to the employer and the employee. It is an opportunity for the supervisor and employee to review and update job descriptions and competencies that clarify job expectations as well as review personal goals and accomplishments. The performance evaluation is documented using statistics and measurable criteria that provide an avenue whereby the employer reviews strengths, weaknesses, areas of achievement, and areas for improvement. This process allows a time of open communication between the supervisor and employee to measure performance by comparing actual results to expectations. Additionally, it is an opportunity to reward employees who exceed expectations as well as motivate employees to strive for outstanding performance. In some cases, the performance evaluation serves as documentation of improvement, when needed, or in making decisions regarding demotions, disciplinary actions, and dismissals (East Carolina University, 2004).

The performance evaluation process begins when the supervisor and the CMC employee meet within the first thirty days of employment to develop a work plan. The work plan is reviewed and updated annually. It is a specific course of action outlining job competencies, responsibilities, employment dimensions, expectations, and methods and sources for measuring the actual results. A standardized rating scale is used to determine the performance level based on the documented actual results. Once the work plan has been developed, a day-to-day monitoring or tracking by both the CMC staff member and the supervisor begins based upon the measuring sources as agreed upon in the initial meeting.

New employees are evaluated once during and at the end of a probationary period, usually six months from the initial hiring, to ensure that job competencies are understood and being met. The probationary period is separate from the first annual performance cycle. During the probation term, new employees are given an opportunity to discuss their job competencies and expectations with their supervisor in order to reach a level of acceptable proficiency prior to the end of the probation term. The probation term serves as a time of learning and comprehension of job competencies. Additionally, this term provides the supervisor an opportunity to observe and make recommendations, if needed, to the new employee on improving performance and adjusting to new job expectations. If the employee is not able to perform at an acceptable level, then the supervisor can dismiss the employee prior to the position becoming permanent. While dismissal of a probationary employee is not the desired outcome, it is necessary when a newly hired candidate is unable to perform the job competencies at an acceptable level.

If the probationary term ends successfully, the employee becomes permanently hired. An annual performance evaluation cycle begins, which includes an interim review every six months with an annual final review at the end of each year. The interim review serves as a midpoint informal discussion between the supervisor and CMC employee regarding progress toward each of the established competencies, expectations, and dimensions (required tasks or duties). Since the interim review is informal, the supervisor communicates to the employee the overall level of performance to date, recording only the date the meeting occurred, topics discussed, and any additions to or deletions from the work plan. A formal rating is not given at this point of the performance cycle. Feedback and communication during the interim review are important elements to encourage acceptable performance.

During the annual or final review, the supervisor and employee meet to review the employee's actual performance as it compares to established expectations and measurable results. The supervisor and employee discuss each competency in conjunction with the dimensions or general scope of the job duties as well as expectations in order to determine the overall performance rating. It is vital that open discussions occur so that the CMC employee understands and has input into their final performance overall rating for the year. Documentation is written on a formal appraisal instrument indicating the actual results based on the established measurement scale. The CMC employee is given the opportunity to make comments on the document as well. Both the supervisor and the CMC employee sign the appraisal to validate that the rating has been discussed and the evaluation was held. If there is a disagreement on the given rating, the employee may write comments on the final appraisal in rebuttal (East Carolina University, 2004).

CMC staff should be highly encouraged to develop three to four personal goals annually. Brian Tracy (2002) states in his book, *Focal Point*, that the difference between successful and unsuccessful people is the way they think. Successful people know what they want and how to obtain it based on their personal goals. Personal goals are simply a way to motivate CMC employees to contribute to the overall success of the center. Successful centers are composed of successful people. For this reason, personal goals should support the vision, mission, and strategic goals of the center. These goals are related to job competencies and are relevant, attainable, timely, and measurable. Setting personal goals establishes direction, productivity, and professional growth, which can play a key role in the success of the employee and the center.

Finally, it is extremely valuable and important to provide continuous skills development and job enrichment in order to increase CMC employee performance. Professional development and training provide increased CMC effectiveness by raising individual competencies among support staff as well as faculty. It allows staff exposure to innovative technology and future trends so that they can better prepare themselves and the center to meet patron needs (Lo, 2008). Such opportunities are formally written in an employee work development plan and personal goals agreed upon between the supervisor and employee. Regardless of the technique, professional development and training are essential if CMC staff members intend to develop and enhance their work-related knowledge, skills, and attitudes to meet future changing technologies and services.

Valuing the CMC Staff

It will take months or even years to secure the number and type of positions needed to efficiently operate a successful CMC. Regardless of the size of the CMC staff, valuing each individual member of the center is crucial in maintaining a motivated, team-driven, self-empowered staff with high morale. Motivating employees changes with the times. Studies report that motivation affects behavior which is directly linked to individual needs and that motivation is not a fixed trait, but varies in relationship to age, gender, employment status, occupational category, and income. Keeping this in mind, several overall factors motivate employees: interesting work, sympathetic understanding relating to personal problems, good working conditions, full appreciation of work done, and a feeling of inclusion in decision making (Wiley, 1997). Unappreciated employees are more likely to search for other employment, resulting in departures that cost thousands of dollars in recruitment, hiring, and training. Absenteeism, tardiness, and lack of motivation abound in undervalued staff; therefore, it is always important to show employees that their contributions are valued. Topper (2009) reports the findings of a survey by the Foundation for Enterprise Development (http://www.fed.org) showing that employees ranked personal congratulations from their supervisor as their number one choice for recognition, with a written note as second, out of sixty-seven potential forms of recognition that were offered to them for doing a good job.

CMC supervisors can motivate staff by regularly reminding them of the importance of their work in achieving the vision, mission, and goals of the center. While teamwork is important in the success of the CMC, valuing the part played by each individual is also important because involvement in the achievement of the center's vision, mission, and goals produces a sense of ownership and contribution. Employees who regularly receive positive feedback regarding their contributions are motivated to seek ways to accomplish even more for their employer (Quinn, 2005). Additionally, administrators must communicate to CMC staff that their work is highly appreciated and that patrons need them more than ever during these ever-changing technological times. Administrators who engage everyone in the mission of the organization and generate a shared vision for success indirectly inspire staff to do their best (Topper, 2009). Engagement is accomplished by developing an effective CMC team whose individual members feel ownership of the accomplishments of the center. Ownership increases morale, allowing staff to realize the influence of empowerment and involvement. Staff involvement enables employees to contribute to continuous improvement and the ongoing success of the center. In a highly effective CMC team, all staff members share in the decision making, an openness that leads to collaboration built on trust and respect, an understanding of the relationship between personal and CMC strategic goals, and a mutual agreement that every-one is important. Each CMC staff member realizes that he or she has an important role in fulfilling and contributing to the overall mission of the CMC. Employees in today's workforce, regardless of their position, must continue to work on their knowledge, skills, competencies, and experience in a changing and sometimes unpredictable environment. Through motivation, teamwork, empowerment, and involvement, staff members develop the ability to dynamically apply their skills to an ever-changing environment, making them even more valuable and essential to the success of the CMC (Metz, 2010). It is crucial that staff members realize their value; this is accomplished by communicating recognition of their accomplishments, providing a team environment in which they understand their purpose and contribute to the overall achievement of strategic goals, supporting them in the challenges that arise in their personal lives, creating good working conditions, and giving them input into decision making.

Summary

CMCs have been a valuable resource for teacher education in America for over a half a century (McGiverin, 1988), and staffing the CMC is an integral part of its overall success. Throughout the history of edu-cation, the classroom teacher has been viewed as the primary element in the teaching/learning process. Melvin Alston (1969) notes that the continual development and integration of CMC services and resources into teacher education has proven to be a second factor in the teaching/learning process, contributing significantly in the development of com-petent teachers.

The quality of CMC services and resources is directly linked to the staffing of the CMC. As technology advances, forcing new services to emerge, challenges in adding and maintaining CMC positions must be addressed to accommodate future changes (Youngman, 1999). Types and number of positions are determined based on the direction of the CMC, analysis of key influential factors, physical location, allocations, and funding. A CMC staff plan projects the needs of the center based on long-range goals and future trends. Once the plan has been approved and has administration support, the hiring process focuses on creating job descriptions and competencies, interviewing, hiring, and orienting the new employee. While the hiring process is an integral part of CMC staffing, it is important to recognize that retention of staff is just as valuable for the CMC in maintaining and developing competent staff members. While performance evaluations serve as means of retention by offering staff members an avenue of open communication to continually improve job performance, developing and accomplishing personal goals and continuous job enrichment through professional development and training opportunities provide additional securities in the retention of staff. Highly trained staff members who fully understand their role in the overall CMC mission possess the ability to perform at a level of satisfaction allowing them to feel confident in their performance at work. Confidence produces pride, which increases retention of employees.

In conclusion, one of the most important aspects in the retention of staff lies in valuing the CMC staff. Motivation, teamwork, and self-empowerment together produce high morale in the work environment. To further cultivate the value of CMC staff, a genuine attempt to listen to, implement, and compliment staff input must be continual and sincere (Quinn, 2005). By reviewing the historical perspective and analyzing current needs in order to prepare for the future, CMCs realize that staffing transitions of the twenty-first century can and must be met in order to effectively and successfully meet the ever-changing needs of patrons.

References

ACRL (Association of College & Research Libraries). 2002. *Recruitment, Retention, and Restructuring: Human Resources in Academic Libraries.* Chicago: Association of College & Research Libraries. Retrieved from http://www.acrl.org/ala/mgrps/divs/acrl/proftools/recruiting/recruiting-wp.pdf.

———. 2009a. *Directory of Curriculum Materials Centers,* 6th ed. Chicago: American Library Association.

———. 2009b. *Guidelines for Curriculum Materials Centers.* Chicago: Association of College & Research Libraries. Retrieved from http://www.ala.org/acrl/standards/guidelinescurriculum.

Alston, Melvin O. 1969. "Foreword." In *The Role of the Curriculum Laboratory in the*

Preparation of Quality Teachers, by Elinor Vivian Ellis, iii. Tallahassee: Florida A & M University.

Bechet, Thomas P. 2000. "Developing Staffing Strategies That Work: Implementing Pragmatic, Nontraditional Approaches." *Public Personnel Management* 29 (4): 465–476.

Burger, Bob, Bart Clark, and Bill Mischo. 1999, June 4. *University Library Staffing Inventory*. University of Illinois at Urbana-Champaign. Retrieved from http://www.library.illinois.edu/administration/services/planning/staffinginventory.pdf.

Carr, Jo Ann, ed. 2001. *A Guide to the Management of Curriculum Materials Centers for the 21st Century: The Promise and the Challenge*. Chicago: American Library Association.

Dols, Jean, Peggy Landrum, and K. Lynn Wieck. 2010. "Leading and Managing an Intergenerational Workforce." *Creative Nursing* 16 (2): 68–74. doi:10.1891/1078-4535.16.2.68.

East Carolina University, Human Resources. 2004. "Policy Statement 3: Performance Management." Greenville, NC: East Carolina University. Retrieved from http://www.ecu.edu/business_manual/Human_Resources_Policy3.htm#pol3.

Ellis, Elinor Vivian. 1969. *The Role of the Curriculum Laboratory in the Preparation of Quality Teachers*. Tallahassee: Florida A & M University. Retrieved from ERIC database (ED031457).

Guion, Robert. 1997. "Criterion Measures and the Criterion Dilemma." *International Handbook of Selection and Assessment*, 2nd ed., edited by Neil Anderson and Peter Herriot, 279. New York: Wiley.

Jakubs, Deborah. 2008. "Out of the Gray Times: Leading Libraries into the Digital Future." *Journal of Library Administration* 48 (2): 235–248.

Lipow, A. 1997. "Thinking Out Loud: Who Will Give Reference Service in the Digital Environment?" *Reference & User Services Quarterly* 37 (2): 125–129.

Lo, Patrick. 2008. "Empowering Your Library: Training and Professional Development, a Library Imperative!" *International Journal of Learning* 14 (12): 41–52.

McGiverin, Roland H. 1988. "Curriculum Materials Centers: A Descriptive Study." *Behavioral & Social Sciences Librarian* 6 (3–4): 119–128.

Mech, Terrence. 1989. "Recruitment and Selection of College Librarians." In *Operations Handbook for the Small Academic Library*, edited by Gerard B. McCabe, 63–78. New York: Greenwood Press.

Metz, Ruth. 2010. "Coaching in the Library." *American Libraries* 41 (3): 34–37.

Musser, Linda R. 2001. "Effective Retention Strategies for Diverse Employees." *Journal of Library Administration*, 33 (1&2): 63–72.

Nevil, Leota. 1975. "A Survey of Curriculum Laboratories in Selected Colleges in Pennsylvania." Master's thesis, Wilkes College, Wilkes-Barre, PA. Retrieved from ERIC database (ED112909).

Quinn, Brian A. 2005. "Enhancing Academic Library Performance through Positive Psychology." *Journal of Library Administration* 42 (1): 79–101. doi:10.1300/

J111v42n01_05

Raschke, Gregory K. 2003. "Hiring and Recruitment Practices in Academic Libraries: Problems and Solutions." *portal: Libraries and the Academy* 3 (1): 53–67.

Spiegleman, Barbara M. 1997. *Competencies for Special Librarians of the 21st Century.* Washington, DC: Special Libraries Association.

Teclehaimanot, Berhane, and Amos Patterson. 1992. "The Nature, Function and Value of the Curriculum Materials Center on Colleges of Education." Retrieved from ERIC database (ED348030).

Topper, Elisa F. 2009. "Keeping Staff Motivated in Tough Times." *New Library World* 110 (7/8): 385–387. doi:10.1108/03074800910975205.

Tracy, Brian. 2002. *Focal Point: A Proven System to Simplify Your Life, Double Your Productivity, and Achieve All Your Goals.* New York: Amacom Books.

Wiley, Carolyn. 1997. "What Motivates Employees according to Over 40 Years of Motivation Surveys." *International Journal of Manpower* 18 (3): 263–280.

Youngman, Daryl C. 1999. "Library Staffing Considerations in the Age of Technology: Basic Elements for Managing Change." *Issues in Science & Technology Librarianship* 24: 1–5.

7 Building a Successful Outreach Program

Hazel J. Walker, East Carolina University

This chapter explores the success of the outreach program of the Teaching Resources Center (TRC) of J. Y. Joyner Library, East Carolina University. The TRC serves as the curriculum materials center for the university and maintains a specialized birth-to-twelfth-grade collection of more than 60,000 volumes. The center serves a diverse population of faculty, staff, and students with a major focus on the College of Education. The College of Education student population totals more than 3,000 undergraduate students, graduate students, and doctoral candidates. Additionally, outreach services are provided to area educators in more than thirty-six eastern North Carolina school systems. The collection includes fiction and nonfiction young adult materials, easy picture books, big books, biographies, state-adopted and supplemental textbooks, mixed media materials, a professional collection, and young adult reference materials. Partnerships with campus, community, and the library profession enable the TRC to offer its resources, materials, and services to area educators at all levels. Each partnership is addressed in this chapter, and the key elements to the success of the outreach program are discussed.

Introduction

Curriculum materials centers (CMCs) may vary in size, title, administrative structure, and physical location on campus, but they share at least one thing in common—a unique collection of instructional materials designed to support the needs of school professionals, particularly those of teachers and preservice teachers (Hagenbruch, 2001, p. 137).

What better way to encourage and support educators as they strive to teach our children than to offer an outreach program that will provide them with materials, services, and resources?

What Is Outreach?

The American Library Association acknowledged the importance of outreach services when it established the Office for Literacy and Outreach Services (OLOS). The mission of OLOS is to identify and promote library services that support equitable access to the knowledge and information stored in our libraries (OLOS, 2011). OLOS focuses attention on providing services to underserved populations. In many instances, educators meet the criteria of an underserved population because the availability and accessibility of services, resources, and materials are limited by lack of administrative support, budget deficiencies, or size and location of facilities. Such limitations directly affect student populations and their academic success.

The Outreach Program of the Teaching Resources Center of Joyner Library, East Carolina University

Established in 1988, the Teaching Resources Center (TRC) of J. Y. Joyner Library, East Carolina University, serves as the curriculum materials center for the university and maintains a specialized birth-to-twelfth-grade collection of over 60,000 volumes, including fiction and nonfiction young adult materials, easy picture books, big books, biographies, state-adopted and supplemental textbooks, mixed media materials, a professional collection, and reference materials. One facet of the university's mission is to create a strong, sustainable future for eastern North Carolina through education, research, innovation, investment, and outreach. The TRC embraced this philosophy by developing and creating the mission to facilitate teaching and learning initiatives by providing resources and services to educators at all levels (TRC, 2011).

Why Was the Program Needed?

One of the main purposes of the TRC is to serve the students and faculty in the College of Education. Providing quality materials, resources, and services to students and faculty helps to ensure their needs are being met. Preservice teachers continually return to the TRC, expressing that the books and materials are invaluable resources integrated into their teaching experience. The TRC is essential to eastern North Carolina because the region has small media centers with limited numbers of textbooks, lack of supporting materials in the centers, and low budgets in the schools. With the majority of eastern North Carolina being rural and falling below the state and national average socioeconomic level, many schools struggle to provide the basic materials due to deficient budgets (Hossfeld, 2003 (Word document)). Based upon the knowledge of these school deficiencies, the need to develop and implement an outreach program by extending TRC resources, services, and materials to eastern North Carolina educators was evident and convincing.

How Was the Program Started?

A proposal for an outreach program was developed and presented to the library administration. Upon approval and support of the proposal, planning for the outreach program began. The outreach program was designed to increase and diversify the center's audience to include area educators, offering innovative programs and services to strengthen relationships and form strong partnerships with eastern North Carolina schools. In order to accomplish this goal, the TRC identified mutual interests and needs that could be addressed by making available to the schools its resources, materials and services. The TRC outreach program partnered with the ECU College of Education's Walter and Daisy Carson Latham Clinical Schools Network to establish the boundaries of the program. The Clinical Schools Network, which continues to expand as the College of Education expands its programs, encompasses a wide area of public school systems in eastern North Carolina. The purposes of the Latham Clinical Schools Network are to

- provide a network in which public schools and East Carolina University can collaborate
- seek to enhance recruitment, retention, and renewal of teachers

from preservice to in-service

+ provide quality field placements and clinical experiences for teacher education candidates

+ facilitate the implementation of innovative practices and new initiatives in both public schools and university partners (ECU College of Education, 2011)

After intensive planning, the TRC outreach program consisted of three significant components: an Educator Library Card, interlibrary loan services to area public schools, and an Enhancing Teachers' Classrooms production center. Once plans were finalized, the new program was presented in a written proposal to the library assembly, a deliberative body that discusses and provides a voice in policy-making processes of the library. The library assembly approved the program unanimously, and work began immediately to implement the outreach program.

Educator Library Card

In November 2003, Joyner Library announced the addition of an Educator Library Card (Bailey, Teel, & Walker, 2006). This card is available, free of charge, to K–12 educators of eastern North Carolina. The card is offered in a thirty-three–county region with thirty-six public school systems that are served by the Clinical Schools Network in the College of Education. Within the network, there are approximately 564 schools with over 22,500 teachers who participate in partnership efforts.

The Educator Library Card is issued at the Access Services desk of Joyner Library and the service desk of the music library. To register, the educator completes a registration form and presents verification of employment as an educator. School IDs, pay stubs, and school contracts are examples of acceptable school employment verification. Once registered, an educator is given a yellow credit card–sized card and a smaller yellow key ring card (figure 7.1), accompanied by a list of the loan periods for the various resources in the library. The Educator Library Card is issued initially for a year. Renewals are available contingent upon educator employment continuation.

Figure 7.1. Educator Library Card and key ring card

The Outreach Librarian visits schools in the Clinical Schools Network to inform educators of the various services offered by Joyner Library and the TRC. During the librarian's visit to the school, educators are encouraged to register for the Educator Library Card, and registration forms are delivered by the librarian to Access Services for processing. Once the forms are processed, the cards are mailed to the school, where school media specialists assist in distributing the cards to the educators.

The goal of Joyner Library in offering the Educator Library Card is to provide area educators with free access to materials in Joyner Library, to increase awareness of the resources and materials in Joyner Library, and to show commitment and support for area educators as a partner in the education process. During the first year of the program, 2,300 educators were registered as new patrons. The circulation of the TRC materials doubled as awareness of the resources and materials increased. The Educator Library Card has proven to be a valuable resource for area educators. It should be noted that the card has proven to be a retention factor for ECU graduates who become teachers in eastern North Carolina to continue contact with the university. Educators appreciate the benefit of the resources, materials, and services of the TRC.

Interlibrary Loan

Free access to circulated materials from Joyner Library is available to the thirty-six public school systems represented in the Clinical Schools Network through interlibrary loan. Each school can register through ILLiad to request materials from Joyner Library. Registration is completed and managed by the media specialists of each school. Only circulated materials from Joyner Library can be requested. Requests for materials from other libraries are not allowed due to university policies and agreements. Educators in public schools are encouraged to borrow materials to help supplement teaching and to aid their professional development. Requests for materials are submitted to media coordinators, who coordinate the interlibrary loan process in each school. Additionally, media coordinators are encouraged to place individual material requests for students who are working on projects. The TRC is also used to supplement resources for high school senior graduation projects.

Enhancing Teachers' Classrooms Room

The Enhancing Teachers' Classrooms room (ETC room) is a production center designed to assist preservice teachers and eastern North Carolina educators as they create materials for use in the classroom. This room contains equipment, software, and supplies needed in the preparation of resources used in lesson units, classrooms, and presentations.

Three computer workstations with Internet access and Microsoft Office are available in the ETC room. Helpful software such as Button Builder Pro, Calendar Creator, Kid Pix Deluxe, Print Shop Deluxe, Art Explosion, Essential Teacher Tools, Graph Master, Mapmaker's Toolkit, Timeliner, MathType, and Adobe Acrobat Professional is available on the computer workstations. This software enables teachers to construct such items as handouts, activity sheets, bulletin board materials, and classroom badges. Each workstation is connected to a scanner and printer.

A manual radial binder machine that binds up to 450 pages is available for use. Educators are limited to five binder combs per semester, but the use of the binder machine is unlimited if the user provides the supplies.

Two die-cut machines with more than 800 patterns are available to help educators prepare their classrooms and create educational aids. Materials such as paper, foam board, mat board, bubble wrap, felt, fur, foil, magnets, tin, and wood can be used. The machines allow users to make multiple copies of letters, numbers, shapes, and other objects, which permits educators to save time. Users must supply their own materials to use with the machines.

Educators can create original buttons or choose from several available templates when using the electronic button maker and cutter. Each person is limited to five buttons per semester, but users who provide their own button supplies may use the machine to make extra buttons. Software is available to create and design original button artwork.

Two laminators are located in the ETC room. Each person is allocated ten free feet of lamination each semester. An Excel document is used to keep track of the lamination used by each person. Access Services sells a Pirate Nation Lamination Card for five dollars that allows the user an additional ten feet of lamination (figure 7.2). A lamination drop-off service is available for students and educators who have time constraints. Upon completing an online form, they leave their materials at the TRC service desk, and the TRC staff will laminate their materials within twenty-four hours.

Figure 7.2. Pirate Nation Lamination Card

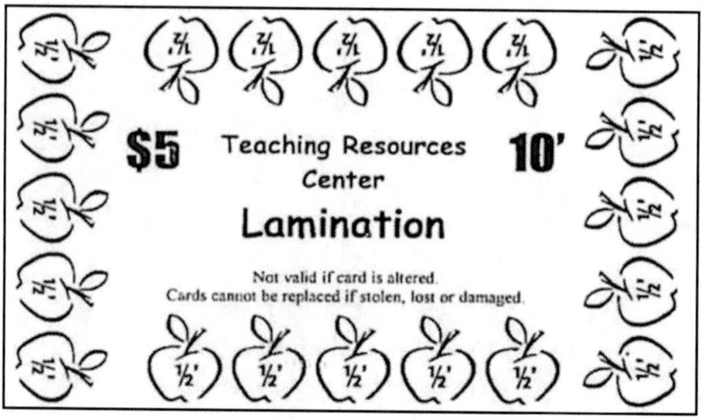

An Artwaxer is located in the ETC room. This machine distributes a thin film of wax on the back of materials. It eliminates the need for tape or staples because the waxed item will stick to all types of wall surfaces. This piece of equipment is very helpful and popular with educators at the beginning of the school year when they are setting up their classrooms. Materials that are waxed have multiple uses within the classroom and may be stored for use at later dates.

Basic office supplies and equipment are available in the ETC room. Tape, staplers, scissors, glue, markers, pens, pencils, staplers, paper clips, rubber bands, paper cutters, and pencil sharpeners can be found throughout the room.

Partnerships

Forming alliances with groups or individuals that share your service philosophy or mission is extremely valuable in the development and implementation of outreach services. Partnerships help reach out to your targeted audience in many ways. Some provide you with personal contacts to reach the targeted audience, and some may also provide financial support. Alliances are strategic resources that enable you to adjust the type of service, its delivery, and its location to meet the needs of your clientele (Trotta, 1993, p. 27).

Faculty

One type of alliance that benefits any curriculum materials center is partnerships with the faculty of the college of education. Activities such as faculty focus groups, office calls, faculty brown bag seminars, bibliographic instruction, and receptions honoring faculty are ways to improve faculty/librarian relations and increase faculty awareness of library services (Reeves et al., 2003, p. 62). The TRC encourages faculty to bring their classes to the curriculum materials center for bibliographic instruction. Librarians often visit classrooms to deliver on-site bibliographic instruction or to share resources and materials on specific subjects. This method of TRC promotion entices students and faculty to visit the library to use the valuable materials for lesson or unit preparations. Workshops are offered to the faculty to keep them abreast of the latest technology or resources that are available and being used in the profession. Librarians from the TRC have been guest lecturers in online classes, enabling the TRC to reach out to the distance education population. Each semester, the *TRC Treasure Chest*, a departmental newsletter, is sent via e-mail to the faculty and staff of the College of Education highlighting new services, resources, materials, and changes. Promotion and communication are essential components in strengthening partnerships, conveying to faculty that their input, in the form of material requests and suggestions for the TRC collection, is valuable and critical to student academic success.

The College of Education hosts several conferences and educational events throughout the year. The TRC supports these conferences and events through presentations, poster sessions, and exhibits of the resources and services of the TRC. Additionally, the center supports and reaches out to the educational clubs that are sponsored by the College of Education by providing guest speakers at meetings or by hosting meetings in the center. The TRC provides specialized support to the GEAR UP NC (Gaining Early Awareness and Readiness for Undergraduate Programs North Carolina) program and the North Carolina Teaching Fellows program, the most ambitious teacher recruitment program in the nation.

Campus

The School of Art and Design hosts a Youth Arts Festival in April each year. The festival brings over one hundred visual and performing artists to campus. Area residents of all ages are encouraged to attend. The festival is offered as a free community outreach event. Children have the opportunity to create their own artwork after viewing artists demonstrating their craft. The TRC collaborates with the School of Art and Design by providing storytellers for this event. What started as staff, faculty, and students reading selected books from the TRC collection has now evolved into professional storytellers from North Carolina telling original stories throughout the day. After hearing a story, children create art to reflect it.

To celebrate Hispanic Heritage Month in 2010, the local art museum, School of Art and Design, department of Foreign Languages and Literatures, and TRC partnered to offer an "Art without Borders" program. Art without Borders introduces the work of local, national, and international Latino artists to the community through several events, with the goal of building and strengthening ties between the diverse groups that make up our community. One of the events was a bilingual storytime and art workshop for children. Hosted by the TRC, the stories, featuring family life of famous Latinos, were read in Spanish and English by the Hispanic studies students. Afterwards, art education students helped children create bilingual autobiographies, which were taken home as souvenirs of an exciting day and event. The event drew more than one hundred participants.

The TRC reaches out to various departments, organizations, faculty and staff members, and students to collaborate on events, activities, and projects. Whether the curriculum materials center serves as a collection site for donated school supplies or a place to hold an organizational meeting, the TRC is ready to serve its patrons.

Community

In addition to special events discussed previously, the TRC serves as a place for community involvement. Lectures celebrating such events as

Constitution Day and Banned Books Week are often held in the TRC. Displays of children's books and exhibits featuring artwork from local schools can be found throughout the TRC, making the area a bright and cheerful place for studying or meeting with colleagues. Students who exhibit artwork in the TRC are recognized with formal certificates of appreciation. Such recognition provides students with a sense of pride in having artwork displayed on the university campus, encouraging them to continue to excel and exposing them to the university.

The TRC is proud to be the base library for many homeschoolers in the county, who use our materials and resources to supplement their teaching. They participate in the free Educator Library Card program by providing proof from the state of North Carolina that identifies them as homeschoolers. The TRC Outreach Coordinator attends regional homeschool meetings to promote the center's services, resources, and materials.

Since our curriculum materials center houses birth-to-twelfth-grade materials, students in several early college high school programs use the TRC to conduct research for papers and projects. Their visits to Joyner Library begin with a bibliographic session on the basics of conducting research, and then students are encouraged to use the available resources to find primary source material on their topics. For many students, this is their first introduction to a research library with various forms of materials, resources, and technology.

Members of the TRC visit area schools to read books to classes, offer storytelling, conduct puppet shows, provide minitalks on specific topics, tutor, and serve as judges in art and science competitions and senior projects. Faculty members of the TRC are heavily involved with the Battle of the Books competitions for middle and elementary schools, serving as judges, scorekeepers, and timekeepers for the local and regional competitions.

Library Profession

In 2006, the TRC partnered with Scholastic Library Publishing on a planning team to develop and implement a professional development opportunity for eastern North Carolina school media personnel (Bailey, Teel, & Walker, 2007, p. 3). The planning committee selected the event title "Librarian to Librarian Networking Summit." The goal of the summit was to create an atmosphere where school media personnel could share their expertise while networking with their colleagues. After conducting a needs assessment with the local school media personnel, it was determined that the conference should be held in Joyner Library and that Saturday would be the most logical day of the week to host the event. The Librarian to Librarian Networking Summit consists of four sessions, with eight roundtable discussions being offered during each of the four sessions. This format allows each participant the opportunity to contribute thoughts and ideas during the forty-five-minute sessions. Through the needs assessment, school media personnel requested that registration cost be minimal and that continuing education units (CEUs) be offered.

The planning committee organized a one-day Saturday summit for the school media personnel of eastern North Carolina. The agenda encompassed registration, opening and closing sessions, four concurrent sessions, morning and afternoon breaks, and an on-site box lunch (Bailey, Teel, & Walker, 2007, p. 5). A keynote speaker set the tone of the summit by addressing the participants during the opening session. The closing session provided a time of reflection and an opportunity to evaluate the day's events.

Based upon evaluation results and comments from participants, the Librarian to Librarian Networking Summit was a successful professional development opportunity for school media personnel. Recommendations for improvement included these:

- Hold the summit annually.
- Provide a continental breakfast.
- Continue the roundtable format.
- Invite a well-known author, illustrator, or librarian to serve as keynote speaker.
- Post large informational signs in areas where sessions are being held.

- Expand the conference to include school media personnel in all of North Carolina instead of just eastern North Carolina.
- Provide backup equipment for facilitators and speakers.
- Provide better driving directions to Joyner Library.

Recognizing the value of this professional development, the planning team realized the need for future summits and committed to providing them annually. Several improvements were implemented the following year. The Librarian to Librarian Networking Summit starts the day with a continental breakfast, and the event is now open to all school media personnel in North Carolina. The keynote speakers for the past three years have been nationally recognized authors. Other suggestions provided via the summit evaluations have been implemented each year to improve the Librarian to Librarian Networking Summit.

In 2011, the Librarian to Librarian Networking Summit added a new component to the event. The guest author agreed to conduct a session with the preservice teachers and faculty from the College of Education. This session was offered as an option and extension to their coursework allowing participants to interact firsthand with an award-winning author.

Workshops

Joyner Library has developed several digital collections, but three of these collections contain an educational component. The Outreach Coordinator serves as the educational consultant for each of these digital initiatives. Focus groups and usability studies were held with area educators to gather needed feedback on the digital initiative as the project began. Once the digital collection was created, workshops were held to introduce area educators to the collection. At the workshops, area educators received a demonstration of the collection and were asked to write a lesson activity or plan that incorporated a book, pamphlet, map, or artifact from the digital collection. These lesson activities and plans were then incorporated in the digital collection under Education Resources. The lesson plans were reviewed and edited by a master teacher who assured that the lesson activities and plans aligned with and integrated state goals and objectives. The educational consultant partnered with Learn NC, a program of the University of North Carolina at Chapel Hill School of Education which provides lesson plans, professional development, and innovative web resources to support teachers and improve K–12 education in North Carolina. The lesson plans and activities were highlighted and featured on the Learn NC website. These projects have provided valuable educational lesson plans that bring excitement along with primary and secondary sources to the K–12 classroom.

The Outreach Coordinator for the TRC is constantly promoting and demonstrating these digital collections to schools and educators throughout the area. Training on the digital collections that have an educational component has been very beneficial for area educators. Demonstrating an activity or lesson plan that incorporates a book, document, artifact, or picture from the digital collections teaches how that resource can be used in the classroom. In addition, presentations at educational conferences help to inform and promote the resources available within these digital collections.

Personnel

The ultimate success of any outreach program will depend upon the level of understanding and the support it gets from the staff implementing it (Trotta, 1993, p. 97). Committed, enthusiastic, flexible people with a positive attitude and vision are essential to any outreach program. The TRC has dedicated staff and faculty who work to provide needed assistance to educators at all levels through instruction, resources, and materials. It is the TRC staff and faculty members who have helped build an atmosphere conducive and open to learning for the center by providing positive customer service to meet the needs and expectations of patrons.

Funding

Most outreach programs are regarded as a value-added service instead of part of the basic library service (Trotta, 1993, p. 1). With this attitude from administrators, most library outreach programs are forced to seek funding from grants or special funds from companies or foundations. Finding a reliable source of funding for an outreach program is crucial and may involve several grants instead of one. Presenting a plan for an outreach program to library administrators, convincing them of the value of the program and seeking funding are the ultimate goals for any library outreach program. A library outreach program has a better chance to be successful if it is supported and funded by the library. However, in tough economic times all funding is closely scrutinized and all programs must be prepared to provide proof of their effectiveness. It is always important to maintain reliable and valid statistics to demonstrate to the administration the success of the program.

Marketing

Promotion is vital to the success of any outreach program. Identify your audience and develop a promotional campaign. Promote and market the program through your local and campus newspapers, radio, and television stations; make presentations to groups, host activities or events, and work closely with the library's marketing department to include the program in library promotions. Traditional outreach products such as brochures, pamphlets, newsletters, posters, and handouts are inexpensive ways to target the intended clientele. Promotional products such as pencils, pens, bookmarks, rulers, stickers, highlighters, and magnets should always have the library's contact information and address on the item. These products provide a nonthreatening introduction to the outreach program. Furthermore, library personnel can develop information packets to be distributed throughout the community. Staff can be creative and brainstorm new and interesting ideas. Current users of particular outreach services and resources are excellent voices for promoting outreach programs. Word of mouth is the most effective promotion for any outreach program.

Advancements in technology have created social networking sites that are valuable marketing tools. Social media such as Facebook, MySpace, YouTube, LinkedIn, Flickr, and Twitter allow direct connections to massive numbers of people. MySpace and Facebook can further the outreach efforts of any university library, much in the same way other technologies have extended the library's presence (Chu & Meulemans, 2008, p. 81).

The TRC, like other departments in Joyner Library, has a Facebook account. It is used to inform students, faculty, staff, and community about events, materials, and services in our department. At the most recent Librarian to Librarian Networking Summit, hosted by the TRC, several participants blogged about sessions they attended. This served to promote the event as well as inform those who were not able to attend the summit. Some summit participants asked that a Twitter account be established so they could tweet about the summit as well. Many patrons use mobile technology to search the online catalog, search databases, check e-mail, and post to Facebook. Having grown up with computers, the Net Generation is very tech savvy, and the Internet is their primary media vehicle (Mi & Nesta, 2006, pp. 415–416). They prefer to communicate through e-mail and instant messaging. They are very comfortable using RSS feeds, wikis, blogs, podcasts, and webpages to find information. It is imperative to keep abreast of the latest technology and utilize the tools of the Net Generation in promoting and informing them of outreach activities. Social media is a highly used form of communication for today's society.

Once a determination has been made on the audience that is to be targeted, then a decision on the best form of communication to use to reach that audience can be made. It should be noted that Internet access is still limited in some rural areas of North Carolina and school systems often have filters on their computers that restrict access to Internet sites. Local educators are the prime audience for the TRC outreach program, and their use of social media is limited. Social media is used to reach TRC students, staff, faculty, and community, but efforts to use social media to reach the local educator population are somewhat restricted.

Assessment

To evaluate the effectiveness of your outreach program, conducting an assessment is key. Libraries are increasingly expected to document their significance, and an assessment tool provides valuable information to prove the worth of the program. Surveys, interviews, and quizzes are assessment tools that provide statistical data and feedback used to gauge the success of outreach efforts. This information proves valuable during tough economic times. Positive feedback and statistics provide powerful arguments for continued funding of an outreach program.

Summary

The keys to a successful outreach program include partnerships, personnel, funding, marketing, and assessment. These facets need to be strong and work together in order to achieve the mission of the outreach program. By forming partnerships with agencies and organizations that share similar goals and objectives, partnerships and collaboration are strengthened. Partners offer community connections and help promote the outreach program. In order to build a successful outreach program, hiring competent people who exhibit positive attitudes allows the outreach vision to be obtained more easily and quickly. Library administration and staff who support and embrace the outreach services feel a sense of pride in the program. It is the responsibility of the outreach coordinator to promote the program so that every member of the library staff has a vested interest in the outreach program. Keeping library administration and staff informed of outreach plans and activities makes them a vital part to the promotion and success of the program. In order to justify the outreach program, it is essential to listen to potential and current users to gather information that supports successful outcomes that lead to achieving goals and visions. Finally, the continuation of any outreach program lies in its ability to assist in the achievement of the overall mission and goals of the library, proving its worth and vitality in these changing times.

References

Bailey, Alan R., Linda M. Teel, and Hazel J. Walker. 2006. "Designing an Academic Outreach Program through Partnerships with Public Schools." *E-JASL: The Electronic Journal of Academic & Special Librarianship* 7 (1). Retrieved from http://southernlibrarianship.icaap.org/content/v07n01/bailey_a01.htm.

———. 2007. "Librarian to Librarian Networking Summit: Collaboratively Providing

Professional Development for School Media Personnel." *Southeastern Librarian* 55 (1): 3–13.

Chu, Melanie, and Yvonne Nalani Meulemans. 2008. "The Problems and Potential of MySpace and Facebook Usage in Academic Libraries." *Internet References Services Quarterly* 13 (1): 69–85. doi:10.1300/J136v13n01_04.

ECU (East Carolina University) College of Education. 2011. "The Walter and Daisy Carson Latham Clinical Schools Network." Retrieved from the East Carolina University's College of Education website: http://www.ecu.edu/cs-educ/teached/ClinicalSchools.cfm.

Hagenbruch, Harriet. 2001. "Outreach and Public Relations in CMCs." In *A Guide to the Management of Curriculum Materials Centers for the 21st Century*, edited by Jo Ann Carr, 137–147. Chicago: American Library Association.

Hossfeld, Leslie. 2003. "Poverty in the East, 1980–2000: What Has Changed?" Retrieved from Eastern North Carolina Poverty Committee website: http://www.povertyeast.org/toolkit/research/PovertyInEasternNC.doc.

Mi, Jia, and Frederick Nesta. 2006. "Marketing Library Services to the Net Generation." *Library Management* 27 (6/7): 411–422. doi:10.1108/01435120610702404.

OLOS (Office for Literacy and Outreach Services). 2011. "Mission." Retrieved from the Office for Literacy and Outreach Services website: http://www.ala.org/ala/aboutala/offices/olos/index.cfm.

Reeves, Linda, Catherine Nishimuta, Judy McMillan, and Christine Godin. 2003. "Faculty Outreach: A Win-Win Proposition." In. *Outreach Services in Academic and Special Libraries*, edited by Paul Kelsey and Sigrid Kelsey, 57–68. Binghamton, NY: Haworth Information Press.

TRC (Teaching Resources Center). 2011. "Teaching Resources Center Mission" and "Teaching Resources Center Goals." Retrieved from the East Carolina University website: http://www.ecu.edu/cs-lib/trc/misgoals.cfm.

Trotta, Marcia. 1993. *Managing Library Outreach Programs*. New York: Neal-Schuman.

8 Evolution of the American Textbook: From Hornbooks to iPads

Nancy P. O'Brien, University of Illinois at Urbana-Champaign and
Judy Walker, University of North Carolina-Charlotte

This chapter explores the development of the American textbook from early origins as a hornbook in colonial America to the present-day implementation of electronic textbooks in the K–12 classroom. The terms schoolbook and textbook are used interchangeably. The chapter also discusses other formats and media found in the curriculum materials center over time, such as filmstrips, kits, and DVDs. The challenges of managing and working with a diverse array of materials are addressed.

When the first European settlers arrived in what was to become the United States of America, they brought with them a desire for an educated population and some of the written tools for teaching and learning. Initially, most textbooks were in the language of the immigrant population and reflected the values held by the country of origin. Latin was also commonly used in textbooks since it was a language for published educational works and for advanced study (Nietz, 1966, pp. 154–155). Typically these resources had a religious viewpoint and were used to simultaneously instill moral values and teach reading. Some of the early textbooks used in the colonies were hornbooks, so named because they were typically printed on a sheet of paper or parchment that was affixed to a paddle that could be held in one hand and covered with thin sheets of horn to protect the document. Most commonly, the hornbook text contained the alphabet, numerals, and, often, a copy of the Lord's Prayer (Carpenter, 1963, p. 21). The importance of education was a common theme among the immigrants, many of whom fled persecution in their countries of origin due to religious or other beliefs.

As the colonies became established, the importation of books to use in schools increased. Books were scarce but valued in the early years. One of the earliest textbooks used in the colonies was the *New England Primer* circa 1686 (Nietz, 1961, p. 47). From that point forward, the publication and proliferation of schoolbooks in America increased steadily. Lack of copyright meant that printers would print and publish texts with little acknowledgement of the original source of publication (Nietz, 1961, p. 7). Frequently texts used in Europe were reprinted by colonial printers without modification other than the name of the printer and sometimes the date of printing. This importation of European texts along with settlers to the New World meant that traditional schoolbooks perpetuated a focus on the history of Europe, and notably England, as well as reference to the various colonies established by England around the globe.

As the American colonies expanded westward to the Ohio territory and beyond, schoolbooks were part of that westward migration. In fact, the publishers of textbooks, particularly in the nineteenth century, also migrated west. As the immigrant populations increased, specialty publishing houses developed, such as Augsburg Publishing House and the Wartburg Press in the Midwest that focused on texts published in Norwegian, German, and English for Lutheran immigrants. In some cases, companies that provided supplies to schools also published textbooks. For example, the Prang Company and Joseph Dixon Crucible Company (a pencil manufacturer) offered textbooks that promoted their products. (Snow & Froehlich, 1922; Clark, Hicks, & Perry, 1898–1900; Joseph Dixon Crucible, 1904). In the case of Prang, drawing books, teacher's manuals, and workbooks emphasized art techniques that would benefit from Prang products such as crayons and watercolors; for the pencil manufacturer, a pamphlet offered a geographical lesson on the locations where the company's pencils were made, the places where the source materials were obtained, and the distribution of the final product. Later, companies such as Bell and Howell would follow similar practices in promoting the purchase of their equipment by selling education films to schools and libraries (Fabos, 2001, p. 12).

Some of the major publishers of schoolbooks in the United States included the American Book Company, Ginn, Heath, Houghton Mifflin, and Scott Foresman. Over time many of these publishers have merged into other companies, and some of these were formed from mergers of earlier companies in the nineteenth century.

The American textbook became more uniform through publication of editions that became familiar as household words, such as McGuffey's Readers. "McGuffey's was… popular and widely used. It is estimated that at least 120 million copies of McGuffey's Readers were sold between 1836 and 1960, placing its sales in a category with the Bible and Webster's Dictionary. Since 1961 they have continued to sell at a rate of some 30,000 copies a year. No other textbook bearing a single person's name has come close to that mark. McGuffey's Readers are still in use today in some school systems, and by parents for home schooling purposes" (National Park Service, 1993). While few textbooks have had the extensive history and popularity of McGuffey's Readers, some, such as the "Dick and Jane" books, have become nostalgic and iconic representations of an era in US history.

Certain authors were synonymous with branches of study such as geography (Ralph Tarr and Frank McMurry), social studies (Harold Rugg), mathematics (Benjamin Greenleaf or George A. Wentworth), or reading (William H. Elson and William S. Gray). The Elson readers, eventually transformed into the *Basic Readers* series published by Scott Foresman, are more popularly known as the Dick and Jane readers. Just as schoolbooks evolved to reflect an American focus, the Dick and Jane readers developed into several different editions to meet the needs of particular regions or populations in the United States. For example, an edition was produced using the Initial Teaching Alphabet (i.t.a.) of 44 characters that offered a phonetic spelling of words; an edition was published for urban areas that included illustrations depicting characters of color; the standard edition with Dick, Jane, and Sally continued to be published; and the *Cathedral Basic Readers* were published for Catholic schools (Robinson et al., 1965a, 1965b, 1965c; McDowell et al., 1963). These developments reflect the social and political movements that were occurring in the larger society.

Initially, schoolbooks followed the format that was familiar in other books, with a great deal of dense text and occasional illustrations. Literature and reading books for the upper grades contained few illustrations in the seventeenth and eighteenth centuries. Arithmetic and mathematics books were very formulaic with extensive examples of mathematical equations, but limited explanations to the student or to the teacher. History texts contained the occasional portrait of major figures or picture of scenes of historical note. Geography books often contained maps, and, as emphasis shifted toward social geography, increasingly contained illustrations and photographs. Social studies, as a development of the twentieth century, reflected that same emphasis on illustrations and photos since it was a relative newcomer to the subject areas taught within the elementary and secondary schools. Its previous incarnation as separate subject areas, such as civics and history, has a long record of being taught within schools using varying methods. Similarly, health schoolbooks such as those in the nineteenth century relied less on illustrations and more on text. The emphasis on including illustrations to aid learning expanded rapidly in the twentieth century and reflected new understandings of the learning process. Improvements in size of font, illustrations, and white space in textbooks began in the 1820s with publications from the Samuel Goodrich publishing company (Carpenter, 1963, pp. 274–275). Some publishers began to adopt similar formatting practices, but many continued to reproduce dense text in small font with little illustrative material well into the early twentieth century. A comparison of nineteenth- and twentieth-century schoolbooks in areas such as mathematics or reading show a significant leap from little illustration to extensive inclusion of illustrative material. Resistance to some of these innovations can be seen in suggestions to teachers such as that found in the *Werner Arithmetic* (1897), which exhorted, "Do not waste time in 'pretty,' useless, namby-pamby number stories in connection with splints or toothpicks." (Hall, 1897, Book One, p. 8).

In the early years of the American colonies, emphasis in schooling was placed on reading, writing, and arithmetic. These were viewed as the basics that were needed for an educated individual. While higher study in any of these areas was possible, having the basic skills in these three areas meant that someone was better able to function within society and had improved opportunities for advancement in work or living conditions. As educational opportunities increased through mandatory schooling across colonies, and later in territories and states, other school subjects became increasingly available. History as a subject of study has always been a staple of education since it offers explanations of current social and political situations, as well as opportunities to point out unpopular systems such as tyranny. Other subject areas that were added to the curriculum include health, art, manual or industrial arts, and civics. As the shift from the basic reading, 'riting, and 'rithmetic curriculum changed to a more expansive course of study, the schoolbooks to support these subject areas also evolved. By the late nineteenth century, graded textbooks to match levels in the graded schools became commonplace (Venezky, 1987, p. 251). These graded books encompassed a variety of subject areas.

As Friedrich Froebel (1782–1852), Maria Montessori (1870–1952), and others promoted teaching methods that included hands-on use of objects and play, the classroom began to routinely include objects that moved beyond textbooks and chalkboards (Peltzman, 1998, pp. 25, 83). Learning theories that focused on the intellectual development of the child began to incorporate techniques that stimulated thinking and making connections rather than rote memorization (Unger, 2007, pp. 244, 247). Similarly, the textbook itself became more visual in nature and included illustrations, greater white space, and less dense text. This was a continuation of the initiatives taken by Samuel Goodrich in presenting material in an attractive and engaging format likely to appeal to students (Carpenter, 1963, p. 275).

Teacher's manuals and editions were uncommon in the nineteenth and earlier centuries. Instructions to teachers might be included in a preface, an introduction, or possibly the back matter of a text, but not necessarily (Venezky, 1987, p. 252). In the late nineteenth and early twentieth centuries, it is not uncommon to find authors of schoolbooks pointing out their innovative inclusion of guidance to teachers and lamenting the lack of the same in competitors' works. In some cases, authors are unapologetic about the fact that their work offers nothing new in substance, but that the presentation is an improvement over the competitors' work. Other innovations that occurred at this time were supplemental materials to aid the student. Heavy card-stock protractors might be found in the back of a geometry or mathematics book such as *The New Mathematics* (Stone, 1927), while workbooks or other consumable texts became more common. As technology became more widely available in the twentieth century, filmstrips, sound recordings on vinyl albums, and multimedia items started to infiltrate the classroom (Fabos, 2001, pp. 2, 4). Teachers had to develop enough technical ability to run filmstrips (possibly in synchronous combination with vinyl albums or, later, audiocassettes) or films in the classroom. In some cases, technical support was provided by school or library staff. These same media appeared in curriculum centers at teachers colleges and required that the staff in those centers have enough knowledge and possibly the equipment to use and read the media in whatever format was provided. The progression of technology in schools followed the patterns in general society, such as films evolving into videocassettes and eventually DVDs. These changes required that curriculum centers and libraries that supported schools and teacher education programs acquire and maintain these formats as well. As early as 1898, curriculum materials centers were collecting these supplemental items (Roberts, 1990, p. 23). Not only media, but also kits and three-dimensional material became a standard part of the classroom. In the early years, these supplemental items might have been as simple as maps, globes, and charts displaying the alphabet or simple words. As educational theories developed about enriching the environment to aid in student learning, other types of items joined the classroom supply of learning tools. Reading charts, flash cards, manipulative items to support mathematical learning, educational games, science sets (sometimes with live specimens such as mealworms), kits containing puppets, and other items that allowed the teacher to engage the student in learning appeared in the classroom. These items were considered fresh approaches to demonstrate science or mathematics or discuss social issues in ways that offer increased understanding by students. "As educational historians have noted, each new technology introduced into schools spurred an enormous amount of enthusiasm among educators, administrators, and technology advocates," according to Fabos (2001, p. 1). Fabos further notes that each new technology was viewed as an "educational panacea" that could alleviate a number of problems with the educational system (p. 9). Rather than being viewed as innovative, by the end of the twentieth century, the acquisition of kits, DVDs, and other media to supplement the learning process was considered routine. For the curriculum materials center, managing this type of material requires unique solutions that often differ from practices in the rest of the library. For example, special containers to store and to circulate kit material are often necessary. Loan periods may differ since the demand for this type of material is high, but the actual length of use is fairly brief. To house plastic tubs of kit items, board games, oversized boxes of reading and language arts material, and so on may require shelving to be adapted or even require nonstandard equipment. For a working collection of curriculum materials, the issues related to acquiring and maintaining a variety of formats requires flexibility and adaptability. It is no wonder, then, that when the next technological step in the form of electronic textbooks made its appearance, further adaptations were necessary.

As print textbooks evolved over time, another revolution was taking place that is now, and will for the foreseeable future, affect K–12 textbooks and curriculum materials collections and centers. Consider these words written in 1945 by Dr. Vannevar Bush, who was known primarily for his work on the Manhattan Project but also worked extensively in the field of analog computing, in which he describes

...a future device for individual use, which is a sort of mechanized private file and library. It needs a name, and, to coin one at random, "memex" will do. A memex is a device in which an individual stores all his books, records, and communications, and which is mechanized so that it may be consulted with exceeding speed and flexibility. It is an enlarged intimate supplement to his memory....

Most of the memex contents are purchased on microfilm ready for insertion. Books of all sorts, pictures, current periodicals, newspapers, are thus obtained and dropped into place....

If the user wishes to consult a certain book, he taps its code on the keyboard, and the title page of the book promptly appears before him, projected onto one of his viewing positions. (Bush, 1945, pp. 106–107)

Although computers were already being used in mathematics and the sciences to do calculations, Bush was taking their use a step further. He saw a future in which computers could help anyone connect quickly with information and interact with knowledge. From a present-day perspective, what he described looks very much like what can be done now via the World Wide Web. Although he may have had the wrong technologies in mind, his vision planted the seed that now has educators talking about students using a variety of digital formats to explore the world of knowledge and teachers tapping into those same resources to enhance their curriculums.

It was another twenty years before the idea began take root. In 1965 the sociologist and philosopher Ted Nelson at the National Conference of the Association for Computing Machinery introduced the word *hypertext* "to mean a body of written or pictorial material interconnected in such a complex way that it could not conveniently be presented or represented on paper" (*OED Online*, 2010b). In this same presentation he also coined the term *hypermedia*, which he referred to as "mixture of media printed text, handwritten documents, photographs, movies and so on linked together in associative networks" (*OED Online*, 2010a).

Then in 1967 he and Andreis van Dam developed the *Hypertext Editing System* at Brown University ("History of Hypertext," paragraph 5) and a new era of interacting with knowledge was born. Just about everything done on a computer and the Word Wide Web today by the average user is based on the concept of hypertext and hypermedia.

However, the advent of the personal computer and the release of the *Tutor-Tech* hypermedia authoring tool in 1983 for the Apple II computers caused educators to finally take notice of this new technology. Then in 1987, Apple released *HyperCard* for the Macintosh ("History of Hypertext," paragraph 7). Shortly after that in 1988 *HyperStudio* was released for the education market ("Hyperstudio"). These two programs, along with shifting philosophies of education from rote memorization and linear curriculum to more individual experiential learning, had a tremendous impact on the types of resources educators used in the classroom.

The advent of hypertext ushered in new possibilities for students and how they could interact with text. Although references to electronic books appeared in the early 1970s, probably the most well-known use of the term and the one that captured the hearts and minds of students was *The Hitchhiker's Guide to the Galaxy* (originally published in 1974), which Douglas Adams described as "a sort of electronic book" (Adams, 1997, p. 47). A synonym now used more often to refer to this new type of book is *e-book*. The American Library Association first used the term in 1988 to describe "a small, hand-held, flat recording device able to replay text as a portable cassette player replays sound" ("Things to Come," 1988).

From their inception there has been some confusion as to what actually constitutes an electronic book or e-book. Purists feel it is a book delivered on a specific device like a Kindle or Nook. Others feel it is any book that is delivered electronically, which could include CDs, DVDs, stand-alone computer programs, etc., or accessed via the World Wide Web to be read on a computer or a separate device. Another much-discussed element has to do with its interactivity. Again, purists see it as another rendering of text with little interactivity, while others believe that just making print books digital is not the most effective use of the format. They believe it should provide the reader a wider range of experience and interactivity by accessing audio, video, or links to additional information. It is this interactivity that is most intriguing for students and educators. Since e-books have been in a state of constant flux since the 1980s, there is probably little that can be said definitively to resolve this debate. The term *e-book* will for the foreseeable future conjure up a variety of ideas, but as Hillesund indicates, "e-books have characteristics that in some ways supersede those of traditional books, being more flexible and accessible than paper books will ever be. E-books are a new, self-contained medium that will have an enormous impact in time on society" (Hillesund, 2001).

In 1992 the first e-books began to arrive in curriculum materials centers in the form of CDs such as Broderbund's *Arthur's Teacher Trouble* and *Just Grandma and Me* and Microsoft's *Encarta Encyclopedia*. They took advantage of the interactive properties of the new format. Broderbund's CDs were a hybrid of text and Saturday morning cartoons. Students could have the book read to them in several languages, or they could read it themselves. If they didn't understand a word, they could click on the word for the definition and pronunciation. Students were also encouraged to click on different objects on the screen to animate the characters and objects, adding new dimensions to the story. Many companies that published encyclopedias and dictionaries were quick to jump on the e-book bandwagon. They saw the advantages of the new medium. It would be easy to update; cost less to produce (no more printing of multivolume sets); include the ability to add animation, audio, and video; and simplify sending readers from one entry to another. Encyclopedias became a source of interconnected information and knowledge through implementation of an electronic format.

Since the mid-80s when hypertext became a reality for the general public, there has been talk of how the technology could transform textbooks, but much of the focus has been on e-textbooks in higher education. One of the primary hindrances to the proliferation of electronic textbooks, and e-books in general, has been the lack of standardization in delivery systems. Traditional higher education publishers have been experimenting for over fifteen years with ways to deliver their products electronically. At first they included CDs with print texts. Then some moved to just selling them as CDs. Others took another path, associating a website with hard copies. A few have taken the leap to providing the text entirely online. Recently, new companies have appeared to challenge the traditional publishers by offering their textbooks exclusively through the World Wide Web. Many of these companies, and a few of the traditional publishers, allow professors to create their own book by picking which chapters they want to include and decide in what order the chapters should be presented.

In the mid-90s, K–12 textbook publishers started incorporating e-books into their reading series, primarily for enrichment or motivation. They also began digitizing supplemental materials such as worksheets, enrichment and remedial activities, and pre- and posttests and delivering them via CD or DVD. Video and audio support materials also moved from VHS and cassette tapes to CDs and then to DVDs. Most recently publishers have been enhancing their textbooks via the World Wide Web with interactive sites that teachers and students can access. Some require passwords and others do not. But even with the addition of all this digital content, the traditional student and teacher editions of textbooks have remained intact until recently.

In 2009, the Texas legislature approved House Bill 4294, which broadened the state's definition of K–12 textbooks, allowing more flexibility for districts and charter schools in the state to adopt electronic textbooks. The bill still requires that electronic textbooks go through the same review process as traditional textbooks. Another Texas bill, House Bill 2488, required the Texas State Board of Education to adopt open source textbooks for secondary courses developed by Texas institutions of higher education or public technical institutes. Of course one of the primary motivations for the passage of these bills was economics since open source electronic textbooks can usually be downloaded for free. The ramifications of the passage of these bills will reverberate throughout the country since Texas is the largest single purchaser of K–12 textbooks in the country. (Wentworth, 2010).

California, for budgetary reasons, is also encouraging school districts to adopt open source electronic textbooks. In 2009 Governor Schwarzenegger, through his Free Digital Textbook Initiative (CLRN, 2008), invited publishers of electronic textbooks to align their texts to state standards. As of April 2010, the California Learning Resource Network has reviewed and approved thirty-one titles. Most of the titles are in the areas of mathematics and the sciences at the secondary level. Riverside Unified School District plans to have at least one class in every high school piloting a digital textbook and reader in the fall of 2010 (Fensterwald, 2010).

Although no electronic textbooks have actually been adopted in Texas as of this writing, in March 2010 Forbes.com reported that with the release of the Apple iPad, a number of major educational publishers, such as McGraw-Hill, Houghton Mifflin Harcourt K–12, Pearson Education, and Kaplan, would be vigorously pursuing the electronic textbook market at both the higher education and K–12 levels. The article indicates "some experts predict that within the next 10 years, most US college students—and many high-school and elementary-school students as well—will probably be reading course materials on an electronic device instead of in a paper book" (Knowledge@Wharton, 2010). This appears to be the consensus opinion within the education community, especially with budget cutbacks and the prospect of a slow recovery from the 2009 recession.

As the electronic textbook has evolved over the past two decades, the debate over advantages and disadvantages of the format for students and educators has remained relatively consistent. The primary advantage for teachers is the opportunity it gives them to customize content in a way they could not with print textbooks (Johnson, 2010). It can be easily updated. If it is interactive with links to audio files, animations, and videos, students benefit because it will address differences in learning styles and maturation. Students will be more engaged in their learning because they too will be able to customize content to meet their needs. Because companies do not have to print thousands of copies, e-texts should be more economical to produce and friendlier to the environment. Electronic textbooks may also have a physical impact on the students themselves by preventing future backaches because students won't have to lug multiple heavy texts home in their book bags (Freedman, 2009)!

Disadvantages are also numerous. Students may get distracted more easily. Because e-texts are flexible, teachers may need more preparation time to develop their instructional plans. Then there is the question of authority with open source texts, not to mention the problem of the digital divide. Even if the text is open source, will economically disadvantaged students have the same access as those from more affluent communities? The same question arises in relation to students with disabilities. Much of this debate is based on opinion and speculation since most educational communities have been slow to adopt e-textbooks. Researchers are only beginning to study the true impact of this new technology on student learning.

From this very brief summary of the evolution of e-books and e-textbooks, one can deduce that curriculum materials centers will need to be incorporating this format into their collections as school districts move from print to digital formats. Maintaining a current print textbook collection has a number of challenges not encountered when building a regular trade book collection. Integrating and maintaining a K–12 electronic textbook collection will add another layer of challenges that will need to be addressed. The challenges revolve around two broad issues: the nature of e-textbooks and access to them. It is difficult to address these issues individually since they are intimately connected to each other. The nature of the e-text influences what type of access is needed, so an understanding of the variety of forms an electronic textbook can take is important. Since these are new arrivals on the scene, curriculum materials centers are just beginning to work through these issues. As with most of the resources found in centers, how they are organized and accessed will depend greatly on the philosophies, policies, and technology resources of the institution in which the center is housed.

How electronic books are published and delivered varies greatly. As mentioned earlier, a number of traditional textbook companies will soon, if they have not already, be marketing electronic books to both the K–12 and higher education market. In addition to these traditional companies, there are a growing number of new companies that are publishing their textbooks only electronically. Exactly how the companies will deliver these texts is yet to be seen. Traditional companies may just expand their websites and require passwords, or they may decide to deliver content via some type of handheld device. Although the cost for producing e-texts will be less than for print versions, most of the companies will develop pricing structures that are tied to a district's student population. This presents acquisition and licensing problems for a curriculum materials center. Many centers rely on publishers donating materials to their collections. Will the publishers be willing to do the same with their electronic versions? Will it be possible for the centers to partner with school districts to have access to the titles being used in the district? How will the companies determine the center's user population for licensing purposes?

Because much of the current push for districts to consider adopting electronic textbooks instead of print editions is rooted in budget issues, many states are encouraging their districts to bypass the commercial publishers and consider adopting open source electronic textbooks being developed by nonprofit entities such as universities and foundations. By definition, open source electronic textbooks are free, although there may be some licensing agreements involved. These e-texts don't present as big an acquisition or access problem as proprietary e-texts, but centers may still encounter some access problems.

There is a third way electronic textbooks can be published. Districts or the teachers within a district can publish their own e-texts. Open source sites like Wikibooks and WITTIE and course management tools like Moodle make it possible for teachers to create their own electronic textbooks with the same bells and whistles (audio, video, animations, graphics, assessment, and interactivity) as a commercial publisher. Although time-consuming for the educators developing the e-texts, the product will be more closely aligned to local standards and very flexible, allowing for a variety of teaching and learning styles. These electronic textbooks will present a unique challenge to curriculum centers. Most school districts do not communicate well with the public. Finding out what e-texts are being developed by districts and how they can be accessed could prove to be a Herculean task for curriculum materials center staff. The issue is compounded by the fact that most curriculum materials centers need to provide materials to college students working at a number of different school districts. It will be imperative that curriculum materials center staff develop a close working relationship with the school districts they serve to insure their students have access to district-developed electronic textbooks.

The structure of a print textbook is relatively standard from one publisher to another. They may vary in size, shape, and binding, but in general they can be cataloged, classified, and arranged on a shelf for students to peruse and check out. Electronic textbooks are another entity entirely. Some e-textbooks reside as pages on a World Wide Web site and can be accessed only via some type of browser. How will students know the center provides access to the e-texts? Should they be classified and cataloged with links in the online catalog? Or should there be a separate access point such as a curriculum materials center webpage with the links organized by subject or grade level? Yet another option would be to create a separate, searchable database.

But that is only the tip of the access iceberg. Curriculum materials centers will need to address the issue of browsers and what type of device the students and faculty will use to run the browser. Although browsers have improved greatly over the years and now utilize standards so that users don't run into display issues, it is still possible that a particular electronic textbook will display correctly in some browsers and not others. Will the students need access to a variety of browsers if they are viewing the text in the confines of the center? Does the center have enough computers or other devices to accommodate a methods class that comes in to evaluate the texts? If the student is not physically in the center, what type of device will he or she use to access the e-text—a desktop computer, a laptop, a netbook, a smartphone, an iPad? How will the different devices impact access?

Another publishing-related challenge is the format of the document. Currently e-texts are being published in over twenty-five different file types. The more common file types like HTML and PDF can be read on a variety of devices. But many of the others, like .azw for the Kindle and .tr3 for TomeRaider, are proprietary. To read them students need either to have the physical equipment such as the Kindle or have an application installed on their computer or handheld device. This presents a tremendous problem for curriculum materials centers. How will they deal with the variety of file types? Libraries have already run into a similar issue with many of the audiobook and video collections they purchased only to discover they will work on a computer or MP3 player but not an iPod. What happens when one of the districts in the center's service area adopts e-texts that must be read on a Kindle and another adopts ones that need to be read on a Nook? Will the center have to, or even be able to, purchase both devices? The arrival of the iPad and Google's eBookstore may help alleviate some of this problem. A number of applications (apps) have been created for the iPad that will allow students to read proprietary documents for the Kindle, Nook, Stanza, and other devices. Google has also created apps that will allow its books to be viewed on multiple platforms and devices. The problem then becomes more of an annoyance; students will have to remember which app will read what titles.

Two additional questions must be addressed by a curriculum materials center if the electronic text must be read on a handheld device. The first, and probably the easier of the two to address, is how the device will be handled physically. Students and teachers are used to being able to walk into the curriculum materials center, go up to the shelves, and leisurely peruse the textbooks. Electronic textbooks do not lend themselves to this type of behavior. They can't be "seen" on the shelf. The expensive nature of the device will necessitate creating some type of checkout system. This of course leads to questions about lending policies. Can they be taken out of the center? For how long? What are the consequences if the devices don't come back? Although these are tricky questions, they are familiar issues for libraries.

The second, more complicated question is what will actually be on the devices. The concept of one electronic text series per device is completely out of the question for most curriculum materials centers because of their slim to nonexistent budgets. So what can be done? One option would be to group the titles by subject and grade level so that all the high school mathematics titles would be on one device. But then what happens when more than one student needs those books? How many devices can a center afford to duplicate? Another option might be to devise some type of system where files can be added to and removed from the device to accommodate the needs of the student. So, if a preservice elementary student will be working with a third-grade class, he or she could ask the staff of the center to upload the appropriate electronic textbook series to a device to be checked out. This will require turn-around time that the student may or may not have. A third option and probably the way technology will drive the issue is to load the materials directly onto the student's personal handheld device. This immediately throws up red flags for most curriculum materials center staff. What about copyright? How will it affect pricing and licensing agreements? If the titles are open source electronic textbooks, it is not a problem. If they are commercial titles, however, there will need to be a lot of negotiating, but it is not an insurmountable problem.

It is possible that some of these issues will work themselves out in the marketplace. The industry may arrive at some core standards, or accept a single format or device. But one thing is certain: academic libraries in general and curriculum materials centers in particular will need to devise a way to accommodate electronic textbooks in order to meet the needs of their students and faculty. The decisions they make in regard to electronic textbooks will need to be flexible in order to keep up with a format that is still in its infancy and will surely continue to evolve in the coming decade.

Conclusion

From its origins as a hornbook in the American colonies to its present incarnation in an electronic format, the textbook has adapted to the needs of the elementary and secondary classroom. Often reflecting social and political influences as well as contemporary theories of pedagogy, the textbook remains a staple element in the classroom regardless of format. Accompanied by various types of media and objects, the textbook adjusts to meet the needs of students in different time periods. The curriculum materials center needs to practice that same degree of flexibility and adaptability in providing resources in whatever format is appropriate to students and teachers in teacher education programs.

References

Adams, Douglas. 1997. *The Hitchhiker's Guide to the Galaxy*. New York: Random House.

Bush, Vannevar. 1945. "As We May Think." *The Atlantic* 176 (1): 101–108. Retrieved from http://www.theatlantic.com/magazine/archive/1969/12/as-we-may-think/3881.

Carpenter, Charles H. 1963. *History of American Schoolbooks*. Philadelphia: University of Pennsylvania Press.

Clark, John Spencer, Mary Dana Hicks, and Walter S. Perry. 1898–1900. *The Prang Elementary Course in Art Instruction*. Boston: Prang Educational.

CLRN (California Learning Resource Network). 2008. "Free Digital Textbook Initiative." Retrieved from http://www.clrn.org/FDTI/index.cfm.

Fabos, Bettina. 2001. "Media in the Classroom: An Alternative History." Paper presented at the annual meeting of the American Educational Research Association, Seattle, WA, April 10–14, 2001. Retrieved from ERIC database (ED454850).

Fensterwald, John. 2010, May 6. "Digital Textbooks Coming, Quickly and Surely." *Thoughts on Public Education* (blog). Retrieved July 11, 2010, from http://toped.svefoundation.org/2010/05/06/digital-texts-coming-quickly-and-surely.

Freedman, Thomas Z. 2009. *A Kindle in Every Backpack: A Proposal for eTextbooks in American Schools*. Washington, DC: Democratic Leadership Council. Retrieved from http://www.dlc.org/documents/DLC_Freedman_Kindle_0709.pdf.

Hall, Frank H. 1897. *The Werner Arithmetic, Oral and Written*, Book One, Parts I, II, and III. Chicago: Werner School Book.

Hillesund, Terje. 2001. "Will E-books Change the World?" *First Monday* 6 (10). Retrieved from http://firstmonday.org/htbin/cgiwrap/bin/ojs/index.php/fm/article/viewArticle/891/800.

"History of Hypertext," *Wikipedia, The Free Encyclopedia*. Retrieved July 11, 2010 from http://en.wikipedia.org/wiki/History_of_hypertext.

"Hyperstudio." *Wikipedia, The Free Encyclopedia*. Retrieved July 11, 2010 from http://en.wikipedia.org/wiki/Hyperstudio.

Johnson, Bryce. 2010. "Bryce Johnson on the Future of Education." *Our Blook*. Retrieved from http://www.ourblook.com/Future-of-Education/Bryce-Johnson-on-the-Future-of-Education.html.

Joseph Dixon Crucible. (1904). *Pencil Geography: Designed for Boys and Girls of All Ages*, 4th ed. Jersey City, NJ: Joseph Dixon Crucible.

Knowledge@Wharton. 2010, March 5. "Electronic Textbooks? You Bet." Forbes. com. Retrieved July 11, 2010, from http://www.forbes.com/2010/03/05/electronic-textbooks-ipad-entrepreneurs-technology-wharton.html.

McDowell, John B., et al. 1963. *The New Cathedral Basic Readers*. Chicago: Scott, Foresman.

National Park Service. 1993, January. "William Holmes McGuffey and His Readers." *The Museum Gazette*. Jefferson National Expansion Memorial. Retrieved from http://www.nps.gov/jeff/historyculture/upload/mcguffey.pdf.

Nietz, John A. 1961. *Old Textbooks: Spelling, Grammar, Reading, Arithmetic, Geography, American History, Civil Government, Physiology, Penmanship, Art, Music—As Taught in the Common Schools from Colonial Days to 1900*. Pittsburgh, PA: University of Pittsburgh Press.

———. 1966. *The Evolution of American Secondary School Textbooks: Rhetoric & Literature, Algebra, Geometry, Natural History (Zoology), Botany, Natural Philosophy (Physics), Chemistry, Latin and Greek, French, German & World History As Taught in American Latin Grammar School Academies and Early High Schools before 1900*. Rutland, VT: C. E. Tuttle.

OED Online. 2010a. "Hypermedia." Oxford University Press. Retrieved from http://www.oed.com/view/Entry/243460.

———. 2010b. "Hypertext." In Oxford University Press. http://www.oed.com/view/Entry/243461.

Peltzman, Barbara R. 1998. *Pioneers of Early Childhood Education: A Bio-Bibliographical Guide*. Westport, CT: Greenwood Press.

Roberts, Francis X. 1990. "An Early Example of a Curriculum Materials Collection in an Institution of Teacher Education." *Behavioral & Social Sciences Librarian* 9 (1): 21–28.

Robinson, Helen M., et al. 1965a. *The New Basic Readers* [standard ed.]. Chicago: Scott, Foresman.

———. 1965b. *The New Basic Readers* [i.t.a. eksperimental edisjhon]. Chicago: Scott, Foresman.

———. 1965c. *The New Basic Readers* [multicultural ed.]. Chicago: Scott, Foresman.

Snow, Bonnie E., and Hugo B. Froehlich. 1922. *Industrial Art Text-Books: A Graded Course in Art, in Its Relation to Industry*, rev. ed. Chicago: Prang.

Stone, John C. 1927. *The New Mathematics*. Chicago: Benj. H. Sanborn.

"Things to Come." 1988. *American Libraries* 19 (5): 391.

Unger, Harlow G. 2007. *Encyclopedia of American Education*, 3rd ed. New York: Facts on File.

Venezky, Richard L. 1987. "A History of the American Reading Textbook." *Elementary School Journal* 87 (3): 246–265.

Wentworth, J. 2010, March 4. "Viewpoint: Electronic Textbooks in Texas Public Schools." *San Antonio Express-News*. Retrieved from mySA.com July 11, 2010, http://www.mysanantonio.com/community/opinion/Viewpoint_Electronic_textbooks_in_Texas_public_schools.html.

Part III: Future

9

The Value of the Curriculum Center's Mission Statement: Meeting the Needs of Evolving Teacher Education

Julie L. Miller and Nadean Meyer, Eastern Washington University

This chapter explores the value of creating a mission statement to help redefine the academic library's curriculum center in the context of the current dynamic teacher education environment. The mission statement and related texts, such as vision, values, and guiding principle statements, define the purpose of the center for its constituents. It acts as a bridge between communities of practice and organizations, demonstrating the relationship of the center to the teacher education program, the academic library, and the college or university. Most importantly, the mission statement provides guidance for making policy and procedure decisions that are proactive. In an evolving education environment, a mission statement affirmed through assessment processes remains relevant to its constituents now and in the future.

In the preface to *Libraries, Mission, and Marketing: Writing Mission Statements That Work* (2004), Linda K. Wallace writes, "Seeing mission statements colorfully written and prominently posted opened my eyes to their power. I began to wonder why more libraries don't make better use of their mission statements.... Librarians complain that their work is undervalued, but they are better at describing what they do—collect, organize, preserve, etc.—than at communicating why their work is important and the difference it makes in people's lives" (pp. v–vi). The same can be said of curriculum centers. Historically defined as a special collection within the academic library or education program, the curriculum center's purpose has been to provide a physical space for curricular materials. In fact, the Association of College and Research Libraries

(ACRL) *Guidelines for Curriculum Materials Centers* defines the term *curriculum materials center* as "a physical location of a curriculum materials collection" (ACRL, 2009b).

This limited definition of the curriculum center, however, does not describe the curriculum centers that our current (and future) teacher candidates need. They are entering a dynamic profession that is being transformed by changes—in government policy, in technology, in our understanding of the biology and psychology of learning, in a professional culture that increasingly emphasizes student learning outcomes. They are expected to be competent in recognizing and adapting to a range of learning styles, to be proficient in the use of multimedia technologies, to have subject expertise, to use classroom assessments to provide evidence of student learning, to be reflective about their own teaching effectiveness, and to grow and improve. In order for the curriculum center to be important in the education of these future teachers—to make a difference in their lives and, through them, in the lives of children—the curriculum center of the twenty-first century is being redefined as more than a physical space housing collections of materials. Curriculum centers still provide quality curricular resources for teacher candidates and the faculty in teacher education programs, as well as other user groups. Increasingly, however, they are a constellation of resources and services beyond their collections, depending upon the unique needs of the educational program they support. As the curriculum center evolves, the mission statement is an essential tool in redefining the curriculum center and its value to teacher education.

This chapter advocates the use of the mission statement as a tool for change. It is not a how-to guide for writing an effective mission statement; many of those guides already exist. Rather, it focuses on the benefits of using the mission statement to identify and affirm the essential work of the curriculum center looking forward. Those benefits include communicating the purpose of the center to the people who need to know, bridging organizations (big and small, internal and external), guiding day-to-day decisions (what Wallace [2004] calls "putting the mission statement to work" [p. 24]), and engaging others in the ongoing transformation of the curriculum center as a vital resource for learning.

Using the Mission Statement to Communicate the Curriculum Center's Purpose

The dynamic environment of academic libraries and the struggle to keep them relevant to students and faculty who have access to a broader range of information resources than ever before have been well documented. As far back as 2004, Stephen Abram listed "sustaining relevance" as the number one concern of libraries in his presentation to the American Library Association (Abram, 2007, p. 119). In order to maintain collections and services, library administrators are being asked to provide evidence of the library's impact on student learning and faculty research. In *The Value of Academic Libraries* (2010), a survey of current practices commissioned by ACRL, Megan Oakleaf writes, "[Academic] librarians no longer can rely on their stakeholders' belief in their importance. Rather, they must demonstrate their value" (p. 11). When budgets do not keep pace with operational costs, administrators allocate resources to the areas whose value to the academic endeavor they know and understand.

An effective mission statement is one tool for communicating the curriculum center's value. An effective statement establishes organizational focus, identifies its constituents (or stakeholders), motivates (or inspires), and indicates measures for success. It should "deliver a clear, brief, and dynamic message" (Wallace, 2004, p. 4). The lack of mission statement—the inability of the curriculum center to deliver a clear, brief, and dynamic statement of purpose—may contribute to misunderstanding or devaluation of the center's institutional role. Surprisingly, many centers do not have mission statements readily accessible on the Web. In preparation for writing this chapter, we surveyed the Web sites of the 204 centers included in the sixth edition of the *Directory of Curriculum Materials Centers* (ACRL, 2009a). While we may have missed some mission statements due to the dynamic nature of Web addresses and the search limitations of content management systems, we found that only thirty-nine centers listed in the directory (19 percent) have posted a mission statement on their websites. (A list of the centers with mission statements posted online is included in appendix 9.1.) A recent study on the research behavior of undergraduate students found the Web (specifically the use of Google as a search tool) was an integral part of their search strategy, whether as part of course-related or everyday life research (Head & Eisenberg, 2009, p. 15). The lack of an identifiable mission statement on the curriculum center's website (or the lack of a website) communicates a strong message that the center is out of date technologically and out of step pedagogically.

An effective statement of purpose provides organizational focus: why the curriculum center is important and the difference it makes to its stakeholders. The mission statement for the MERIT (Media, Education Resources, and Information Technology) Library at the University of Wisconsin–Madison communicates its organizational focus:

> Our Mission: "We provide creative and personalized solutions that make your work possible." [MERIT] …offers information and technology services to the School of Education and UW–Madison community partners. MERIT is designed as a collaborative and comprehensive cluster of service and support for the School of Education, the UW–Madison and beyond. Staff play an active role in the design and implementation of programs which connect the K–12 community to UW–Madison. (University of Wisconsin–Madison, 2010)

MERIT focuses on offering services that make a difference to the education community at UW–Madison, emphasizing collaboration ("personalized solutions" and "programs which connect the K–12 community" with the university) and a dynamic environment (a "creative" environment in which staff "play an active role in the design and implementation of programs"). The statement speaks directly to its user groups ("We… make your work possible"), offering creative solutions tailored to meet their information needs. The result is a motivational

Figure 9.1. The MERIT Library at University of Wisconsin-Madison features user-oriented, open spaces with integrated services. (Photograph provided by Anna Lewis, University of Wisconsin-Madison)

statement. Even the inclusion of media and technology in its name demonstrates MERIT's commitment to the integration of research and technology tools into teacher preparation, supporting National Council for Accreditation of Teacher Education (NCATE) Standard 6e (NCATE, 2008, p. 45). Although the MERIT library offers extensive physical and virtual collections, the mission does not include collections as a defining characteristic of the center. The MERIT library's mission statement describes a very user-focused, contemporary curriculum center meeting the information needs of educators in the twenty-first century.

Because a curriculum center serves multiple constituencies, an effective mission statement often identifies stakeholder groups and clarifies its purpose for each. The Kalikow Curriculum Materials Center at the University of Maine Farmington (UMF) provides a good example of a mission statement that clearly identifies its stakeholders as primary users of its services:

The Kalikow Curriculum Materials Center provides materials and educational experiences for pre-service teachers at UMF to enrich their teaching of children and youth, birth through age 20, supports the professional development and pedagogy of practicing teachers in western Maine, and is available to education and special education professionals in the community, individuals with disabilities, and their families. (UMF, 2007)

The statement provides a hierarchy of roles and relationships. Teacher candidates at UMF are the primary user group for the center, as indicated by their position (first in the series) in the statement and the scope of resources and services available to them ("materials and educational experiences... to enrich their teaching of children and youth, birth through age 20"). The word *enrich* describes the value the center adds to this user group. The practicing teachers of western Maine are the second-most-important user group; by stating its relationship to this group, the center is identifying its strong, supportive relationship to public education in the region. The scope of service to practicing teachers is defined as support for "professional development and pedagogy." The scope of service ("support for") is much less defined for practicing teachers in the region than for the primary user group, allowing more flexibility for the curriculum center to expand or limit services to this group as resources are available. Finally, the center is "available" to other "education and special education professionals in the community, individuals with disabilities, and their families." The word *available* indicates the most passive level of service provided to the third user group.

In both examples, the mission statement clearly articulates the purpose of the curriculum center to the people who need to know—its stakeholders. Both statements extend beyond the ACRL (2009b) definition of the curriculum center ("a physical location of a curriculum materials collection") to describe dynamic environments where collaboration and "educational experiences" occur. Both place the center within the context of the broader educational community. Although relatively short, these mission statements capture some of the big changes occurring in today's curriculum centers.

Using the Mission Statement as an Organizational Bridge

The curriculum center is a bridge between two different (but closely related) communities of practice, the library and education communities. Sometimes the center resides within the academic library, sometimes within the education program. In some institutions, both the library and the education program feel "ownership" for the center. At other institutions, the center is more closely aligned with one organization than the other. An effective curriculum center mission statement demonstrates the relationship of the center to the teacher education program, the academic library, and the college or university, and it can be used to align and integrate with them.

Two important documents for curriculum centers, one from the professional library community and one from the education community but both issued in February 2010, illustrate this intersection. *Information Literacy Standards for PK–12 Pre-Service Teachers* from the Educational and Behavioral Sciences Section (EBSS) of the ACRL division of American Library Association, provides standards for education librarians. This document uses the vocabulary of the library community (e.g., "information literacy") to describe information and research competencies for teacher education (EBSS Instruction for Educators Committee, 2010). *Educator Preparation: A Vision for the 21st Century*, prepared for American Association of Colleges of Teacher Education and Partnership for the 21st Century, provides guidance in teacher education reform (Greenhill, 2010). While discussing a range of literacies (information, communication, technology, or ICT, as well as media, financial, and economic literacy), this document does not mention libraries or librarians. One key statement from the document, "find good information quickly" (Greenhill, 2010, p. 10), is the closest to direct information skills librarians practice. While the library community assumes that libraries are the resource for developing these literacies, the education community often does not. Therefore, an effective curriculum center mission statement will explicitly make the connection between library services and the development of effective teachers so that both communities of practices see the center as a place where they intersect.

Some curriculum centers are using *Empowering Learners* (formerly *Information Power*), the recently updated standards for school libraries developed by the American Association of School Librarians (AASL), to articulate this intersection. The mission of school libraries articulated in *Empowering Learners* is to "insure that students and staff are effective users of ideas and information" (AASL, 2009, p. 8). Several curriculum center mission statements incorporate this language to demonstrate their link to the school library. For example, the mission statement for the curriculum center of Kutztown University of Pennsylvania states, "In combining these materials with appropriate instruction, we hope to ensure that students, faculty, staff, and local patrons are effective users of ideas and information" (Kutztown University of Pennsylvania, n.d.). The phrase "effective users of ideas and information" clearly creates a connection between the curriculum center and the school library that teacher candidates will encounter in their education curriculum and fieldwork.

The center's mission statement clarifies the broader relationship between the education and library communities by using the vocabularies of both. For example, the Curriculum Materials Center at Minnesota State University–Moorhead begins its mission statement, "The Curriculum Materials Center supports the mission of the Library and the University, as well as the Conceptual Framework of the Education Unit" (MSUM, 2008). By referencing the conceptual framework of the institution's education program, the center signals its support for the standards for accreditation from NCATE—it uses the vocabulary of the education community of practice. The center's mission statement interprets for the academic library the current praxis within the education community and vice versa, thereby strengthening the relationship between the two. As a result, the curriculum center is better positioned to help today's students and faculty successfully use a full range of information competencies.

Some mission statements are even more direct in connecting the two communities of practice. The mission of the curriculum center at Chicago State University states: "With the primary aim of meeting the practice-oriented information needs of its users, the Center collaborates with the university's academic library and its College of Education to provide services and products that develop content knowledge, increase awareness of instructional options, and encourage innovation in curriculum development and teaching methods" (CSU, 2006, p. 1). Whether through subtle use of vocabulary or direct statements of relationship, the mission statement can be very effective in articulating the role of the center as a bridge between the library and education program.

The mission statement and clarifying documents such as vision and values statements, goals, and guiding principles provide tools for building and clarifying relationships between the center and its constituents. By articulating both shared purpose and significant difference, the center's mission statement demonstrates the "value added" by the center. The mission statement for the Curriculum Resource Center at Bowling Green State University (BGSU) illustrates this point:

> The Curriculum Resource Center (CRC) supports the undergraduate and graduate teaching programs in the College of Education and Human Development and other BGSU education-related areas by maintaining a collection of high quality preschool through grade twelve materials reflecting innovation in teaching practices and standards-based instruction. Materials held by the CRC comprise The Frances F. Povsic Collection, so named on March 30, 2001, in honor of Professor Povsic's significant, enduring and distinctive contributions to the CRC, University Libraries and BGSU. (BGSU, n.d.)

The statement uses descriptive language to illustrate the qualities the center shares with specific programs it supports: "high quality... materials reflecting innovation in teaching practices and standards-based instruction." In other words, by being selective and remaining current with and modeling best practices in education, the center shares the values of the teaching programs at BGSU. Additionally, the center makes a unique contribution to the university by housing the Povsic Collection in honor of a valued professor's contributions to the center.

The curriculum center is sometimes a bridge between the institution and the local community, including outreach to area teachers and other educational practitioners as part of the center's mission. The center at Appalachian State University states that "to lay the foundation for the development of professional collaboration patterns between teachers and librarians/school media specialists, and to model an exemplary school media center" is part of its mission (ASU, n.d.). The current higher education environment often emphasizes community outreach, service learning, and collaboration with community partners as strategies to enhance student learning and to strengthen the institution. In institutions that employ these strategies in support of the institutional mission, the curriculum center mission statement can reflect alignment between the institutional and center missions.

Figure 9.2. Student and community children engage in active learning at the Instructional Materials Center at Appalachian State University. (Photograph provided by Margaret Gregor, Appalachian State University)

In addition to acting as a bridge between the center and organizations outside of the academic library, the curriculum center's mission statement can also bridge organizational units within the library. As a special collection within the academic library, the center's collection sometimes represents challenges for other units within the library. For example, it may use a different classification system (Dewey Decimal rather than Library of Congress), requiring that circulation staff and student assistants receive special training for the reshelving materials or that the center have separate staff for processing and managing materials. The mission statement bridges the gaps between the organizational units by showing how the center aligns with the mission of the library while clarifying its reasons for the diverging practice.

In our own experience developing a mission statement and other foundational texts for the Curriculum Center at Eastern Washington University (EWU), the process provided an opportunity to align the center with the mission of the library and the mission of the teacher education program while maintaining the distinction of the center's specialized programs and services (Miller & Meyer, 2008). Learning Resource Librarian Nadean Meyer was hired in 2006 to turn an outdated collection of curricular materials into a curriculum center for the twenty-first century. Her first task was to develop a foundation document to clarify the mission of the "new" center. Working with Associate Dean Julie Miller and meeting with faculty and students in the education programs, Meyer drafted a foundation document that included vision and mission statements, a statement of values, and guiding principles for the center. The mission statement is a succinct statement of purpose: "The Curriculum Center promotes excellence in teaching through the use of quality resources" (EWU, 2007). Among the guiding principles, she included two principles that clarify the center's relationship to EWU Libraries, the "parent" organization:

+ "While providing specific practical materials for teachers and prospective teachers in the EWU community, the Center is an integral part of EWU Libraries' services and collections."
+ "As a special collection, the Curriculum Center includes resources that are used for teaching while EWU Libraries' main

collections contain a range of materials about teaching and education." (EWU, 2007)

The first statement makes it clear that the Curriculum Center is not an unrelated unit that happens to be housed within the library. It implies that library policies apply to the center as well as to other units of the library, that center staff participate in library governance and employee development activities, and that other units of the library provide support for the center. This principle has been very important in developing procedures for the Curriculum Center that diverge from procedures supporting the general circulating collections. Providing current, high-quality resources—"specific practical materials"—is essential to meet the needs of the teacher candidates preparing to enter the classroom. While deselection is seldom done in the general circulating collection at EWU, the Curriculum Center's collection must be weeded regularly in order to fulfill its mission. Meyer has worked with the Cataloging and Acquisitions unit to change expectations and develop procedures to accommodate a different practice within the Curriculum Center. As a result, the center has a more rigorous program for deselection than the collection management of the general circulating collections.

The second guiding principle cited above defines the Curriculum Center's collections. Prior to the development of this statement, the Curriculum Center at EWU had no collection development policy, which had led to a hodgepodge of dated resources. A focus on practical resources "used *for* teaching" defines the relationship between the Curriculum Center's collections and the library's general education collection. This definition was a catalyst for discussions about the role of historical children's literature at EWU Libraries and allowed selective weeding of literature that was no longer appropriate for the Curriculum Center, but also not appropriate for the general circulating collection of education resources. Ultimately, we sent hundreds of these books to a regional historical children's literature collection at the University of Washington.

These examples demonstrate the use of the Curriculum Center's mission statement and guiding principles to clarify the organizational relationship between the library and the Curriculum Center. The process of using these statements to define the scope of the collections improved understanding and strengthened the relationship between the Cataloging and Acquisitions unit of the library and the Curriculum Center staff. These examples also demonstrate the use of the mission statement and supporting documents to guide decisions in a practical way.

Using the Mission Statement to Guide Decisions

One of the primary benefits of articulating a mission for the curriculum center is to guide decision making. As a part of the strategic planning process, the mission statement can help decision makers "make today's decisions in light of their future consequences. It can help them develop a coherent and defensible basis for decision making… and exercise maximum discretion in those areas under their organization's control" (Bryson, 1995, p. 7). In short, the mission statement guides resource allocation.

Surprisingly, very few current curriculum center mission statements allude to resource limitations. The curriculum center at Western Illinois University follows its mission statement with the goal "to build as fine a collection of teaching materials as funds and efforts permit" (Western Illinois University Libraries, 2008). The University of British Columbia's curriculum center uses the words "cost effectiveness and coordination with the Faculty of Education" in its goal statements (UBC, 1996). In both these examples, the goal statements acknowledge limitations. In a time of generally decreasing resources at the university level, a mission statement that establishes priorities for resource allocation supports the center's ability to fulfill its core functions. Whether the purpose of the center is traditional and focused on collections or evolving to encompass additional resources and services, an effective mission statement guides decisions about resource allocation, including decisions about collections, technology, environment, staffing, and services.

The traditional definition of a curriculum materials center is its collection, as evidenced by the ACRL definition, the ACRL Curriculum Materials Center collection development policy, and the mission statements of several curriculum centers. The mission statement is a powerful tool for decision making with regard to scope and depth of collections.

When opportunities for collection development occur—such as large donations, new types of resources, or a particular emphasis on genre or language—the direction provided by the mission statement determines whether to proceed. The mission statement for the Learning Resource Center at Baylor University provides a good example of a mission statement that guides decisions about the collection:

> The mission of the Learning Resource Center of the School of Education is to meet the needs of both faculty and students by providing materials related to the subject fields, to child and adolescent learning, and to professional knowledge that support the SOE curriculum, and to offer students experience in using equipment and materials similar to those they will use when they begin teaching. Maintaining excellence in service, environment, and resources, the LRC will adapt to the changing needs of students and faculty, to the goals of the 2012 Vision, and to the continually developing teacher education program. (Baylor University, n.d.)

The statement is broad enough to allow flexibility to collect a range of types of materials, but specific enough to develop a selection checklist. Figure 9.3 shows a mock selection checklist based on this example.

The mission statement provides guidance in terms of the content of the collections, the format or medium ("using equipment and materials similar to those [teacher candidates] will use when they begin teaching"), and the currency and accuracy (excellent resources that meet the changing needs of faculty and teacher candidates). This example demonstrates how a mission statement can guide decisions about collections in a practical way that insures the collection will adapt and evolve as the education environment changes.

One obvious use of the mission statement for determining the scope of the collection is in defining the diversity of materials. NCATE standards and school reform emphasize diversity, but institutional definition of and emphasis on diversity of resources may vary. An effective mission statement clarifies how diversity of resources is mani-

Figure 9.3. Mock Selection Checklist for Donations Based on the Mission Statement of the Learning Resource Center at Baylor University

Content	Criteria
	Is the resource in a subject field relevant to teacher candidates?
	Is the resource about child and/or adolescent learning?
	Is the resource about professional knowledge that supports the SOE curriculum?
Format or Medium	Criteria
	Is the resource in a format or medium that teacher candidates will use when they begin teaching?
Currency and Accuracy	Criteria
	Does the resource provide current information appropriate to the teaching environment?
	Does the resource provide accurate information appropriate to the current teaching environment?

fested in the individual curriculum center. As stated in its mission, the curriculum center at Berry College includes an "outstanding collection of children's works as well as books that reflect diverse culture and perspectives" (Berry College, n.d.). The mission statement for the center at the University of West Georgia defines diversity of resources to include "children's and young adult books that have been cited for controversy or censorship problems to show the cultural diversity of society, thus widening the students' horizons and increasing their sensitivity" (UWG, n.d.). For this curriculum center, *diversity* refers not just to cultural diversity but also to controversial materials, enabling teacher candidates to explore issues of censorship prior to working in the school.

An effective mission statement provides guidance for resource allocation beyond collection development. The increase in technology within academic libraries and the K–12 environment creates a need for technology access and equipment in the curriculum center in order to prepare teacher candidates. In this dynamic environment, many curriculum centers use the mission statement to address the role of technology in fulfilling the center's purpose. The Educational Technology & Media Center (ETMC) at James Madison University emphasizes technology as central to its purpose, as reflected in its mission statement:

> ETMC is committed to preparing all students in the College of Education and Professional Education Unit to be knowledgeable users of educational technology.... ETMC promotes the use of emerging technologies for learning and is responsive to educational technology needs of faculty and students in these programs. (JMU, n.d.)

Not only does the statement acknowledge the importance of instructional technology, it directs the center to identify and make available "emerging technologies for learning." Based on this statement, one expects the budget allocation for ETMC to reflect the emphasis on technology. Additionally, the selection process for technologies focuses on "emerging technologies for learning," providing teacher candidates with access to current instructional technologies they can expect to use in classroom. Current curriculum center mission statements use a range of terms to address technology resources, including "multimedia" and "assistive technology devices."

As instructional technologies continue to shape K–16 education, the mission statement can also guide decisions about the curriculum center's physical and virtual environments. The allocation of physical space at a university is very important and should be aligned with its mission. "Statements of purpose bring structure and culture into tangible form, and physical space makes mission imperatives—and thereby structure and culture as well—even more concrete" (Fugazzotto, 2009,

Figure 9.4. The International Children's Digital Library, a free children's e-book collection, is an example of a technology-based resource that curriculum centers are beginning to include in their collections.
(Poster created by Nick Brown, University Graphics, Eastern Washington University)

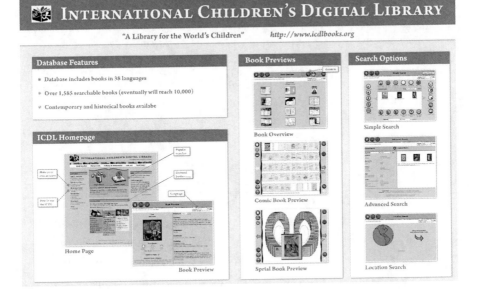

p. 293). With the traditional focus on materials collections, the curriculum center has primarily been a physical location where collections are housed and specific activities may take place. The mission statement provides a guide for the allocation of this space. Mission statements for curriculum centers sometimes include descriptive terms such as "model school library," "laboratory," or even the more general "active area" to communicate this element of the center's purpose. For example, the mission statement for the center at Appalachian State University describes the Idea Factory, "a media production facility designed exclusively for education students and area educators" (ASU, n.d.). If the center is located within an academic library where quiet study spaces are the norm, then it becomes even more important to include some language about the active use of the space in the center's mission.

As the curriculum center evolves to include digital resources and virtual services to meet the needs of teacher candidates in twenty-first-century classrooms, its statement of purpose must also evolve to include the virtual environment. In their Project Information Literacy Progress Report *Lessons Learned: How College Students Seek Information in the Digital Age,* Head and Eisenberg (2009) found that students used research strategies that "leveraged scholarly sources and public Internet sites and [they] favored brevity, consensus, and currency in the sources they sought" (p. 3). The challenge for the curriculum center is to create a blended physical and virtual environment to support and enhance students' research strategies. By addressing this challenge in the mission statement, the curriculum center has a guide for developing the blended physical and virtual environments to meet the specific needs of its stakeholders.

The mission statement for the education library at the University of British Columbia (UBC) provides an example of a center that integrates both physical and virtual resources and services throughout its statement of purpose. Its mission is to "provide outstanding access to the universe of recorded knowledge and information in the field of education." Strategies to accomplish this mission include linking "faculty and students to the very best information resources available and to provide electronic access to specialized BC and Canadian education resources" and providing a library instruction program "to develop those competencies necessary to use changing information technologies and to develop an awareness of the world of information" (UBC, 1996). The UBC education library's mission statement provides a guide to resource allocation to insure its users have access to the best education resources and services to meet their needs.

Although human resources are the most important (and expensive) consideration in resource allocation, relatively few mission statements for curriculum centers include this vital resource. With a few exceptions, the people responsible for fulfilling the mission of the curriculum center are silent partners in its statement of purpose. The Cooperative Children's Book Center (CCBC) at the University of Wisconsin–Madison vision statement is notable for stating the center "has staff expertise in book arts, book evaluation, multicultural literature, alternative press publishing, and intellectual freedom" (University of Wisconsin–Madison, 1999). The curriculum center at the University of British Columbia expands its basic mission statement to include a reference to human resources: "Librarians and staff will strive to do the following," with a list of activities for implementing the mission (UBC, 1996).

Because the mission statement guides decision making, the danger in excluding human resources from the mission statement means making them invisible when establishing priorities for resource allocation. In *The Value of Academic Libraries* (2010), Oakleaf describes a "shift in library emphasis from collections to experience, from resources to educational impact.... [L]ibrary value is increasingly invested in service aspects and librarian expertise" (p. 23). A recent survey of curriculum centers in Australia finds the same shift occurring in those centers: "Curriculum collections were perceived as more than just a collection of resources—often the real value lay not just in the resources, but also in the staff knowledge and expertise and services offered, all of which added value for students and academics" (Locke, 2007, p. 205). For curriculum centers making this transition from a collections-based to a service-based center, the mission statement should explicitly address the realignment of resources to include the librarians and staff providing expertise and service.

The emphasis on service is beginning to be reflected in the library literature for curriculum centers. The 2009 revision of the ACRL *Guidelines for Curriculum Materials Centers* includes the same services as the 2003 version: reference, instruction, faculty liaison, outreach, and production. The 2009 version, however, redefines outreach services to encompass services to students from other institutions, educators in the community, homeschoolers, and others, and adds a new service category for distance learning, focused more narrowly on faculty and students in the institution's distance programs. Additionally, the 2009 guidelines for delivery of instruction have been revised to insure virtual instruction includes a range of appropriate techniques (ACRL, 2009b). Of the online mission statements for curriculum centers listed in the sixth edition of the *Directory of Curriculum Materials Centers* (ACRL, 2009a), most of the statements still focus primarily on collections to define their purpose. (See appendix 9.1 for the list of curriculum centers whose mission statements were reviewed for this chapter.) Eight of the mission statements, however, refer to provision of resources and services about equally (phrases include "resources and services," "services and products," "instructional materials, equipment, and services," "resources, programs, and services," "services and materials," and "services and collections"). A few of the mission statements specify the information services provided by the curriculum center. Appalachian State University, for example, cites reference services, reader's advisory, and instruction as three information services provided by the curriculum center (ASU, n.d.). The MERIT Library at the University of Wisconsin–Madison seems to be unique in focusing its mission on information and technology services and excluding collections from its mission statement (University of Wisconsin–Madison, 2010). It remains to be seen whether the MERIT Library is a predictor for things to come and information and technology services—not collections—become the primary focus for future curriculum centers.

Used strategically, the mission statement guides decisions in support of the curriculum center's purpose. It can also be used to anticipate, prepare for, and respond to change. This use of the mission statement is particularly beneficial for helping the curriculum center remain relevant to its users in a rapidly changing environment.

Using the Mission Statement to Remain Relevant

Information about how curriculum centers are adapting to the evolving conditions of the educational community and academic libraries is scarce in the library literature. Some current challenges are summarized in Rae-Anne Locke's survey of thirty Australian curriculum centers (2007), which provides a snapshot of current practice in Australia. The survey includes open-ended questions including, "What challenges and issues do you see facing Curriculum Collections?" and, "Briefly comment on the future directions of Curriculum Collections as a resource for future educators, staff and students" (p. 212). In her findings, Locke identifies the following challenges as emergent themes:

+ need to make spaces vibrant and integral to the teaching and learning environment
+ need to integrate print and digital collections to raise students' awareness and use of all resources
+ need to demonstrate a link between the collections and services and the student learning experiences
+ difficulties caused by the reduced resource and staffing budgets
+ need to actively engage academics in the collection (p. 194)

Some of the mission statements at American institutions (such as the Instructional Materials Center at Appalachian State University and both the MERIT Library and CCBC at University of Wisconsin–Madison) indicate that American curriculum centers are facing similar challenges. The mission statement is an effective tool for anticipating changes in the education environment while remaining focused on the center's purpose. A mission statement that is user-centered, focused on the future, and grounded in assessment insures the center will remain a vital contributor to the educational mission of the institution.

A user-centered mission statement requires that the curriculum center respond to—or (even better) anticipate—the needs of its constituents. The Education Resource Center (ERC) at Chicago State University, for example, explicitly states that meeting users' information needs is its purpose:

> With the primary aim of meeting the practice-oriented information needs of its users, the Center collaborates with the university's academic library and its College of Education to provide services and products that develop content knowledge, increase awareness of instructional options, and encourage innovation in curriculum development and teaching methods. (CSU, 2006)

This statement holds the center's staff accountable for the center's success based on student learning outcomes. The center is responsible for insuring teacher candidates develop content knowledge, are aware of

Figure 9.5. College students interact with Robert Reid Laboratory School students at the El día de los niños/El día de los libros (Día) Celebration hosted by the Curriculum Center at Eastern Washington University Libraries, April 2008. (Photograph by Ielleen Miller, Eastern Washington University Libraries)

instructional options, and become innovative teachers. These outcomes are central to the ERC's purpose. Resources and services that do not contribute to these outcomes may be extraneous or no longer relevant and therefore candidates for elimination. A user-centered mission statement helps to keep the center aligned with its purpose when external forces exert pressure to change. Sometimes the external force is negative (e.g., cutting the budget), but sometimes the external force comes in the form of an opportunity (e.g., hosting a traveling exhibit, partnering on a large grant, accepting a donation of materials). When faced with such pressures, applying the user-centered mission statement to the situation insures the decision will be the one most beneficial to the center's users and therefore most likely to insure the center's relevance.

A mission statement that incorporates measurable outcomes or strategies for assessment will help the curriculum center remain true to its purpose. In the goals accompanying the mission statement, the curriculum center at University of British Columbia deliberately incorporates the assessment process:

> Central to an effective teaching and research environment are friendly and knowledgeable staff with a sustained commitment to continuous improvement of information services and programs. Advisory committees, focus groups, performance measures and other strategies will aid in determining client needs. The overall purpose is to facilitate the best use of information technologies to advance scholarship, teaching and learning at UBC. (UBC, 1996)

This statement directly addresses the current challenges reflected in the Australian survey. The staff is directed to "sustained commitment of continuous improvement." The UBC statement also lists specific methods for "determining client needs." The wording implies integration of collections by stating "best use of information technologies" to advance the center's mission. This part of the goals gives specific direction to the assessment process (by listing specific forms of constituent input and measures), and the goal statements imply the importance of the assessment process for keeping a curriculum center relevant.

In addition to incorporating the assessment process into the mission statement itself, the mission statement can be used with other strategies to insure the curriculum center remains relevant to its stakeholders. One strategy is to include revision or affirmation of the mission statement as part of the center's (or academic library's) strategic planning cycle. Including the approval or revision dates, along with the approving or endorsing authority, insures continuity within the organization. The approval date also serves as a reminder to review, modify, or affirm the purpose of the center as the organizational environment evolves over time. The mission and goal statements for the curriculum center at UBC, for example, are dated 1996, and their relevance to the current education environment illustrates how effectively the center and its stakeholders anticipated change.

Another strategy is a data collection model called "Monitoring Our Mission" that places the mission statement at the center of the assessment process for the curriculum center. The model was developed for results-oriented educational planning (Holcomb, 1999) and has been adapted for evaluation of school library media centers (McGriff, Harvey, & Preddy, 2004). It can be easily adapted for the curriculum center. Monitoring Our Mission uses a grid to determine "what evidence, if any exists to prove that the stated mission is being accomplished" (McGriff, Harvey, & Preddy, 2004, p. 26). A three-column data collection grid helps to identify existing evidence for fulfillment of the mission as well as gaps in the evidence. The columns are headed (from left) "what we say," "evidence we have," and "evidence we need." Phrases taken directly from the mission statement are listed in the left column, and sources of data for each phrase are listed in middle column. Missing evidence, if any, is listed in the right column (Holcomb, 1999, pp. 30–32). The gaps in evidence can be as revealing as the evidence itself. Sometimes missing evidence reflects the difficulty of assessing a particular outcome. More importantly, the gap may indicate that an outcome has become a low priority and resources are no longer allocated to accomplish it. This model is useful because it focuses only on data related to the mission (McGriff, Harvey, & Preddy, 2004)—the most meaningful data for insuring the curriculum center remains relevant to its users.

Positioning for a Vital Future: The Changing Mission

In the context of a dynamic teacher education environment and increasing demand for accountability within higher education, a clear articulation of the purpose of the curriculum center is a powerful tool. Put another way, "mission statements make explicit the structural purposes of their organizations" (Fugazzoto, 2009, p. 289). Our Web review of curriculum center mission statements indicates many curriculum centers do not have a mission statement or are not posting the statement on the Web. Perhaps these curriculum centers believe their stakeholders understand the center's mission based on the traditional definition of the center as a physical location housing curricular materials. Indeed, this definition is still common in the library literature (ACRL, 2009b; Fabbi, Bressler, & Earp, 2007). We believe that curriculum centers that have not articulated their purpose within the context of the current education environment are risking their own demise.

As teacher education environment evolves, the curriculum center must evolve as well in order to remain vital to its users. We have highlighted mission statements (in some cases, portions of mission statements) that reflect the variety of purpose and organizational focus in curriculum centers today. This variety is essential given the unique mission of each institution of higher education within its community of service and the unique role of the education program and the academic library within the college or university. A good mission statement makes explicit the curriculum center's distinctive contributions in meeting the needs of its stakeholders (Wallace, 2004, p. 7), so each center's statement of purpose should, of course, reflect its unique circumstance and reason for being.

Change in the labor force is an urgent reason to revisit the curriculum center's mission. Frequently, special collections such as the curriculum center are directed by champions and catalysts—librarians with the vision, expertise, and focus who drive its mission. As these champions for the curriculum center retire or are reassigned within the organization, the center may lose its voice for articulating the value of the center. A strong mission statement that has been approved or endorsed by stakeholder groups insures continuity and provides clarity for the new director and staff, who can then use it to address future challenges and to implement change collaboratively. Engaging stakeholders—education faculty, library colleagues, administrators, teacher candidates, practitioners, and other key constituents—in the mission review process will insure the curriculum center remains a vital learning resource.

References

AASL (American Association of School Librarians). 2009. *Empowering Learners: Guidelines for School Library Media Programs*. Chicago: American Association of

School Librarians.

Abram, Stephen. 2007. *Out Front with Stephen Abram: A Guide for Information Leaders*, compiled by Judith A. Siess and Jonathan Lorig. Chicago: American Library Association.

ACRL (Association of College & Research Libraries). 2009a. *Directory of Curriculum Materials Centers*, 6th ed. Chicago: American Library Association.

———. 2009b. *Guidelines for Curriculum Materials Centers*. Chicago: Association of College & Research Libraries. Retrieved from http://www.ala.org/acrl/standards/guidelinescurriculum.

ASU (Appalachian State University). N.d. "Mission Statement." Retrieved Aug. 11, 2011 from http://www.library.appstate.edu/imc.

Baylor University. N.d. "Learning Resource Center (LRC)." Retrieved Aug. 11, 2011 from http://www.baylor.edu/soe/index.php?id=65432.

Berry College. N.d. "CMC Mission and Purpose." Retrieved Jan. 5, 2011 from http://www.berry.edu/library/cmc/mission.asp.

BGSU (Bowling Green State University). N.d. "Collection Statement." Retrieved Jan. 5, 2011 from http://www.bgsu.edu/colleges/library/crc/page38567.html.

Bryson, John M. 1995. *Strategic Planning for Public and Nonprofit Organizations: A Guide to Strengthening and Sustaining Organizational Achievement*, rev. ed. San Francisco: Jossey-Bass.

CSU (Chicago State University). 2006. "The Education Resource Center." Retrieved from http://library.csu.edu/erc/MatCenPoliciesAndproceduresRevDec2006.pdf.

EBSS Instruction for Educators Committee. 2010. *Information Literacy Standards for PK–12 Pre-Service Teachers*, February 2010 draft, rev. June 2010. Chicago: Association of College & Research Libraries. Retrieved from http://connect.ala.org/files/39851/ebssstandardsrvsdjune0610_pdf_16275.pdf.

EWU (Eastern Washington University). 2007. "Mission." Retrieved from http://research.ewu.edu/aecontent.php?pid=87256&sid=837496.

Fabbi, Jennifer, Darla Bressler, and Vanessa Earp. 2007. *A Guide to Writing CMC Collection Development Policies*. Chicago: Association of College & Research Libraries. Retrieved from http://www.ala.org/ala/mgrps/divs/acrl/aboutacrl/directoryofleadership/sections/ebss/ebsswebsite/ebsscommittees/curriculum-materials/guidetowritingcmc.pdf.

Fugazzotto, Sam J. 2009. "Mission Statements, Physical Space, and Strategy in Higher Education." *Innovative Higher Education* 34 (5): 285–298. doi:10.1007/s10755-009-9118-z.

Greenhill, Valerie. 2010, February 15. *Educator Preparation: A Vision for the 21st Century*, draft. Washington, DC: American Association of Colleges of Teacher Education and Partnership for the 21st Century. Retrieved from http://aacte.org/email_blast/president_e-letter/files/02-16-2010/Educator%20Preparation%20and%2021st%20Century%20Skills%20DRAFT%20021510.pdf.

Head, Alison J., and Michael B. Eisenberg. 2009. *Lessons Learned: How College Students Seek Information in the Digital Age*. Project Information Literacy Progress Report. Seattle, WA: University of Washington Information School. Retrieved from http://projectinfolit.org/pdfs/PIL_Fall2009_finalv_YR1_12_2009v2.pdf.

Holcomb, Edie L. 1999. *Getting Excited about Data: How to Combine People, Passion, and Proof.* Thousand Oaks, CA: Corwin Press.

JMU (James Madison University). N.d. "Mission." Retrieved Aug. 11, 2011 from http://www.jmu.edu/coe/etmc.

Kutztown University of Pennsylvania. N.d. "About the CMC." Retrieved Aug. 11, 2011 from http://kucmc.wordpress.com/about.

Locke, Rae-Anne. 2007. "More Than Puppets: Curriculum Collections in Australian Universities." *Australian Academic & Research Libraries* 38 (3): 192–215.

McGriff, Nancy, Carl A. Harvey II, and Leslie B. Preddy. 2004. "Collecting the Data: Monitoring the Mission Statement." *School Library Media Activities Monthly* 20 (6): 26–29.

Miller, Julie L., and Nadean Meyer. 2008. "Transforming a Curriculum Center for the 21st Century at Eastern Washington University Libraries." *Education Libraries* 32 (2): 18–29.

MSUM (Minnesota State University–Moorhead). 2008. "Mission Statement." Retrieved from http://www.mnstate.edu/cmc/MissionStatement.cfm.

NCATE (National Council for the Accreditation of Teacher Education). 2008. *Professional Standards for the Accreditation of Teacher Preparation Institutions.* Washington, DC: National Council for Accreditation of Teacher Education. Retrieved from http://www.ncate.org/documents/standards/NCATE%20Standards%202008.pdf.

Oakleaf, Megan. 2010. *The Value of Academic Libraries: A Comprehensive Research Review and Report.* Chicago: Association of College & Research Libraries. Retrieved from http://www.ala.org/ala/mgrps/divs/acrl/issues/value/val_report.pdf.

UBC (University of British Columbia). 1996. "Mission Statement." Retrieved from http://www.library.ubc.ca/edlib/nav/mission.html.

UMF (University of Maine Farmington). 2007. "Mission Statement." Retrieved from http://kcmc.umf.maine.edu/mission.php.

University of Wisconsin–Madison. 1999. "CCBC Vision Statement." Retrieved from http://www.education.wisc.edu/ccbc/about/vision.asp.

———. 2010. "MERIT: Our Mission." Retrieved from http://merit.education.wisc.edu/Home/About.aspx.

UWG (University of West Georgia). N.d. "Our Mission." Retrieved Aug. 8, 2011 from http://tmc.ed.westga.edu/mission.asp.

Wallace, Linda K. 2004. *Libraries, Mission, and Marketing: Writing Mission Statements That Work.* Chicago: American Library Association.

Western Illinois University Libraries. 2008. "Curriculum Library Information." Retrieved from http://www.wiu.edu/library/units/curr/curr_web.sphp?id=135.

Appendix 9

The mission statements for the following curriculum centers were found online and reviewed for this chapter (in alphabetical order by institution).

Name of Institution	Name of Curriculum Center	Location	Web Address
Adelphi University	Curriculum Materials Center	Garden City, NY	
American University	Curriculum Materials Center	Washington, DC	http://www.american.edu/library/collections/cmc.cfm
Appalachian State University	Instructional Materials Center	Boone, NC	http://www.library.appstate.edu/imc/
Asbury College	King Curriculum Lab	Wilmore, KY	http://www.asbury.edu/academics/departments/education/overview/king-curriculum-lab
Baylor University	Learning Resource Center	Waco, TX	http://www.baylor.edu/soe/index.php?id=65432
Berry College	Curriculum Materials Center	Mt. Berry, GA	http://www.berry.edu/library/page.aspx?id=8662
Boston College	Educational Resource Center	Chestnut Hill, MA	http://www.bc.edu/libraries/collections/erc.html

Name of Institution	Name of Curriculum Center	Location	Web Address
Bowling Green State University	Curriculum Resource Center– The Frances F. Povsic Collection	Bowling Green, OH	http://www.bgsu.edu/colleges/library/crc/
Brevard College	Curriculum Materials Center	Brevard, NC	http://www.brevard.edu/Academics/Library/Collections/CurriculumMaterials/tabid/449/Default.aspx
Bridgewater State College	Educational Resource Center	Bridgewater, MA	http://www.bridgew.edu/library/erc.cfm
Central Connecticut State University	Curriculum Lab	New Britain, CT	http://web.ccsu.edu/library/curriculumlab/
Chicago State University	Education Resource Center	Chicago, IL	http://library.csu.edu/erc/
East Carolina University	Teaching Resources Center	Greenville, NC	http://www.ecu.edu/cs-lib/trc/index.cfm
Eastern Michigan University	Educational Resource Center	Ypsilanti, MI	http://www.emunix.emich.edu/~abednar/erc/
Eastern Washington University	Curriculum Center	Cheney, WA	http://research.ewu.edu/content.php?pid=87256&sid=837496
Elon University	Curriculum Resource Center	Elon, NC	http://www.elon.edu/e-web/academics/education/crc/default.xhtml

Name of Institution	Name of Curriculum Center	Location	Web Address
Fayetteville State University	Curriculum Laboratory	Fayetteville, NC	http://www.uncfsu.edu/soe/CURLAB.HTM
Gonzaga University	Curriculum Center	Spokane, WA	http://www.gonzaga.edu/Academics/Libraries/Foley-Library/Departments/Curriculum/default.asp
Harvard University	Monroe C. Gutman Library	Cambridge, MA	http://www.gse.harvard.edu/library/index.html
Illinois State University	Teaching Materials Center	Normal, IL	http://www.gse.harvard.edu/library/index.html
James Madison University	Educational Technology & Media Center	Harrisonburg, VA	http://www.jmu.edu/coe/etmc/
Kansas State University	Curriculum Materials & Juvenile Literature	Manhattan, KS	http://www.lib.k-state.edu/services/cmc.html
Keene State College	Curriculum Materials Library	Keene, NC	http://www.keene.edu/cml/
Kutztown University of Pennsylvania	Curriculum Materials Center	Kutztown, PA	http://kucmc.wordpress.com/

Name of Institution	Name of Curriculum Center	Location	Web Address
Liberty University	Curriculum Library	Lynchburg, VA	https://www.liberty.edu/informationservices/ilrc/library/curriculumlibrary/index.cfm?PID=409
Minnesota State University - Moorhead*	Curriculum Materials Center	Moorhead, MN	http://www.mnstate.edu/cmc/AboutCMC.cfm
Missouri State University	Curriculum Resource Center	Springfield, MO	http://library.missouristate.edu/meyer/crc/index.htm
Mount Vernon Nazarene University	Educational Resource Center	Mount Vernon, OH	http://library.mvnu.edu/screens/ercservices.html
Radford University	Patricia Langford Roughton Teaching Resources Center	Radford, VA	http://trc.asp.radford.edu/Shannon/mission.htm
University of British Columbia	Education Library	Vancouver, BC	http://www.library.ubc.ca/edlib/nav/mission.html
University of Maine -Farmington*	Kalikow Curriculum Materials Center	Farmington, ME	http://kcmc.umf.maine.edu/
University of North Carolina - Greensboro	Teaching Resources Center	Greensboro, NC	http://www.uncg.edu/soe/trc/index.htm
University of West Georgia	Teaching Materials Center	Carrollton, GA	http://tmc.ed.westga.edu/

Name of Institution	Name of Curriculum Center	Location	Web Address
University of Wisconsin - La Crosse	Alice Hagar Curriculum Resource Center	La Crosse, WI	http://www.uwlax.edu/murphylibrary/departments/curriculum/about.html
University of Wisconsin -Madison	Media, Education Resources & Information Technology (MERIT)	Madison, WI	http://merit.education.wisc.edu/Library/Overview.aspx
University of Wisconsin -Madison	Cooperative Children's Book Center (CCBC)	Madison, WI	http://www.education.wisc.edu/ccbc/
University of Wisconsin - Oshkosh	Educational Materials Center	Oshkosh, WI	http://www.uwosh.edu/library/emc/
Washburn University	Curriculum Resource Center	Topeka, KS	http://www.washburn.edu/mabee/crc/
Western Connecticut State University	Curriculum Collection	Danbury, CT	http://www.washburn.edu/mabee/crc/
Western Illinois University	Curriculum Library	Macomb, IL	http://wiu.edu/libraries/curriculum_library/index.php
York University	Education Resource Centre	Toronto, ON	http://edu.yorku.ca/erc.html

*Indicates center is not included in the Directory of Curriculum Materials Centers 6th ed.

10

Staying Relevant: Re-engineering for the Future

Shonda Brisco, Oklahoma State University

This chapter discusses how the perceptions of librarians by the academic faculty affect the role that they play in education. It defines functions, services, and resources offered in CMCs with the intent of moving into a twenty-first-century model of collaboration with preservice teachers, K–12 media specialists, and college of education faculty as an instructional team. Teaching students how to develop critical-thinking skills, become effective researchers, and develop the skills necessary for academic achievement is at the forefront of this discussion. A key component for achieving overall academic success is bridging the gap between K–12 school library information literacy programs and those offered in academia. The chapter also suggests opportunities for achieving this collaboration, identifies stakeholders, and stresses the importance of a relationship with school libraries for academic success.

Despite nearly a century since the establishment of the first curriculum materials centers (CMCs) within the colleges of education across the nation, today's CMC continues to face the challenge of staying relevant to both preservice educators and the academic faculty. As educational programs and practices are scrutinized for evidence of scientific research–based effectiveness, teachers are also faced with the need to provide evidence that the instructional content that they teach will significantly impact student achievement.

As CMC librarians work toward meeting these specific instructional needs among preservice educators, they also have the opportunity *and the responsibility* to create dynamic intellectual partnerships with education faculty, staff, students, K–12 library media specialists, school administrators, and public librarians, all of whom will at some point have a significant impact upon the careers of these future professionals. Each of these groups has the potential to influence how the preservice teacher perceives educational theories, instructional methods, cultural influence, collaborative efforts, information literacy, and access to information within the educational community.

Perhaps at no other time in the history of education has the CMC been more important to preservice educators in their preparation for presenting instruction in the classroom. As information continues to bombard us from all directions and technology becomes more accessible to students of all ages, the CMC librarian is charged with assessing not only the needs of preservice teachers and their academic curriculum, but also the instructional curriculum being presented within the schools throughout the state and around the nation. Understanding how students, educators, and even college faculty access and utilize information for instruction is imperative for the CMC librarian who will need to provide instructional guidance in the best practices in educational research.

Staying current in once-traditional content areas such as curriculum guides, textbooks, or children's literature can no longer be the primary function of the CMC librarian. Learning ways to collaborate with the education faculty in order to introduce information literacy skills to preservice teachers, collaborating with preservice teachers to discover the best methods for developing lesson plans that meet instructional objectives, and building bridges between high school librarians and academic librarians to help high school students / incoming freshmen better understand what types of research skills are required to successfully complete academic assignments are key components to ensuring that future educators and their students have a strong foundation from which to continue building academic success. These skills, as well as the ability to access and utilize new technology applications as they relate to education and library instruction, are imperative to the success of the twenty-first-century CMC.

Relevant Services

Today's preservice teacher cannot remember a time when school libraries were not an integral part of the public school program. Depending upon where these educators began their college degrees, those students enrolled in education courses who have CMCs available to them generally don't question how these unique programs began or why they might have been needed. Most preservice teachers know only that these libraries, resources, and services are available if they are needed—but do these future educators take full advantage of what is being made available to them?

As school libraries continue to face budget cuts and even the elimination of certified school librarians within hundreds of districts around the nation (AASL,"School Library Funding Crisis Press Kit," 2010), it is imperative that academic librarians—especially CMC librarians—step up in support of these educational partners, not only to encourage interaction and continual growth between these two programs, but also to ensure that future generations of college students are adequately prepared for the rigors of academic research.

From a professional standpoint, it might seem that the CMC and the school library are essentially mirror images of the same program at different stages in development. The school library, while providing for the needs of the K–12 student, also plays a significant role in the continual growth and development of the classroom teacher. In turn, preservice teachers who utilize the resources and services provided by the CMC and its librarian will learn to expect some of the same types of resources and services once they begin their professional careers. A well-developed and properly managed CMC can provide the preservice teacher with the opportunity to work within a model school library while developing the skills needed to make the transition between the practicum experience and actual classroom teaching much easier.

Historically, the function of the CMC has been to introduce preservice teachers to the types of educational materials, resources, services, and collaborative partnerships that await them once they began teaching. However, many CMCs have slowly transformed from active instructional programs to simply collections of books. Unfortunately, those academic libraries that merely provide a collection of K–12 textbooks, theoretical print materials, and curriculum guides housed separately within the library's main collection are not properly providing for the educational needs of today's preservice educators or the school environment that awaits them. Materials alone do not adequately provide preservice teachers with the skills necessary in developing lessons that require evidence of curriculum correlations to instructional objectives.

Today's CMC must meet the needs of preservice teachers by providing the services of a knowledgeable education librarian who understands the current methods of instruction and is capable of modeling the various collaboration methods for information literacy instruction. Ideally, the CMC librarian should have had classroom teaching experience and should understand the process of lesson plan development, as well as evaluation. Other areas of importance to consider for the CMC librarian should be the ability to utilize the various technology applications and equipment currently available in the K–12 classroom.

Because technology is used in nearly all subject areas in schools today, despite their tech-savvy skills in searching the Internet, most preservice educators have no experience with the technology resources currently available and used in the classroom (Uhl, 2007, p. 44). This lack of experience in the appropriate use of educational technology, coupled with the need to develop lessons that include evidence of academic success upon instruction, places preservice teachers at a disadvantage unless they have the opportunity to work with an experienced CMC librarian.

Subscription databases, e-books, iPhones, Smart Boards, and cloud computing systems have become more and more popular in today's classroom, but the effective use of these resources by students and teachers is still questionable. In order to adequately prepare preservice teachers for the types of technology applications that they will need to understand and accurately use for classroom instruction, the CMC librarian must be versatile in a wide range of technology tools and applications, as well as their potential use in the classroom.

Although subscription databases and e-books have been integrated into most academic library programs and most incoming freshmen are provided with the basic bibliographic instruction during their first year of college, the instruction provided to preservice teachers by the CMC librarian often exceeds these basic elements of research. As preservice teachers begin developing lesson plans to meet the needs of different types of learners, the CMC librarian will need to highlight the more unusual features within many of these resources and demonstrate ways in which preservice teachers might be able to use them with their own students.

For example, most subscription databases provide online tutorials, instructional guides, and even lesson plans for the classroom; however, these tutorials and other instructional materials may not be easily found without the assistance of the CMC librarian. Techniques for using e-books effectively for research, as well as methods for utilizing online database tools and 2.0 resources to bookmark, cite, collaborate, share, and save electronic resources can also be shared by CMC librarians who work extensively with these resources and can help preservice teachers learn ways to teach these techniques once they begin teaching.

Relevant Technology

Aside from the wide range of resources that might be available to preservice teachers within today's CMC libraries, the attention to technology is extremely important in order to remain relevant in the field of education. Despite the cost for some of these pieces of equipment, the CMC library that provides preservice teachers with the ability to utilize new technology such as LCD projects and Smart Boards will be seen as much more progressive than those that provide older instructional equipment such as overhead projectors and videotape players. Changes made to the CMC's equipment holdings should include a wide variety of instructional resources to support today's preservice teacher in the development of instructional content. Opportunities to utilize new pieces of technology for instruction will help the preservice teacher in learning what does or doesn't work well with that particular piece of equipment but also how to utilize the equipment effectively while providing instruction. Among some of the more common educational technology equipment and resources currently being used in today's classrooms and libraries are

- e-books for elementary students (such as BookFlix, Tumble-Books, or Capstone Interactive)
- MP3 players for audiobooks (such as Playaway)
- video streaming programs (such as Discovery Education or Learn360)
- subscription databases specifically designed for children and young adults (such as World Book Online, SIRS, EBSCO's Searchasaurus, etc.)
- laptop computers or iPads
- digital cameras
- digital audio recorders
- video gaming equipment and games
- geocaching equipment

As new technology continues to find its way into the mainstream—especially among teens and college students—be assured that it will soon find its way into the classroom. It will be important for the CMC librarian to learn ways to evaluate these resources in order to determine their possible application and use by teachers and students in the classroom. Some of the more popular technology applications currently used in K–12 classrooms and libraries include

- online chat or IM services embedded into library websites for homework assignments
- resources (such as Delicious) that use tagging to create special book lists or websites for reading or student research
- real-time video tools (such as Skype) to connect students in the classroom with authors and special guest speakers from around the world
- podcasting by students as a form of sharing book reviews, research work, and assignments or providing information about school-related activities to parents and the community

- wikis for use by teachers and students to generate online collaboration projects and to share research, resources, and instructional content
- blogs for use by teachers and students to create an online forum for the discussion and feedback of specific topics in areas such as literature, history, science, technology, book reviews, etc.
- online presentation programs such as Prezi, Glogster, or Google Docs to create classroom projects for instruction or presentation
- the introduction of Google Lit Trips (through Google Earth) to allow for visual literacy while teaching other subject matter including literature, geography, social studies, and technology
- the integration of Creative Commons tools into the classroom to not only encourage student creativity in remixing and designing new content but to also provide preservice teachers and librarians the opportunity to introduce issues of copyright into the K–12 instructional curriculum.

As the CMC librarian begins to consider the various methods for utilizing technology for instruction, it is important to investigate some of the publications used by educational technology instructors as well as by school librarians. By reviewing not only professional library journals, but also educational technology publications, the CMC librarian will gain a better idea of the latest trends taking shape and how new technology is being implemented in the classroom.

Reviews of new technology applications and the integration of these resources into the K–12 classroom and library can often be found in professional journals and trade magazines such as these:

- *Learning and Leading with Technology.* http://www.iste.org/store/product.aspx?ID=24
- *Journal of Research on Technology in Education.* http://www.iste.org/store/product.aspx?ID=25
- *Journal of Digital Learning in Teacher Education.* http://www.iste.org/store/product.aspx?ID=26
- *Tech & Learning.* http://www.techlearning.com

- *Information Today.* http://www.infotoday.com/IT/default.asp
- *ONLINE: Exploring Technology & Resources for Information Professionals.* http://infotoday.stores.yahoo.net/onlinemagazine.html
- *Computers in Libraries.* http://infotoday.stores.yahoo.net/cominlibmags.html
- *Searcher: The Magazine for Database Professionals* http://infotoday.stores.yahoo.net/searmagforda.html
- *EContent.* http://www.econtentmag.com
- *Internet@Schools.* http://www.internetatschools.com
- *KMWorld.* http://www.kmworld.com

Another possible method to ensure that the CMC reflects the current status of the school library and instructional classroom is to actually visit some of the more popular school library programs around the country—either physically or virtually—in order to learn how teachers and librarians are using these resources and how they might correlate to the instructional curriculum.

Some of the more innovative school librarians and their library programs that CMC librarians might want to consider visiting online include these:

- Springfield High School
  http://bit.ly/3enL61
  Dr. Joyce Valenza
  1801 E. Paper Mill Road
  Erdenheim, PA
- McKillop Library
  http://bit.ly/8okZdo
  Doug Valentine
  McKillop Elementary School Library
  Melissa, TX
- Rundlett Middle School Learning Commons
  http://bit.ly/e5nIAB
  Nancy J. Keane, MLS, MA
  144 South Street
  Concord, NH

- Petaluma High School Library
  http://bit.ly/fpQeKo
  Connie Williams, Teacher Librarian/National Board Certified
  Petaluma, CA
- Horace Mann Elementary Library
  http://bit.ly/dOBR4e
  MaryAnn Karre, School Librarian
  Horace Mann Elementary School
  Binghamton, NY
- Colquitt County High School Media Center
  http://bit.ly/fMCyI1
  Cheryl Youse, MLS
  Media Specialist
  Colquitt County High School
  Moultrie, GA

Relevant Resources

As varied as are individual CMC librarians, so are the resources that they provide. According to the data collected by the Education and Behavioral Sciences Section of the American Library Association, there are more than one thousand curriculum materials centers across the nation. During the latest survey of those CMCs, approximately 204 institutions responded in detail to provide information about their curriculum materials or collections in universities across the country (ACRL, 2009). Based upon this survey, most, if not all, of the CMCs responded that they provide examination textbooks and supplemental resources that would normally be used in the K–12 classrooms (ACRL, 2009). In addition to textbooks, the CMCs reported that they also provide additional resources such as:

- children's and young adult literature
- foreign language materials
- kits, games, and puppets
- posters and maps
- DVDs and videos

- computer software
- professional materials
- testing instruments
- reference materials
- periodicals (ACRL, 2009)

However, depending upon the size and location of the CMC within the particular university campus, these resources may vary in quantity, quality, and availability. Although several university libraries may offer the resources typically found within a CMC, once again, not all of these libraries provide the services of a CMC librarian who is an expert in the areas of K–12 education, information literacy, and collaborative instruction.

CMCs without a vibrant, interactive library program that includes the services of a CMC librarian who is able to collaborate with students enrolled in the education programs cannot meet the information literacy needs of today's preservice teacher. Unfortunately, many CMC libraries and their collections are being eliminated—much like many of the K–12 school library programs—only because there is a lack of understanding of the importance of these programs and the impact that these librarians have in the academic success of students. Educators, administrators, and even academic faculty who do not understand the importance of these libraries and the librarians who work with educators and their students often discount the need for these resources, especially during lean financial periods, despite their insistence that today's preservice teachers and high school students do not have adequate critical-thinking skills and do not understand the information literacy skills that are necessary for instruction or research.

Providing evidence of academic impact of the CMC within the preservice teachers' curriculum must be the guiding principle for the CMC librarian in order to help meet the needs of educators and students. Because of the significant shift from the original design of libraries and in how librarians were taught to address the needs of their patrons, many academic libraries are scrambling to meet the needs of today's students and educators. These changes, however, have provided CMC librarians with a rare opportunity to reinvent these libraries to meet the needs of tomorrow's classroom teacher—to transform their traditional curriculum-support-only program into a learning commons that allows for the integration of technology, research, collaboration, and project development by various groups and individuals working within a single space that does not limit itself to a physical location.

In other words, the CMC library and its staff must become more responsive to the needs of the preservice teachers, as well as of the education faculty, in terms of providing services and resources. Reinventing the CMC to meet the needs of today's preservice teacher may include investigating different types of libraries and classrooms that have begun the movement forward in meeting these goals and are working with new technologies and resources in order to make their services and resources available to their users on demand. By taking the opportunity to learn the types of resources, equipment, and services preservice teachers will soon have available to them as professionals, the CMC librarian will feel more comfortable in preparing preservice teachers to learn ways of utilizing a wide range of instructional resources for their own classrooms.

Relevant Growth

While the CMC must maintain solid footing within both the academic and public education arenas, the opportunities for change can often bring about the implementation of new techniques and methodologies that may not be quickly embraced by the academic library. As an instructional lab for preservice teachers to begin developing the skills necessary for the classroom, the CMC must be responsive to the needs of its patrons. In the process of making these changes, it is imperative that the academic library be open to the opportunities that may result from the implementation of new technology, new services, and new methods in providing for the instructional needs of CMC patrons. As these changes are implemented within the CMC for preservice teachers, the academic success and confidence that these patrons have in their coursework will reflect positively on the CMC for providing resources that replicate today's classroom environment. This positive impression of the CMC will then also transfer to the academic library as a whole.

Relevant Perceptions

While educators might agree that the library is an important component of the preservice curriculum and experience, most academic faculty members fail to include the CMC or even the school library as a part of the academic instruction. To make matters worse, most academic textbooks written for preservice teachers fail to even mention the value, resources, or services provided by the school library or the school librarian in relation to the instructional curriculum and classroom teaching.

In a speech given at the White House Conference on School Libraries in 2002, Dr. Gary Hartzell, professor of Educational Administration and Supervision at the University of Nebraska, summarized the coverage of libraries in education courses for preservice teachers and those studying school administration by stating, "Most often, libraries surface only in school law class discussions of copyright or censorship—leaving administrative students with the impression that school libraries are legal time bombs—instead of with the impression that the library and librarian can make significant contributions to their success. It fosters... a view of negativity... [that] the 'good' librarian is the one who doesn't get me into trouble" (p. 2).

Hartzell (2002) goes on to state that teachers are still predominantly trained to be the primary instructor within the classroom and are not taught to develop collaborative models for classroom instruction, unlike the collaborative team formations that are often found in other professions. As a result, most preservice teachers don't come to think of librarians as potential partners in curriculum and instruction.

Unless the CMC librarian becomes an integral part of the academic instructional team, there is a high probability that most academic courses in education will not include the discussion—or the collaborative model—of the librarian as an instructional partner in education courses.

Although research studies have shown that students are more academically successful in schools where teachers and librarians work collaboratively to accomplish instructional goals, most professional teachers and principals do not maximize student learning by fully utilizing their library programs (Roberson, Applin, & Schweinle, 2005, p. 45).

For nearly two decades, research to determine the impact that school libraries and the school librarian have on student achievement has been done in various school districts across the nation (Library Research Service, 2011). Unfortunately, most of the research has been ignored by those outside of the K–12 library programs. Even among school administrators and classroom teachers, the influence that the librarian can have in areas of information literacy, collaboration, and instruction has essentially been missed.

The CMC librarian's job must include the teaching of information literacy skills and the evaluation of those skills as demonstrated by preservice teachers through various instructional projects that take place within the CMC. The recent inclusion of information literacy skills in the national education guidelines demonstrates the need for teachers to become information-literate as a part of their preservice education program (Asselin & Lee, 2002, p. 10). However, work done by instructional librarians with various groups of preservice teachers shows that the majority of today's classroom teachers do not know what the school librarian can do to help them with instruction or with their students' learning. In fact, most preservice teachers are not being taught the benefits of collaborative partnerships with school librarians. If that is the case, then the omission of this instructional component within the academic coursework of education majors will result in neither the practicing teacher nor the preservice teacher seeing the librarian as a teacher or instructional partner (Church, 2006, p. 20).

Even while working with the CMC librarian is perhaps the first experience that many preservice teachers have in working with a professional librarian in the development of instructional materials, the importance of the teacher/librarian relationship at either the academic or the K–12 level should not be ignored by education faculty. Studies show that preservice teachers who have been exposed to a well-defined and integrated program of information literacy instruction will move into the profession better equipped to engage in significant instructional partnerships with their school librarians and to teach information literacy skills to their students (Johnson & O'English, 2004, p. 130).

Because CMC librarians are unique professionals within the academic library, they are often multidegreed subject specialists. In addition to their knowledge of information literacy, these individuals are acquainted with both state and national instructional standards, as well as instructional methods, educational technology, and testing and certification requirements. If the preservice teacher is encouraged to collaborate with the CMC librarian in the development of lesson plans or other real-life projects to be implemented or taught, student teachers will discover that they are able to create much more effective instructional projects than if they had worked alone (Floyd, Colvin, & Bodur, 2008, p. 369).

The importance of the CMC as the foundation in the development of new instructional plans and ideas can also provide preservice teachers with the opportunity to reflect on the various resources that they have had the opportunity to explore during their academic training and to begin working toward gathering those same resources for use once they begin their professional careers.

Teachers faced with potentially fewer resources available to them in the classroom due to budget cuts will often find that school librarians are the gatekeepers to a wealth of informational resources and knowledge. These expectations can be drawn from their earlier experiences working with the CMC librarian and the resources made available to them within the library, including

+ educational standards for subjects taught
+ tests and measurements
+ curriculum resources
+ textbooks
+ educational software
+ multimedia resources and equipment
+ children's and young adult literature

The potential for the CMC librarian to assist preservice teachers in their understanding, development, and implementation of instructional content is significant specifically because many student teachers have indicated that they found the theories and concepts that they learn in coursework too abstract to help them adequately address specific problems that they encountered in the real classroom (Floyd, Colvin, & Bodur, 2008, p. 369). By providing these students with the opportunity to practice working with these various theories before they attempt to use the theories in the classroom, they will become more confident in their ability to become successful classroom teachers.

Relevant Collaborations

While collaboration and teamwork among teachers is encouraged in most educational settings, it is still difficult for many faculty members within the colleges of education to work collaboratively with the CMC librarian. Some of this behavior could be the result of the instructor's own lack of interaction with librarians as instructional partners, while some can be related to the cultural hierarchy within the academic community. Regardless of the reason, the lack of collaborative interaction between the education faculty and the CMC librarian in the development and instruction of preservice teachers may well be an outdated and ineffective method of exclusion based upon cultural ideals from the past that has now created an environment that makes it more difficult for collaboration to occur between the preservice or classroom teacher and the school librarian.

To maximize student learning and to assist in better lesson plan development and collaboration among educators and librarians, there is a need for curricular development in higher education to advance the attitudes and practices of preservice teachers, teachers, and principals in areas of teacher/librarian collaboration (Roberson, Applin, & Schweinle, 2005, p. 45).

Collaborating with education faculty to determine what changes have been made to the educational curriculum is imperative to influencing both the faculty's and the students' perception of what the CMC provides to enhance the instructional unit and the educational process. By maintaining close faculty contact and involving key individuals in the process of sharing not only their course syllabi, but also their input into the selection of library resources that would be useful for their instruction or their students' research, the CMC librarian demonstrates that the CMC and its collection belong to each individual within the education program. This creates a community relationship among users who identify the CMC as "their space" and not the CMC librarian's space.

Methods for encouraging collaborative partnerships between the CMC librarian and the academic faculty include the development of the CMC's collection through input by the faculty and by working with the CMC librarian. Through the development of integrating new resources and materials into the collection, the CMC librarian also has an opportunity to provide instruction in the use of these resources to preservice teachers (Witt & Dickinson, 2004, p. 80).

The development of a CMC advisory committee made up of some of the strongest users of the CMC, including both professors and students, may provide an opportunity to learn more information from various viewpoints. Advisory members would then be able to provide any information, ideas, and suggestions regarding the instructional curriculum, while making the CMC librarian aware of recent proposals for new courses that might be added, changes to existing syllabi, or new instructional methods (such as distance education courses replacing face-to-face courses).

Other methods to involve both faculty and students in the collaborative process of making the CMC a program that embraces *their* interests and research is to provide online one-question surveys to gather information about the users' interests, opinions, and ideas about how the CMC is providing resources and services. While these simple surveys may not address all issues or suggestions, they do provide a method for feedback that, if addressed by the CMC librarian, will help to increase the positive working environment among the users and the CMC librarian in meeting their needs.

Studies suggest that the experience that teachers have with the library as students themselves will impact their use of the library as professionals (Earp, 2009, p. 168). In fact, Nancy O'Hanlon (1987) surmises in her study of library instruction since 1897 that "librarians have attempted to convince educators of the value of bibliographic instruction for teacher education for more than eighty years, without much success" (p. 32).

Based upon this research, it is apparent that the failure in librarian/faculty collaboration at both the academic and K–12 levels is the result of the lack of experience that these educators have had with librarians as students. Unfortunately, this lack of collaboration often results fewer positive examples of academic achievement in students at both the K–12 and the academic level because many teachers do not understand the importance of the work done by the librarian or the results of collaboration. As a result, teachers who have not internalized the skills necessary for library research during their own training are unlikely to value such skills or pass on the value of those skills to their own students (Earp, 2009, p. 168).

These findings indicate a need for higher education programs to develop and align curricula in professional education programs to ensure instruction relating to the role and value of school libraries and the inclusion of strategies that allow for greater collaboration between all members of the school's educational team (Roberson, Applin, & Schweinle, 2005, p. 51). The ability to utilize the CMC as the "model school library" for this type of instruction and the CMC librarian as the collaborative partner for both the education faculty and the preservice teacher increases the probability that educators, as well as students at all levels, will have a better understanding of information literacy.

As teacher education programs are faced with federal mandates, such as those in No Child Left Behind that require teachers to be able to design and implement evidence-based practices in their classrooms, collaborative partnerships between the CMC librarian and the education faculty are essential (Emmons et al., 2009, p. 140). Despite the studies and surveys published within the professional literature for higher education that focus on the library skills needed by teachers and the complaints that teachers lack these skills, as well the models and methods for providing these skills to preservice teachers, the value of bibliographic instruction for teacher trainees has remained unsuccessful simply because these skills are often taught by the librarian who must, in one short class session, share as many research skills as possible all at once, rather than being allowed to integrate these skills into the instructional component and teach them throughout the academic curriculum. (Emmons et al., 2009, p. 142).

Despite the value seen in the CMC library and its librarian, the lack of collaboration between the education faculty and the CMC librarian remains one of the more difficult bridges to cross primarily for the education faculty, who may view the act of collaboration with the CMC librarian as an acknowledgment of ignorance in subject area content less familiar to them.

College of Education Faculty Collaboration

Although collaboration may take on various forms within the educational environment, it is important that the CMC librarian be aware of the education faculty's perception of their collaboration with individuals whom they may view as support staff rather than highly qualified educational partners. Regardless of the academic status of the CMC librarian or the number of courses taught, the number of years of instruction in either the K–12 or academic fields, or the popularity of the librarian viewed by the many patrons who visit the CMC, the perception of most education faculty members is that *the librarian is not an instructional partner.*

Most academic librarians have complained that faculty may insist that their students need to understand research skills in order to be successful in college, and yet these faculty members provide only limited opportunities for students in their courses to develop those skills. The false assumption is that the students will develop these abilities simply by being sent to the library to use its resources (Badke, 2005, p. 64). Unfortunately, this assumption, along with the lack of instruction time given to academic librarians to provide instruction to students in these areas, only compounds the problem. In fact, even when education faculty members do give librarians an hour of their teaching time, they often do not attend the class themselves despite the fact that the faculty member is less aware of the new technologies than the average student (Badke, 2005, p. 64).

According to studies relating to academic librarians working with education faculty members in areas of information literacy, there appears to be an aversion on the part of the education faculty members to being taught by one's own colleagues, and particularly by those perceived as being less adequate than the intended learner. As a result, faculty members are hesitant to reveal that they lack current skills and knowledge in this aspect of the academic process (White, 2003, p. 324; Badke, 2005, p. 65). In other words, teaching the importance of information literacy instruction to the college of education faculty will be much more difficult if the faculty member does not perceive the CMC librarian as an instructional partner or equal and is not willing to allow the CMC librarian to opportunity to work with the faculty member in order to teach these skills.

Rather than trying to encourage faculty members to understand that there *might be a deficiency* in their own knowledge of educational content, it best to work toward finding ways to introduce information literacy to preservice students through methods that fall in line with the teaching faculty's interests and professional goals. As the CMC librarian provides instruction in the methods by which preservice teachers might determine if the resources being used are accurate and correlate with the instructional objectives of the lesson or subject being taught, the CMC librarian might demonstrate methods for utilizing these information literacy skills in a manner that will meet the teaching faculty's professional goals in the process. Despite our best intentions to become collaborative partners with our education faculty, any academic instruction *to faculty* needs to be geared to meeting the faculty's academic objective in order to succeed (White, 2003, p. 331).

Other methods for encouraging faculty to engage in information literacy instruction as a collaborative partner or for impressing upon the teaching faculty the ability of the CMC librarian to provide information instruction that meets the instructional objectives are:

- to present information literacy content that is tied to a specific assignment given by the professor
- to provide in-depth reference assistance to students in the class being taught

◆ to allow for hands-on experience working with the print or electronic resources being used to teach the concept (Manuel, Beck, & Molloy, 2005, p. 150).

By including the university faculty in the instructional process being used by the CMC librarian for preservice teachers, it becomes more likely that the professor will want to be involved. University faculty tend to be more involved as a learning group when the design of instruction is such that they can have regular input regarding the content or can make a contribution to the learning of others simultaneously with their own learning process (White, 2003, p. 329).

Even though the CMC librarian is perhaps more attuned to the needs of the preservice teachers and the faculty who utilize the CMC resources, the results of studies relating to the impact that academic librarians make with education faculty concludes that in order to impress teaching faculty, librarians should be competent and be willing to go above and beyond (Manuel, Beck, & Molloy, 2005, p. 152).

Of course, most CMC librarians would agree to nothing less.

Relevance through K–12 Collaboration and Higher Education

Perhaps one of the more ambitious initiatives for CMC librarians in the effort toward staying relevant involves providing outreach programs that incorporate information literacy skills instruction through partnerships with K–12 school librarians and subject area teachers. These partnerships would include sharing with high school students, teachers, and even parents the academic expectations of college faculty for high school students preparing to enter college after graduation.

In 2000, the AASL/ACRL Task Force on the Educational Role of Libraries released a report entitled "Blueprint for Collaboration," which essentially laid the foundation for the collaborative partnerships between the academic and school librarians working together to meet the needs of not only the preservice teacher but also that of the current classroom teacher and K–12 students. This report encouraged both academic and school librarians to recognize that they shared the responsibility for information literacy instruction to ensure the academic success of incoming freshmen. As a result, the American Association of School Librarians (AASL) and the Association of Colleges and Research Libraries (ACRL) have worked to encourage collaboration between school and academic librarians in meeting the needs of their constituents through information literacy instruction (ACRL/AASL Task Force, 2000).

In order to ensure that students at the K–12 levels have the necessary skills for academic success, it is imperative that the CMC librarian and the education faculty collaborate to guarantee that library instruction is meaningful and that preservice teachers understand the importance of the CMC and their school library within the construct of their curriculum (Earp, 2009, p. 168).

Moreover, to ensure that the information literacy needs of students at all levels are being met, it is necessary for all educators to become more aware of the librarian's expertise. One method for addressing this issue is for librarians at all levels to advocate for an information literacy course in teacher education programs and the requirement of collaboration by preservice teachers with both the CMC librarian *and then* with the school library media specialists (Zoellner & Potter, 2010, p. 198). Partnerships between the CMC librarian and the school library media specialists in schools where preservice teachers are beginning their teaching experience will not only help to make the transition from the academic library/CMC library experience easier, but also provide preservice teachers with a familiar contact person to assist them in locating resources that may not necessarily be available within the school's library.

CMC librarians who have worked closely with preservice teachers being assigned to begin teaching in the classroom can provide the K–12 school librarian with information regarding the collaborative projects that have been performed within the CMC and the level of coordination, cooperation, or collaboration that has occurred between the preservice teacher and the librarian. Much like the education faculty sharing information with the supervising teacher regarding the preservice teacher, the CMC librarian can provide similar information needed by the school librarian. By understanding the preservice teacher's level of collaboration with the CMC librarian, the K–12 school librarian will then have a starting point from which to begin working with the preservice teacher in the development of more in-depth collaborative projects as an instructional partner.

In addition to helping preservice teachers make the transitions necessary for classroom instruction, CMC librarians can begin collaborating with high school librarians and classroom teachers in areas of research and information literacy instruction for college-bound students. A study conducted by Zoellner and Potter (2010) showed that high school librarians expressed an interest in collaborating with university librarians in methods other than the current model of inviting high school groups to visit the library for research and instruction. Some of the ideas suggested included these:

- ◆ university librarians presenting at high schools
- ◆ university students discussing with high school students the research expectations at the university
- ◆ university librarians holding workshops for high school teachers and school librarians (p. 197)

The need for this collaboration is becoming more evident as students enter college lacking the necessary information literacy skills to be successful. Oftentimes they discover too late that using the resources necessary for academic research is much more difficult and much more involved than locating information online for high school projects. Students who have not been exposed to the information literacy skills needed for academic research often find themselves struggling to navigate the strenuous assignments required and expected of them during their first year of college.

The formation of a collaborative partnership between the CMC librarian, the preservice teacher, and the high school librarian is the first step in improving high school students' information literacy skills and increasing their potential for academic success in college. A study done in 2008 of the syllabus for incoming freshmen at North Carolina State University showed that the level of inquiry-based assignments required of freshman students included the use of multiple source types and, if the use and interaction with these resources had not been taught in high school, the possibility of them being taught at the academic level was even more limited based upon the student-to-librarian ratio at the academic levels (Oakleaf & Owen, 2010, p. 53).

Over the years, school librarians have seen a significant change in the how students use the library for research projects. Instead of the traditional research-based writing assignments that, in the past, covered the steps necessary to conduct a research assignment generally found in college, today's high school students are producing senior projects that include PowerPoint presentations, brochures, pamphlets, posters, or videos. As a result, the traditional research process and the methods by which students are expected to conduct college research are generally unknown to many students until their junior or senior year (Zoellner & Potter, 2010, p. 196).

These unique research projects, while creative in many ways, often fail to include any evidence that the teacher has incorporated or taught the information literacy skills necessary for their own students to utilize. It is the CMC librarian's responsibility to move beyond simply helping preservice teachers become more information literate themselves to preparing the preservice teachers to integrate information literacy skills into their own teaching (Branch, 2004, p. 43). By requiring preservice teachers to identify methods of embedding information literacy skills into their lesson plans, the CMC librarian will then be able to illustrate how students in the classroom are then challenged to use critical-thinking skills in order to complete the assignment. It is through the use of these types of information literacy skills that high school students begin to develop the necessary skills that are essential for academic success. But in order for this to occur, preservice teachers need to learn how to rethink methods for incorporating these skills into their subject areas and then teach their students how to utilize new technologies to locate, organize, synthesize, and present information (Branch, 2004, p. 45).

"Blueprint for Collaboration" (ACRL/AASL Task Force, 2000) includes several examples of high school and academic librarians working together to help bridge the gap for students entering college. A list of these examples appears in appendix I of the report, and a list of grants for implementing new projects appears in appendix II, both found at http://bit.ly/cnkiOO.

Even at the K–12 levels, information literacy skills should be considered an essential component within the educational curriculum. It is imperative that the process of acquiring those skills and the development of assignments that require the use of these skills be embedded within the instructional units (Zoellner & Potter, 2010, p. 198). The CMC librarian can be instrumental in supporting this instructional concept by working with the librarians at schools where preservice teachers are placed during their practicums to encourage them to seek out preservice teachers in order to show how school libraries can advance student achievement and add creative energy to classroom programs (Asselin & Doiron, 2004, p. 30).

Educational resources, instructional tools, and technology integration are essential elements, but they are only the beginning. In order to remain relevant in the ever-changing educational programs of the future, the CMC librarian must learn methods of interacting with the stakeholders involved. This includes working with preservice teachers, education faculty, classroom teachers, school administrators, and school librarians, as well as incoming freshmen, through collaborative partnerships at each level within the educational continuum. By providing outreach opportunities beyond the perimeters of the academic setting; extending services, resources, and instructional collaboration with educators at all levels; and utilizing technology in ways that will enhance student learning and academic achievement, the CMC librarian is ensuring the relevance of the CMC library program for the next century's educators.

References

ACRL (Association of College & Research Libraries). 2009. *Directory of Curriculum Materials Centers*, 6th ed. Chicago: American Library Association.

ACRL/AASL Task Force. 2000. "Blueprint for Collaboration." Retrieved from http://www.ala.org/acrl/publications/whitepapers/acrlaaslblueprint.

American Association of School Librarians. 2010. "School Library Funding Crisis Press Kit." Retrieved from http://www.ala.org/ala/newspresscenter/mediapress-center/presskits/schoollibrariesincri/index.cfm

Asselin, Marlene, and Ray Doiron. 2004. "Whither They Go: An Analysis of the Inclusion of School Library Programs and Services in the Preparation of Preservice Teachers in Canadian Universities." *Behavioral & Social Sciences Librarian* 22 (1): 19–32. doi:10.1300/J103v22n01_03.

Asselin, Marlene M., and Elizabeth A. Lee. 2002. "'I Wish Someone Had Taught Me': Information Literacy in a Teacher Education Program." *Teacher Librarian* 30 (2): 10.

Badke, William B. 2005. "Can't Get No Respect: Helping Faculty to Understand the Educational Power of Information Literacy." *The Reference Librarian* 43 (89): 63–80. doi:10.1300/J120v43n89_05.

Branch, Jennifer L. 2004. "Teaching, Learning and Information Literacy: Developing an Understanding of Preservice Teachers' Knowledge." *Behavioral & Social Sciences Librarian* 22 (1): 33–46. doi:10.1300/J103v22n01_04.

Church, Audrey. 2006. "Catch Them (Preservice Teachers) While You Can!" *Teacher Librarian* 33 (5): 20–23.

Earp, Vanessa. 2009. "Integrating Information Literacy into Teacher Education: A Successful Grant Project." *Behavioral & Social Sciences Librarian* 28 (4): 166–178. doi:10.1080/01639260903275748.

Emmons, Mark, Elizabeth B. Keefe, Veronica M. Moore, Rebecca M. Sánchez, Michele M. Mals, and Teresa Y. Neely. 2009. "Teaching Information Literacy Skills to Prepare Teachers Who Can Bridge the Research-to-Practice Gap." *Reference & User Services Quarterly* 49 (2): 140–150.

Floyd, Deborah M., Gloria Colvin, and Yasar Bodur. 2008. "A Faculty-Librarian Collaboration for Developing Information Literacy Skills among Preservice Teachers." *Teaching and Teacher Education* 24 (2): 368–376. doi:10.1016/j.tate.2006.11.018.

Hartzell, Gary. 2002, June. "What's It Take?" Paper presented at the White House Conference on School Libraries, Washington, DC. Retrieved December 14, 2010, from http://www.laurabushfoundation.org/Hartzell.pdf.

Johnson, Corey M., and Lorena O'English, L. 2004. "Information Literacy in Preservice Teacher Education: An Annotated Bibliography." *Behavioral & Social Sciences Librarian*, 22(1), 129–139. doi:10.1300/J103v22n01_09.

Library Research Service. 2011. "School Library Impact Studies." Retrieved from Library Research Service website: http://www.lrs.org/impact.php.

Manuel, Kate, Susan E. Beck, and Molly Molloy. 2005. "An Ethnographic Study of Attitudes Influencing Faculty Collaboration in Library Instruction." *The Reference Librarian* 43 (89): 139–161. doi:10.1300/J120v43n89_10.

Oakleaf, Megan, and Patricia L. Owen. 2010. "Closing the 12–13 Gap Together: School and College Librarians Supporting 21st Century Learners." *Teacher Librarian* 37 (4): 52–58.

O'Hanlon, Nancy. 1987. "Library Skills, Critical Thinking, and the Teacher-Training Curriculum." *College & Research Libraries* 48: 17–26.

Roberson, Thelma J., Mary Beth Applin, and William Schweinle. 2005. "School Libraries' Impact upon Student Achievement and School Professionals' Attitudes

That Influence Use of Library Programs." *Research for Educational Reform* 10 (1): 45–52.

Uhl, Jean O'Neill. 2007. "The Curriculum Materials Center: Library Support for a Teacher Education Program." *Collection Building* 26 (2): 44–47.

White, Marjorie V. 2003. "Information Literacy Programs: Successful Paradigms for Stimulating and Promoting Faculty Interest and Involvement." *The Reference Librarian* 38 (79): 323–334. doi:10.1300/J120v38n79_22.

Witt, Steven W., and Julia B. Dickinson. 2004. "Teaching Teachers to Teach: Collaborating with a University Education Department to Teach Skills in Information Literacy Pedagogy." *Behavioral & Social Sciences Librarian* 22 (1): 75–95. doi:10.1300/J103v22n01_06.

Zoellner, Kate, and Charlie Potter. 2010. "Libraries across the Education Continuum: Relationships between Library Services at the University of Montana and Regional High Schools." *Behavioral & Social Sciences Librarian* 29 (3): 184–206. doi:10.1080/01639269.2010.498761.

11 Curriculum Access and Creation in the CMC of the Future

Jo Ann Carr, University of Wisconsin-Madison, Emeritus
with Anna K. Lewis, University of Wisconsin-Madison

Curriculum materials centers (CMCs) have evolved over their long history from places in which curriculum could be constructed to also include places in which sample curricula could be accessed. The future of CMCs will continue this evolution as access to new tools for curriculum construction and a wider range of curriculum materials will support the development, adaptation, and distribution of curriculum targeted to individual needs. This chapter explores the impact of new technologies for accessing, creating, and distributing curriculum information.

Introduction

As detailed in chapters one and two of this volume, the "twentieth century phenomenon" (Clayton, 1989, p. 51) of curriculum materials centers (CMCs) has evolved from "a laboratory in which pre-service teachers might study, experiment with and construct curriculum materials for use in their K–12 classrooms,... into a multifaceted service point that houses unusual material types... serves a diverse but well defined clientele... and enters into collaborative work with allied agencies... not often identified with academic library work (Walter, 2001, p. 2). This identification of collaboration beyond the realm of academic libraries contrasts with Theodore Yuhas's 1952 recommendation that "CMC's planning be in harmony with the general university library and research facilities" (Yuhas, 1952, p. 241). This change in viewpoint from 1952 to 2001 should serve as a touchstone for the role that CMCs will play in the next decades of the twenty-first century.

To successfully respond to these changes and challenges, CMCs must adopt a new vision of their role. The new vision of the CMC requires that the CMC's planning be in harmony with the vision of the school, college, or department of education (SCDE) as well as with state and national education reform and revitalization movements. Embracing this new vision will facilitate CMCs' leadership role in building coordination across the P–20 educational environment. New collaborative partners for CMCs will include agencies and entities responsible for technology as well as those responsible for teaching and learning at the PK–12 and higher education levels. The development of these new collaborations will support CMCs as they expand user access to materials to also include user access to software programs, equipment, and learning environments.

CMCs must respond to forces of changes in higher education, especially teacher education, as well as in PK–12 education. These forces of change encompass changing measures of success including certification and accreditation requirements and the development of specific learning standards as well as a changing political climate. In addition, the increasing development of technologies that blend information access, distribution, and creation are redefining the roles of teacher and student. Despite the "parallel and intertwined paths" of these forces, there has been "little coordination" in the transformation or reform of teacher education and PK–12 education (Futrell, 2010, p. 432). Adopting a new vision, developing new collaborations, and expanding user access will enable CMCs to complete the circle and embrace equal roles as places in which curriculum materials are accessed as well as places in which curriculum materials are created and distributed.

Influences on CMC Development since 1950

In chapter 1 of this volume, Rita Kohrman has described the development of CMCs until 1940. As detailed by Suzan Alteri in chapter two, the development of CMCs since 1940 has been impacted by a changing political climate for education with an increased emphasis on accountability. A second major factor in the development of CMCs in the last seventy years has been the move beyond the textbook to a wide range of audiovisual, electronic, and virtual materials.

Calls for reform of education have been a recurring refrain in both PK–12 and teacher education since the mid-twentieth century. In the 1950s, the race for space led to greater emphasis on math and science and an increase in the number of titles and types of materials that were available to CMCs, including Cuisenaire Rods and Unifix Cubes. In the 1960s, materials with a greater emphasis on race, gender, and special needs became part of the CMC realm of responsibility. This emphasis was characterized by the development of series such as Man a Course of Study (MACOS) that taught children to investigate the question "What is human?" (*Time*, 1970). This series included texts, charts, and films, thus also expanding the types of materials to be used in classrooms.

The standards movement began in the 1970s, a decade that also saw the creation of the Department of Education and a larger federal emphasis on education, "especially at the K–12 level" (Futrell, 2010, p. 433). The development of standards has been closely connected to the "back to basics" movement, leading to the development of such series as Saxon Mathematics (Kohn, 1999).

The 1980s can be seen as the policy and standards decade with the publication of *A Nation at Risk: The Imperative for Educational Reform* in 1983 (National Commission on Excellence in Education, 1983) and *A Nation Prepared: Teachers for the 21st Century* in 1986 (Task Force on Teaching as a Profession, 1986). These reports led to a stronger role for state government in education standards as the National Governors Association (NGA) proposed national goals for our public education system (Futrell, 2010, p. 433). Although the governors proposed national goals, America's commitment to local education resulted in the development of state-level standards to provide specific criteria for the national standards. The National Board for Professional Teaching Standards, established in 1987, has developed national standards for teachers (Futrell, 2010, p. 433). In 1994, the NGA standards became law with the addition of two other goals including the professional development of teachers.

The first decade of the twenty-first century was marked by legislation that focused on issues of accountability. The No Child Left Behind (NCLB) act, passed in 2001, brought an expanded era of testing into PK–12 schools. These tests were often aligned with state standards and focused on reading, mathematics, and science. NCLB also required that every child be taught by highly qualified teachers. This call for highly qualified teachers was articulated by Title II of the Higher Education Act (HEA), which "mandated that all core subjects be taught by highly qualified teachers by the conclusion of the 2005–06 school year" (Spellings and Manning, 2006, p. iii). The 2006 report on teacher quality demonstrates the impact of the HEA reauthorization on teacher education as SCDEs reported on "completion rates for traditional and alternative route teacher preparation programs, state teacher assessments and certifications." States reported that "Ninety-five percent of the new teachers completing preparation programs passed their state licensing exams." In addition, the number of teachers prepared through alternative certification increased by 40 percent from 2000 to 2004. Forty-four of the fifty states had taken steps to align their teacher certification programs with PK–12 education standards (Spellings and Manning, 2006, p. iii). These mandates affected CMCs as they responded to the need to support students preparing for subject area assessments and examined the alignment of their collections with state PK–12 education standards. In addition, the increase in individuals obtaining teacher certification through alternative programs provided a challenge to CMCs, which found themselves either out of the loop with teacher certification candidates or needing to work with individuals beyond "the diverse but well defined clientele" identified by Scott Walter (2001, p. 2).

The changes in expectations for teacher education during the time period from 1950 to 2000 were also reflected in changes in the requirements of the National Council on the Accreditation of Teacher Education (NCATE). NCATE's 1960 accreditation standards required that a "materials center or laboratory should be maintained either as part of the library or as a separate unit" and that "it be directed by a faculty member well informed in the various instructional media and materials at different grade levels." By 1990 this requirement had been changed to the need for an "identifiable and relevant media and materials collection [that is] accessible to education students and faculty." In the 2001 NCATE revision, the need for access to materials was greatly expanded to "The unit... secures resources... serves as an education technology resource center.... Faculty and candidates have access to exemplary, library, curricular, and/or electronic information resources that serve not only the unit but also a broader constituency" (Hagenbruch, 2001, pp. 137–138).

The new emphasis by NCATE that the SCDE's resource unit serve "as an education technology resource center" reflects the expanded formats for collections housed by CMCs. An examination of the *Directory of Curriculum Materials Centers* published by Education and Behavioral Sciences Section (EBSS) of ACRL in 1985, 1996, and 2009 demonstrates the changes in formats for which CMCs provide access as well as the growing impact of technology for the creation of materials (ACRL, 2009; Anderson, 1996; Lehman & Kiewitt, 1985). These editions of the directory were published shortly after the time periods in which personal computers, the Web, and Web 2.0 became parts of the education environment. The term *microcomputer* was added to the *Thesaurus of ERIC Descriptors* in 1980 (ERIC, 2004); the term *Internet* was added in 1996 (ERIC, 1996); *Web 2.0* was popularized when O'Reilly and Associates hosted the first Web. 2.0 conference in 2004 (O'Reilly, 2005).

Each of the surveys on which these directories were based also reveals an increasing interest in technology. The survey for the 1985 edition is not appended to the directory, but only general yes/no information about the inclusion of AV materials was included (Lehman & Kiewitt, 1985). The 1996 survey included specific questions on the number of "A/V, Software, and other non-print" and the availability of "'an audiovisual production facility in the CMC" but no specific question on the availability of a computer lab (Anderson, 1996, p. 154). The survey for the 2009 directory included questions on the range of numbers for specific types of audiovisual materials and software, specific types of equipment, and circulation information for audiovisual materials and software (ACRL, 2009, p. 142–143).

The first *Directory of Curriculum Materials Centers* was published by EBSS in 1981 following a 1979 survey of CMCs. Eva Kiewitt and Lois Lehman, cocompilers of this first directory, provided a synopsis of the results of their 1979 survey of 187 CMCs in an ERIC document. Seventy-one percent of these centers were administratively part of the library, and 26 percent were part of the SCDE. The main purpose of the centers was stated as to "provide a variety of multimedia resources to support the education curriculum for students and faculty" (Kiewitt & Lehman, 1979, p. 4). The transition from the curriculum *laboratory* of the early twentieth century to the curriculum *library* of the late twentieth century is revealed by Kiewitt and Lehman's discussion of the cataloging of the collection (p. 6) as well as by their statement that "Few centers contain much audiovisual equipment" (p. 7). This change in role is also reflected in the 58 percent of respondents who reported that previewing and evaluation of materials was a service provided, contrasted with 35 percent of the centers that reported the production of teaching materials as a service (p. 5).

The 1985 edition of the *Directory of Curriculum Materials Centers* includes entries for 170 CMCs, 67 percent of which were administratively a part of the library, 29.5 percent a part of the SCDE, and another 3.5 percent reporting other administrative homes. One hundred forty of these centers reported holding audiovisual materials, although only 46 centers enumerated their holdings. The role of the CMC in providing access to materials as a library rather than as a preview or production facility is again reflected, as only 21 centers reported having AV equipment. However, the impact of computers and software as important resources in education also began to be demonstrated, as 20 of the responding institutions reported collections of computer software and 14 reported the presence of computers or computer labs (Lehman & Kiewitt, 1985).

In the 1996 *Directory of Curriculum Materials Centers*, one third of the centers reported having an audiovisual production facility, while almost all of the centers reported having collections of "A/V, Software, and other non-print." However, the relative unimportance of "A/V, Software, and other non-print" versus print materials is demonstrated by the fact that 45 percent of the CMCs reported having fewer than 500 items in this category. Ninety-three centers reported they had "AV equipment," but only 10 of the centers included information about computers or computer labs in their comments. An era of collaboration between the library and the SCDE may have been reflected by the 23 centers (8 percent) that indicated they reported both to a library administrator and to an education administrator, with 58 percent of centers administratively part of the library compared to 26 percent being part of the SCDE. Two CMCs reported they were responsible for the management of model classrooms, an access role that will be key to the future of CMCs (Anderson, 1996, pp. 56, 69). A new vision of the CMC was articulated by James Madison University (Virginia's) Educational Media Labs as "a teaching facility where students learn how to operate equipment and software and then use those skills in their classes" (Anderson, 1996, pp. 126).

As noted above, the survey for the 2009 edition reflected a growing interest in the role of audiovisual materials, computer software, and supporting equipment. This directory presented information for 204 institutions; however, many centers presented incomplete information. Of the 146 centers that reported on their administrative home, 82.8 percent were in the library, 12.3 percent were in the SCDE, and 5 percent reported to both the library and the SCDE. More centers reported having audiovisual materials, with multimedia kits being held by 135 centers. The impact of software on education that had occurred in the thirteen years since the 1996 directory was reflected in an increase to 99 centers holding instructional software (ACRL, 2009).

The collection of more detailed information on the types of equipment available in each center provides a deeper picture of the transition to CMCs as centers for curriculum creation as well as for curriculum access. The range of equipment included audio recorders and players (67 centers), cameras (38 centers), Macintosh computers (42 centers), PC computers (103 centers), scanners (43 centers), and video recorders and players (72 centers). Although many of these types of equipment can serve to access the content of materials or to create materials (audio recorders and players, Macintosh computers, PC computers, and video recorders and players), others, notably cameras and scanners, are used for the creation of materials, not for access. It is also interesting to note the preponderance of PCs versus Macs despite the dominant role that Macintosh computers have historically played in PK–12 education. The availability of dual boot systems for Macintosh computers may impact this ratio in the future (ACRL, 2009).

Centers whose variety of "A/V, Software, and other non-print" materials and availability of equipment indicate that they have embraced the recommendation from NCATE to be "an education technology center" include Francis Marion University, which has 40 cameras for a student population of 101–500 (ACRL, 2009, pp. 43–44); Slippery Rock University of Pennsylvania, which has over 500 software applications, 30 cameras, and 3 scanners for a student population of 1,001–5,000 (ACRL, 2009, pp. 83–84); the University of Calgary, which has 57 PCs and 30 cameras for a student population of 501–1,000 (ACRL, 2009, pp. 100–101); and the University of North Carolina Charlotte, which has 150 PCs, 6 Macintosh computers, and 50 cameras for a student population of 1,001–5,000 (ACRL, 2009, pp. 116–117). The University of Wisconsin–Madison Center for Instructional Materials and Computing (now part of Media, Education Resources, and Information Technology) has one of the most diverse collections of equipment with 59 each of PC and Macintosh computers, 13 scanners, and 67 cameras for a student population of 501–1,000 students (ACRL, 2009, pp. 124–125).

Future Influences on the Development of CMCs

Changes in the educational policy climate, accreditation standards, and the role of CMCs in housing and creating a wider variety of materials and equipment impacted the post-1940 development of CMCs. Projections of the future of technology in education and new views of twenty-first-century standards for PK–12 and teacher education reveals the elements that will help to define the future definition of access for CMCs.

Among the premier resources for identifying the future of technology in education are the annual *Horizon Reports*. The New Media Consortium has developed these annual reports since 2002 to "chart the landscape of emerging technologies for teaching, learning and creative inquiry" (NMC, 2006).

From 2004 to 2008, a *Horizon Report* was issued for higher education only, but in 2009 and 2010, reports on technology in K–12 education were also issued. The authors of the 2009 K–12 report identify the overlap in emerging technologies for K–12 and higher education. However, they also note, "Assessment and filtering greatly impact the degree to which some technologies can be adopted in schools, which helps to explain the considerable variation in adoption time frames between the two sectors." The current reliance on standardized tests makes it difficult to translate assessments using new media and collaborative work to measures of student learning. The authors also recognize the need for new filtering tools that keep "objectionable content out of the way while allowing useful tools and content to be accessed" (Johnson et al., 2009, p. 2).

Implementation of many Web 2.0 technologies and personalized learning technologies is also hampered because of individual school district restraints on using online tools, the lack of personal laptops or other mobile computing devices owned by students, and policies that restrict Internet access in schools. The lack of mobile computing devices is especially true at the elementary level, while student access to mobile computing devices (e.g., smartphones) in middle and high schools is often restricted by school district policy. However, CMCs that serve as curriculum access and creation units for SCDEs need to prepare future teachers for projected changes for the time when policy and access to mobile computing are aligned with twenty-first-century learning standards and metrics.

The K–12 editions of both the 2009 and 2010 *Horizon Report* were produced in collaboration with the Consortium on School Networking. Each *Horizon Report* presents key trends and challenges and identifies those technologies that will become part of the mainstream for schools within the next twelve months, within the next two to three years, and within the next four to five years. Each report also highlights practical models, innovative work, and future reading for each of the emerging technologies.

Key trends for K–12 over the next five years enumerated in these reports are these:

- Technology skills and the digital divide are a factor of education—those who learn technology skills will succeed.
- Technology is a means for empowering and connecting students, a method for communicating and socializing, and a ubiquitous, transparent part of their lives.
- The Web is an increasingly personal experience.
- Innovation and creativity must be embraced in schools
- Learning is increasingly "just-in-time, alternate, and non-formal."
- Learning environments are changing, becoming more community-driven, and "supported by technologies that engage virtual communication and collaboration." (Johnson et al., 2009, pp. 5–6; Johnson et al., 2010, pp. 5–6)

The 2009 report identifies two challenges of particular relevance to the role and development of CMCs. The first is the need for "formal instruction in key new skills, including information literacy, visual literacy, and technological literacy" (Johnson et al., 2009, p. 6). Another is the need that technology tools "that are part of everyday life for many students and working professionals should be seen as core tools of the teaching profession that teachers are required to master as any professional would master the tools of his or her trade" (Johnson et al., 2009, p. 7). In the 2010 report two additional challenges of particular relevance to CMCs were identified. The first was the gap between the types of materials being used in the classroom and the ways in which K–12 students learn. The second is the availability of learning materials, including games and social networks, to students outside the classroom environment (Johnson et al., 2010, p. 5).

The six "technologies to watch" in K–12 education over the next five years are summarized in table 11.1.

Table 11.1. Technologies to watch	
2009 Report	2010 Report
Near term (within 12 months): • Collaborative environments • Online communication tools	Near term (within 12 months: • Cloud computing • Collaborative environments
Mid term (2–3 years): • Mobiles • Cloud computing	Mid term (2–3 years): • Game based learning • Mobiles
Far term (4–5 years) • Smart objects • Personal web	Far term (4–5 years): • Augmented reality • Flexible displays
(Johnson et al., 2009, pp. 5–6)	(Johnson et al., 2010, pp. 6–7)

CMCs can assist SCDEs in preparing future teachers to integrate these technologies into their work in a variety of ways. Access to cloud computing, collaborative environments and online computing tools, augmented reality, flexible displays, and some game-based learning is an adjunct to access to other Internet resources. Collections of AV equipment can be supplemented with mobiles such as iPads to support access to tools beyond those personally owned by faculty, staff, and students. Many CMCs have already ventured into support of the personal web by providing access to citation organization tools, adding access to Ning, Flickr, blogging tools, and Picasa as an extension of the use of citation organization tools. With their long history of providing access to children's fiction and nonfiction, adding access to books compatible with LeapFrog Tag (see http://www.leapfrog.com/tag) is a natural extension into support of smart objects.

CMCs can address and are addressing the key trend of learning environments. Support of model classrooms was identified as a role by two institutions in the 1996 directory (Anderson, 1996, pp. 56, 69). The University of Wisconsin–Madison's MERIT Library is part of a larger service unit—Media, Education Resources, and Information Technology—that also includes network and desktop support, media development, and classroom support. The Education Resources area of MERIT includes library services, classroom support, information and technology literacy instruction, and assistance to faculty in the integration of technology in their teaching. This marriage of multiple aspects of education resources provides to the School of Education staff members who plan and implement classroom spaces, instruct faculty and students in the use of these spaces, and integrate information resources into teaching and learning. MERIT staff members have supported access to library resources in online learning through providing electronic reserves and course-specific library resources pages as well as working with faculty to design virtual learning spaces in the Second Life environment. During the past three years, implementation of interactive whiteboards has involved library staff in teaching students and faculty basic operation of the equipment but, more importantly, providing instruction that emphasizes access to online resources supported by the manufacturers of the boards as well as to other Internet resources and tools compatible with the use of this equipment.

As CMCs support an expanded role with providing access to and through virtual and physical learning environments, Northrup's (1997) criteria for teaching labs can serve as a guide:

a. multiple platforms
b. adherence to current industry standards
c. connectivity to the Internet
d. current software titles for productivity tools, integrated software, desktop publishing, and graphics
e. one or more multimedia development stations
f. point-to-point and multipoint desktop videoconferencing
g. authoring tools (p. 4)

Efforts to adapt the standards movement to the needs of the twenty-first century were addressed by Education Secretary Arne Duncan in a video on the US Department of Education blog on February 7, 2011, noting that NCLB has led to a "dummying down of standards and a narrowing of the curriculum" (Duncan, 2011). Multiple national efforts on standards revision are addressing these concerns about the "dummying down of standards." Major efforts impacting the development of CMCs include the Partnership for 21st Century Skills (P21), the Common Core State Standards Initiative, and revisions of information and technology literacy standards by the American Association of School Librarians (AASL) and the International Society for Technology in Education (ISTE).

P21 is a national organization that "advocates 21st century readiness for every student" (P21, 2004). P21 began in 2002 as a collaboration among industry, government, and educational organizations and now has established partnerships with fifteen states. Its framework for twenty-first-century learning includes core subjects; twenty-first-century themes, learning, and thinking skills; ICT (information and communications technology); life skills; and twenty-first-century assessments. Although the late-twentieth-century standards movement served as an impetus for CMCs to collect in the core subjects of English/language arts, mathematics, and science, implementation of the vision that is articulated by P21 also requires providing access to the full range of core subjects:

+ English, reading or language arts
+ world languages
+ arts
+ mathematics
+ economics
+ science
+ geography
+ history
+ government and civics (P21, 2009, p. 2)

In addition, P21 recognizes twenty-first-century themes as

+ global awareness
+ financial, economic, business, and entrepreneurial literacy
+ civic literacy
+ health literacy
+ environmental literacy (P21, 2009, pp. 2–3)

With their traditional emphasis on information literacy, CMCs have a strong role to play in supporting the learning and thinking skills of information and media literacy, ICT literacy skills, and the life skills of ethics, personal productivity, and self-direction. CMCs can also make the resources and publications of P21 in print and electronic forms accessible to all of their client groups.

The Common Core State Standards Initiative is an initiative of the National Governors Association, whose earlier work following the publication of *A Nation at Risk* was central to the development of state-level standards. Forty-one states and the District of Columbia have adopted these standards (Washington, Montana, Virginia, Texas, Minnesota, Maine, North Dakota, Alaska, and Nebraska are the exceptions). These standards, developed in collaboration with the Council of Chief State School Officers, are designed to provide consistent standards across all adopting states while including both college and career readiness standards and K–12 standards for elementary through high school. The first standards to be developed are English language arts (including literacy in history/social studies, science, and technical subjects) and in mathematics. The English language arts standards reflect an understanding of learning that goes beyond factual knowledge, with an emphasis on research, evaluation of complex information, participation in formal and informal discussions, and analysis and production of media. Given the widespread adoption of these standards, CMCs will need to provide access to resources that support content knowledge, learning skills, and analysis and production of media (Common Core State Standards Initiative, 2010).

AASL and ISTE have also embraced the movement toward more rigorous standards. In 2007, AASL presented *Standards for the 21st-Century Learner*, which transformed the AASL standards from information literacy standards to learning standards that recognize the social context of learning. The four standards are

- Inquire, think critically and gain knowledge.
- Draw conclusions, make informed decisions, apply knowledge to new situations, and create new knowledge.
- Share knowledge and participate ethically and productively as members of our democratic society.
- Pursue personal and aesthetic growth.

In addition to providing skill-based standards, *Standards for the 21st-Century Learner* also reflects twenty-first-century learning through the identification of dispositions, responsibilities, and assessments for each standard (AASL, 2007). This revision of the AASL standards moves them farther away from alignment with the *Information Literacy Competency Standards for Higher Education* that was developed by the Association of College and Research Libraries (ACRL) in 2000. However, the Education and Behavioral Sciences Section of ACRL is currently developing information literacy standards for educators that mirror the stronger emphasis on learning that is inherent in the 2007 AASL standards.

ISTE has developed National Educational Technology Standards (NETS) for students, teachers, and administrators. These standards, first developed in 2000, were "refreshed" in 2007–2008. The latter standards continue the new focus on digital-age learning that requires higher level thinking rather than skills. The first NETS for students were

+ basic operations and concepts
+ social, ethical, and human issues
+ technology productivity tools
+ technology communication tools
+ technology research tools
+ technology problem-solving and decision-making tools (ISTE, 2000a, pp. 15–16)

The first iteration of *NETS for Teachers (NETS-T)* listed

+ technology operations and concepts
+ planning and designing learning environments and experiences
+ teaching, learning, and the curriculum
+ assessment and evaluation
+ productivity and professional practice
+ social, ethical, legal, and human issues (ISTE, 2000b, p. 9)

In contrast, the 2007–2008 standards recognize that technology is putting new demands on students and teachers that reach beyond skills. "NETS for Students 2007" promotes higher-level thinking and learning abilities rather than skills:

- creativity and innovation
- communication and collaboration
- research and information fluency
- critical thinking, problem solving, and decision making
- digital citizenship
- technology operations and concepts (ISTE, 2007)

"NETS for Teachers 2008" reflects the new role of the teacher as an instructional guide and leader for the digital age:

- Facilitate and inspire student learning and creativity.
- Design and develop digital-age learning experiences and assessments.
- Model digital-age work and learning.
- Promote and model digital citizenship and responsibility.
- Engage in professional growth and leadership (ISTE, 2008).

Judy Walker wrote presciently regarding the role of CMCs in supporting the new learning standards promoted by all of these organizations: "Since the CMC's function is to support the education curriculum, any type of instruction the CMC undertakes with educators… should incorporate instructional experiences that will help students meet technology competencies." She adds, "Students should be able to set up an instructional consultation with CMC staff during which CMC staff can help the student choose appropriate instructional technologies for their particular unit" (Walker, 2001, pp. 152–153). The role of the teacher in "designing and developing digital-age learning experiences and assessments" aligns closely with the role of the CMC in supporting access to physical and virtual learning environments as well as the tools to create and present curriculum (ISTE, 2008).

Embracing the New Role for the CMC

Continuing to expand the responsibilities of the CMC beyond access to materials to access to tools and resources to create, distribute, and test learning materials will require closer alignment with the vision of the teacher-librarian embraced by our K–12 counterparts and a re-examination of the appropriate academic background for the professional staff of CMCs.

Highly qualified school librarians have embraced their role as teacher-librarians. CMC librarians need to be not only the teachers' librarian but a teacher-librarian who models team teaching, serves as a leader in project-based teaching and learning, and prepares future educators for their role as partners in the instructional process with school library media specialists, with other educators, and with students.

The creation of new partnerships and collaborations can be more easily developed if CMC librarians share the same professional enculturation as their teacher education colleagues and their primary clients. The development of an interdisciplinary program "that brought future academic librarians together with future children's librarians, school librarians, and school teachers would allow the preservice CMC librarian to more fully appreciate the network of education information professionals who are responsible for helping to meet information needs of CMC user groups" (Walter, 2001, p. 16).

As we look to the future of access in CMCs, we can find inspiration in the past. A 1947 study of CMCs identifies this role for CMCs: "A curriculum laboratory is a dynamic entity, including not only a 'laboratory,' traditionally defined as a place—room or rooms—with equipment and materials for research and experimentation, but also providing 'leaders' who use the facilities, materials and equipment available for curriculum study and development" (Drag, 1947, p. x). "Obviously, this type of curriculum endeavor requires continuous growth in service if teachers are to cope with constantly arising problems, if they are to be prepared to set new educational goals, and if they are to provide more socially significant education for children" (Drag, 1947, p. 7).

References

AASL (American Association of School Librarians). 2007. *Standards for the 21st-Century Learner*. Chicago: American Association of School Librarians. Retrieved from http://www.ala.org/ala/mgrps/divs/aasl/guidelinesandstandards/learningstandards/AASL_Learning_Standards_2007.pdf.

ACRL (Association of College & Research Libraries). 2000. *Information Literacy Competency Standards for Higher Education*. Chicago: American Library Association. Retrieved from http://www.ala.org/ala/mgrps/divs/acrl/standards/standards.pdf.

———. 2009. *Directory of Curriculum Materials Centers*, 6th ed. Chicago: American Library Association.

Anderson, Beth G., ed. 1996. *Directory of Curriculum Materials Centers*, 4th ed. Chicago: Association of College and Research Libraries.

Clayton, Victoria. 1989. "Curriculum Libraries at Institutions of Higher Education: A Selective Annotated Bibliography." *Behavioral & Social Sciences Librarian* 8 (1/2): 51–66.

Common Core State Standards Initiative. 2010. "Common Core State Standards." Retrieved from http://www.corestandards.org.

Drag, Francis L. 1947. *Curriculum Laboratories in the United States: A Research Study: San Diego County Schools.* San Diego, CA: Office of the Superintendent of Schools.

Duncan, Arne. 2011, February 7. "Secretary Duncan on Fixing NCLB and Elevating the Teaching Profession," video file posted on *ED.gov Blog*. Retrieved from http://www.ed.gov/blog/2011/02/secretary-duncan-on-fixing-nclb-and-elevating-the-teaching-profession.

"Education: Teaching Man to Children" *Time* 1970, January 19. Retrieved from http://www.time.com/time/magazine/article/0,9171,878677-2,00.html

ERIC (Education Resources Information Center). 1996, February 23. "Internet." In *Thesaurus of ERIC Descriptors*. Retrieved from http://eric.ed.gov/ERICWebPortal/gotoThesaurusDetail.do?term=Internet.

———. 2004, January 5. "Microcomputers (1980 2003). In *Thesaurus of ERIC Descriptors*. Retrieved from http://eric.ed.gov/ERICWebPortal/gotoThesaurusDetail.do?term=Microcomputers+%281980+2003%29.

Futrell, Mary Hatwood. 2010. "Transforming Teacher Education to Reform America's P–20 Education System." *Journal of Teacher Education* 61: 432–440. doi:10.1177/0022487110375803.

Hagenbruch, Harriet. 2001. "Outreach and Public Relations in CMCs." In *A Guide to the Management of Curriculum Materials Centers for the 21st Century*, edited by Jo Ann Carr, 137–147. Chicago: American Library Association.

ISTE (International Society for Technology in Education). 2000a. *National Educational Technology Standards for Students (NETS-S)*. Eugene, OR: International Society for Technology in Education.

———. 2000b. *National Educational Technology Standards for Teachers (NETS-T)*. Eugene, OR: International Society for Technology in Education.

———. 2007. "NETS for Students 2007." Retrieved from http://www.iste.org/standards/nets-for-students/nets-student-standards-2007.aspx.

———. 2008. "NETS for Teachers 2008." Retrieved from http://www.iste.org/standards/nets-for-teachers/nets-for-teachers-2008.aspx.

Johnson, Larry, Alan Levine, Rachel Smith, and Troy Smythe. 2009. *Horizon Report: 2009 K–12 Edition.* Austin, TX: New Media Consortium. Retrieved from http://wp.nmc.org/horizon-k12-2009.

Johnson, Larry, Rachel Smith, Alan Levine, and Keene Haywood. 2010. *Horizon Report: 2010 K–12 Edition.* Austin, TX: New Media Consortium. Retrieved from http://wp.nmc.org/horizon-k12-2010.

Kiewitt, Eva, and Lois Lehman. *Curriculum Materials Centers: A Survey of Their Poli-*

cies and Practices. 1979. (ERIC 194 110)

Kohn, Alfie. 1999, October 10. "A Look at... Getting Back to Basics: First Lesson: Unlearn How We Learned." *The Washington Post*. Retrieved from http://www.alfiekohn.org/teaching/alagbtb.htm.

Lehman, Lois, and Eva Kiewitt.. *Directory of Curriculum Materials Centers* 2nd ed. Chicago, IL: Association of College and Research Libraries.1985.

National Commission on Excellence in Education. 1983, April. *A Nation at Risk: The Imperative for Educational Reform*. Washington, DC: Government Printing Office.

NMC (New Media Consortium). 2006, August 11. "Horizon Project." Retrieved from http://www.nmc.org/horizon.

Northrup, Pamela Taylor. 1997, February. "Instructional Technology Benchmarks for Teacher Preparation Programs and K–12 School Systems." In *Proceedings: Selected Research Presentations at the 1997 National Convention of the Association for Educational Communications and Technology*, edited by Abel O'Malley, Nancy J. Maushak, and Kristen Egeland Wright, 263–270. Washington, DC: Association for Educational Communications & Technology. Retrieved from ERIC database (ED409858).

O'Reilly, Tim. 2005, September 30. "What Is Web 2.0? Design Patterns and Business Models for the Next Generation of Software." O'Reilly Media website. Retrieved from http://www.oreillynet.com/pub/a/oreilly/tim/news/2005/09/30/what-is-web-20.html.

P21 (Partnership for 21st Century Skills). 2004. Partnership for 21st Century Skills website. Retrieved from http://www.p21.org/index.php.

———. 2009. *P21 Framework Definitions*. Washington, DC: Partnership for 21st Century Skills.

Spellings, Margaret, and James F. Manning. 2006. *The Secretary's Fifth Annual Report on Teacher Quality: A Highly Qualified Teacher in Every Classroom*. Washington, DC: US Department of Education. Retrieved from http://www2.ed.gov/about/reports/annual/teachprep/2006-title2report.pdf.

Task Force on Teaching as a Profession. 1986. *A Nation Prepared: Teachers for the 21st Century*. Carnegie Forum on Education and the Economy.

Walker, Judith. 2001. "Technology and the CMC." In *A Guide to the Management of Curriculum Materials Centers for the 21st Century: The Promise and the Challenge*, edited by Jo Ann Carr, 148–163. Chicago: American Library Association.

Walter, Scott. 2001. "Professional Education." In *A Guide to the Management of Curriculum Materials Centers for the 21st Century: The Promise and the Challenge*, edited by Jo Ann Carr, 1–24. Chicago: American Library Association.

Yuhas, Theodore F. 1952. "The Curriculum Laboratory in the University." *Educational Administration & Supervision* 38: 235–242.

12

A Look to the Future of Curriculum Materials Centers

Kathy Yoder, Bowling Green State University and
Linda Scott, The University of Mount Union

Curriculum materials centers (CMCs) are faced with the same challenges that academic libraries experience: lack of funding, staff, and resources. Despite that, the future of many CMCs remains strong because of an increased need for strong clinical training for preservice teachers. To remain vital, established CMCs must be prepared to share in the goals of their institutions, promote themselves, embrace emerging technologies, and keep a strong commitment to the foundations of librarianship through excellent reference, instruction, and collection development. As shown by the example of the Curriculum Resource Center at the University of Mount Union, not only can established centers do this, but it is possible for new centers to be developed and thrive.

A Look to the Future
Kathy Yoder

Making do with less has been standard operating procedure in many curriculum materials centers (CMCs) for so long that most who operate them have little memory of working in an adequately staffed and funded atmosphere. While budgets decline or at best remain flat, the price of materials continues to rise and inevitably fewer new items can be added to the modest collections that are so lovingly maintained by those who remain. Staff members are transferred to other departments or are lost through retirement and soon, even without layoffs, the few who remain are faced with the challenging task of providing service once given by many. Student employment budgets are also affected as work-study money dries up and departments are asked to pay a greater share of wages. In short, CMCs suffer the same turmoil and upheaval experienced by the greater university community when economic uncertainty threatens. Despite the gloomy economic picture faced by most CMCs, the future doesn't have to be dismal.

CMCs, whether part of the main collection operated through a university library, a branch, or even a special collection, have long had to shout loud and often to be recognized as the valuable asset they truly are to the many students who depend on them. The future of CMCs will be governed by the ability to frame CMCs as the vital component of teacher education that they are. Despite the tendency of the librarians who make the magic happen to do it quietly and efficiently, I've come to realize that we must step out of our comfort zones and be the enthusiastic and vocal leaders in our own promotion. In particular, CMCs must market themselves in the very things that the university at large is focusing on: promotion of teacher education programs as centers of excellence, recruitment of new students and quality faculty, retention of current students, and community outreach. While we may be out of our comfort zones when we engage in these areas, CMC librarians are right at home when we focus on what we do well. In order to remain vital organizations that serve teachers in training and the university at large at a top-notch level, we must also pay attention to the fundamental components of reference, instruction, and collection development. In a climate of "something's gotta give" as we continually make do with fewer resources, a vigilance that does not allow that something to be our ability to provide high-quality reference service, instruction, and collection development is required.

Quality teachers will always be in demand, and training those teachers will also be necessary. As universities attempt to market their teacher training programs as centers of excellence, a well-equipped and active CMC is impressive evidence of a university's commitment to teacher education. Teacher preparation programs are currently undergoing fundamental change. A clear commonality of many recent studies and reports on teacher preparation programs points out the disconnect between the coursework provided to preservice teachers and their experiences in the classroom. The result is a demand that programs increase clinical experiences at all levels of teacher training and integrate practice-based experiences along with pedagogy and content. In its June 2010 presentation to Capitol Hill, the American Association of Colleges for Teacher Education stated the imperative need for strong clinical experiences necessary for training innovative educators (AACTE, 2010). A Blue Ribbon Panel on Clinical Preparation and Partnerships for Improved Student Learning was commissioned by the National Council for Accreditation of Teacher Education (NCATE) in January 2010, and its initial work emphasizes a similar message (NCATE, 2010). Teachers in training will be in classrooms more than ever. The tools that allow students to have strong field experiences are the very hands-on materials that CMCs provide. This recent call for classroom experiences makes the CMC a necessity rather than a luxury in order to provide the education demanded by the profession.

Competition between institutions of higher education over the population of college-bound students increases as the providers of that education expand their markets through distance education, branch colleges, and even the explosion of for-profit higher learning institutions. In this climate of competition, recruitment of students to campus is a task no longer reserved for admissions offices. Rather, all who serve in any capacity at a university are part of the recruitment experience, and CMCs should welcome the opportunity to be part of this process. While the connection might not be obvious at first glance, a visit to a CMC by a potential student and family may be the tipping point when comparing institutions that often offer similar programs.

When a traditional senior high school student, usually accompanied by one or two parents and toting the complimentary school-colored bag of goodies, enters my center, I don't lurk behind the reference desk and wait for inquiries. Instead I see this as an excellent opportunity to share information on the CMC, the teacher training program, and the university as a whole. As I walk around on a minitour of the collection, pointing out the wealth of materials that we offer for use, there are two points to include. First, I assure future students and parents that the teacher training program provides many wonderful opportunities for required clinical experiences such as microteaching, tutoring, field experiences, internships, and student teaching. I explain that the puppets, manipulatives, and children's books that are offered on our shelves are all provided at no cost to the students to borrow so that their practice teaching experiences can be rich and authentic. I like to point out that students who do not have access to a CMC often feel compelled to purchase resources at the local big box stores to be able to create effective and innovative lessons. The second thing I encourage the family to do is make sure, when they make their campus visits to other universities, to ask to see the CMC, as it will help a future student determine how much the institution values its teacher training program.

Fortunately there are other opportunities to work with prospective students besides the occasional student who wanders in. Libraries are often asked to have a presence at special college visit programming, and while many busy librarians aren't eager to stand and chat with prospective students in a large, drafty multipurpose room, I find this to be the perfect opportunity to inquire about academic major interests followed by enthusiastic directions to the CMC. Preview Days are set aside on the campus calendar, and those that coincide with school holidays, such as Veterans Day or Presidents' Day, often bring in large numbers of families. By offering to stand at the main entrance to welcome families and give directions to the highlights of the library, I'm able to find the future education majors and direct them up the steps to our center. Not all strategies for recruitment have to be time-consuming. A bookmark with CMC details can be tucked into information packets, displayed at college fairs, and distributed to visiting high school students with the recommendation, "Education Majors—Always ask to see the CMC when visiting a campus!"

Student retention is a concern on many campuses, and reasons students don't complete their degree requirements cover a broad span. One reason, however, often starts as homesickness and then snowballs into isolation. CMCs often create an atmosphere of friendliness and intimacy because of their size and clientele. It is common for cadres of students working on group projects to get to know each other over colorful round tables. In the relaxed atmosphere created by children's books, posters, and puppets that is reminiscent of a school or public library from childhood, many students walk in for the first time and comment on the familiarity of the space. It is not unusual for a student to be sitting quietly at a table studying while all around the sounds of creativity and laughter ricochet between groups of students engaged in projects. I've often suggested to that student that he might be more comfortable in a quieter spot, only to be rebuffed with the explanation this place reminds the student of home or his youth. A CMC provides a chance for those with similar majors to find others of like interests from different classes and years. Conversations and suggestions flow freely between tables, and peer mentoring is abundant. Discussions of classes, professors, and assignments bloom spontaneously between previously unintroduced students, and frequently encouragement and empathy are offered.

Often CMC staff are former classroom teachers who not only excel at the many readers' advisory questions, but are also available to listen and brainstorm ideas, talk through assignments, and pull helpful books. Encouragement through challenging terms of methods courses allows student patrons and staff to get to know each other personally and celebrate accomplishments. Unlike users of a small special collection that is quietly used for individual research, CMC patrons often feel like they are in the trenches together, and they are loyal to the staff of librarians who are there with them night after night. At our center, we have a "Free Shelf" of teaching materials that we've accumulated from a variety of sources such as retired teachers, duplicate donations, or pullouts from journals. This popular shelf is closely watched by our regular students to raid for treasures for their own soon-to-be classrooms. For those centers that are housed with the education department, some are equipped with comfortable chairs and couches, microwaves, and refrigerators that allow them to be popular meeting spaces that merge the academic and social aspects of student life. CMCs have been doing for years what so many campuses are now trying to create with learning commons. The personal connections created so commonly at a CMC surely go far in combating the isolation and loneliness that can drive students away from completing their academic curriculum.

CMC vitality as we look to the future cannot be assured without considering the community outside of the campus. Community outreach can be difficult for the typical academic library, as topics of interest to the campus and outside community don't always overlap. In a CMC the connections are much more evident. The materials themselves ask to be handled by patrons much younger than the college students who regularly use them. Opportunities to bring children and children's books and educational resources together can be pursued through avenues that bring kids to the center and take the center out to the kids. Not uncommonly, universities offer summer day-camps to elementary-age schoolchildren. CMCs can offer story hours that bring the kids into the library, add a literacy component to an active day-camp program, and use stories and resources that tie in to the camp's theme. Using donated carpet squares and a minimum of materials, story hours are excellent low-cost opportunities to interact with the community. For the younger set, campus child development centers can enjoy a visit from the CMC library lady, who brings puppets, stories, and songs for a special visit. Taking materials out to the community is a larger undertaking, but the benefits of the community engagement are often worth it. At my CMC, we house the Cooperative Services for Children's Literature's Children's Book Center, a review site for recently published children's books. This collection, which includes an exciting selection of picture books, is used in the outreach program Bringing Books to Life: Engaging School Age Children in Picture Book Reviewing. It features school visits to classrooms by a storyteller who takes one of the new picture books and brings it to life through interactive storytelling artistry. Following the story, each student is left with a new book to borrow from the Children's Book Center's collection. The following week, I return to the classrooms and discuss the picture books with the children, lead the children in a book review writing lesson, and post their writing to our book review blog. This outreach program provides a reading- and writing-rich activity for the students that teachers love to host and allows the university to engage with schools and students in a highly positive manner.

Attention to student recruitment and retention and community outreach are excellent ways to promote the CMC throughout the campus, but keeping a CMC vital into the future must happen through a focus on the fundamentals of good librarianship. A strong CMC will withstand an uncertain future by providing excellent reference service, relevant instruction, and an up-to-date standards-based collection.

User-centered service invites students to return for more than just their information needs. Students will have traditional needs, such as help with finding an article in a database or materials on a particular topic, and the ability to provide those is important. However, in a CMC, students are just as likely to need readers' advisory services, help with state education standards, reading-level discussions, and brainstorming sessions as they plan their lessons and units. CMC librarians with teaching backgrounds and classroom experience also find themselves drawing on technical expertise as many demonstrate and facilitate impromptu lessons in lamination, die-cut techniques, document projectors, and interactive whiteboards. The availability of computers and other educational equipment, along with staff knowledgeable in all aspects of classroom technology, instruction, and management, is required for CMCs to remain vital.

A frequently called-upon service for students that is unique to CMCs is providing children's book suggestions and grade-level recommendations. Students are frequently uncomfortable selecting books for children, particularly when they are required to match an age or reading level. A common complaint from student patrons is that children's books are rarely labeled with a suggested age or grade. This is a wonderful opportunity to discuss with students the range of abilities and interests that children possess within a classroom, and that a single title can be appropriate for third-grade students or sixth-grade students depending on their reading skills and maturity. Similarly, a request for a book for first grade is always countered with a return question regarding whether the story to be read to or by a first grader. There are many variables in matching a book to a child, and just as many in matching a book to a student teacher. The reference interview in a CMC is often a valuable exchange in which future teachers can learn to select books appropriate for their students.

The face-to-face reference interview isn't the only way to meet these specialized reference needs. Traditional bibliographies still line our shelves, but students like to take advantage of online resources such as the Children's Literature Comprehensive Database (http://www.childrenslit.com) to help them identify children's books both by topic and grade level. To make that database even more user-friendly, a link to the university's catalog from the database records can be added so that local availability can be determined as the student patron searches the database. The popular *Something about the Author* and *Children's Literature Review* are available as e-books from Gale, as traditional reference works no longer need to be accessed from within the CMC. Another tool for reference that students can access remotely is electronic pathfinders. Frequently requested subjects that can sometimes be difficult to narrow in a catalog lend themselves to guides that can be browsed and searched. Using the popular electronic library guide product from Springshare, LibGuides can be created to address common questions and can be accessible not only from the CMC's webpages, but also linked through online syllabi and course management systems such as Blackboard or Moodle. Some examples of these helpful webpages include guides to primary sources, math manipulatives, easy-reader suggestions, and fairy tales and folktales available in our center. Each page can combine information on books, teacher resources, activity books, teaching aids, links to digital resources, and state standards. Incorporating digital resources into the treasures of the collection is paramount for a CMC that hopes to remain significant in a time when libraries are no longer confined to a building.

The CMC of the future will also have a strong Web presence, allowing students to not only search the catalog remotely and access e-books, but also to tour and gain instruction through video and slide presentations. Simply being listed as a special collection or branch collection or identified on a map is not enough of a Web presence for a CMC. Faculty and students should be able to use the center's website both as a guide to what the collection holds and as a resource for what is available digitally in the world of education. The skills of the center's librarians in organizing and presenting easy access to the rich resources available for classroom teachers are particularly valuable for the viability of CMCs. Those websites must be visually appealing and intuitive to show off the collection beyond a dry description. Book jackets have long been seen as a necessity in the catalog, and now rotating slide shows can feature realia such as culture kits and puppets that are much better seen than described and can be added to a website relatively easily. The CMC's website should be seen as the front door to a collection that can be visited both virtually and in person. Both ways should be welcoming and easy to use by both students and faculty.

A key to attracting patrons at our facility has always been through cultivating good relationships with faculty and instructors. When they perceive the CMC as indispensable to their goals, use of the facility remains high. A good method for attracting faculty is providing quality instruction. Instruction sessions guide the preservice teachers through information on our services and resources, both physical and digital. Because of the teaching background of our staff, we use our sessions as opportunities to model the skills and techniques that the students are learning. We pull ideas out of the very activity books that we hope they will check out, and we make displays and bulletin boards, noting the sources and call numbers, to inspire them. By minimizing boring lectures and making instruction sessions interactive and appealing to different learning styles, we can be one more positive influence on their path to becoming highly effective teachers.

In order to discourage students from feeling bored by attending similar instruction sessions, faculty are encouraged to create assignments that are content-specific to their class, and an effort is made to individualize each session so it doesn't feel canned. Students who attend a session for an assessment class will have a very different experience from those who are there for art education or tutoring tips. Meaningful assignments also increase attendance and promote a more authentic learning experience over a generic tour.

Librarians should get to know the needs of the faculty and make them aware of the materials in the collection. This can be done by traveling to them and presenting at a faculty meeting, or inviting content-area instructors to come for a field trip during a regularly scheduled meeting time. Encourage them to create assignments based on items in the collection, which ideally they have had a voice in selecting, and maybe even donated. Professors often have great collections of materials that they have acquired over the years and want to be able to share with their students. However, keeping track of those materials is incredibly difficult for them. Remind them that as librarians we are excellent at the very thing they hate, and that we have a whole mechanism for keeping track of the materials.

While promoting the CMC to faculty, it is good to remember those outside of the education department. Consider other majors and programs that have an education component, and see if the faculty is aware of materials that apply. Nursing students have such a component, communication sciences and disorders use many of the same materials, English departments offer children's and young adult literature classes, general studies writing has been known to use children's books as writing prompts, and art students should be aware of available picture files and die-cut options. Human development and family studies majors often have requirements involving parent workshops, character education, or counseling that are best served with a CMC's curriculum resources. For a CMC to thrive in the future, finding and educating faculty across campus is imperative.

Instruction is not limited to academic coursework. Offices across campus can use the resources of a CMC. Resident advisors are huge users of our center because of the large selection of die-cut machines and dies. We charge individual students $2 for a semester subscription and departments and offices $10, which enables students and staff to use the equipment as much as they like. The money is then used to buy more dies and maintain the machines. This not only brings many different majors into our center, but it also makes them aware of the other services and resources such as lamination, board games, and DVDs. We feel resident advisors do such a good job of getting the word out to the student body that we attend their training each summer to pitch our services and invite them to visit. Another collection that we've been promoting to the entire student body is our extensive selection of YA titles. Ever since Harry Potter and *Twilight* have made young adult literature cool for college kids to read, we've ramped up the promotion of authors like John Green and Suzanne Collins and connected popular titles to happy students.

Growing a collection during uncertain economic times can be a challenge, but librarians are usually very resourceful. Curriculum materials such as textbooks are often donated by textbook adoption committees at area schools, but they rarely think about such a donation without being solicited for it. Make a connection with curriculum directors and be ready to arrange for the transport of nonadopted texts. Put together culture kits by asking international programs, students, and faculty for donations of items from their culture of interest. Be specific about what is desired, create a kit and display it on the CMC website, then advertise for similar international items on faculty lists, e-mails to language programs, and international clubs. Another group of generous professionals are retiring area teachers and campus faculty members. Ask if they would like to donate materials to the CMC, with the promise that items not added to the collection will be given to future teachers.

CMCs will continue to serve teachers in training as long as quality teacher education with a strong emphasis on clinical experience is in demand. Extensive student use of the CMC will continue as long as our centers are welcoming, demonstrate value to faculty, and are recognized as indispensable to student success. Our reach will continue to grow as our centers meet users on their computers and mobile devices, allowing for discovery of our resources, both physical and digital. As established CMCs attempt to grow with the emerging technology, worrying about viability from one semester to the next, one university library recently made a commitment to create a center from scratch. Like all large projects that are successful, an enthusiastic and committed leader must step up. At the University of Mount Union, that person came from a most unlikely place: the technical services department.

Starting a Curriculum Materials Center from Scratch: One Library's Story
Linda Scott

Despite the recent nationwide trend of CMC closures, there remain some academic institutions whose CMCs have just begun operations. The University of Mount Union opened the doors of a new CMC in October 2009, just one week prior to a scheduled visit from NCATE. The university passed accreditation quite easily, in part due to the new center, which was fully constructed, furnished, and stocked within a matter of three months.

This short time frame does not, of course, reflect the massive preparation that occurred the entire year prior to completion, which was primarily dependent upon the enthusiasm and devotion of one of the library's staff members. The University of Mount Union may be in a somewhat unique position in that the main thrust of its CMC development was undertaken by the head of technical services in the library instead of education personnel, a consultant, or a retired principal or teacher who would subsequently serve on the CMC staff. Instead, it was the head cataloger who, in April 2008, urged the university to move forward with its planning for this new facility, and the administration responded with full support for all aspects of planning and construction.

Since plans for the center began after the current fiscal year's budget had been approved, the center's projected cost failed to be allocated to any single department's budget line, and consequently the center was required to be constructed and furnished at the very lowest possible cost. Instead of approaching the board of trustees to consider new construction, it was decided that the center needed to occupy an existing space somewhere on campus, which would necessarily mean displacing some other campus functions. It was discussed that ideally the center would be either in close physical proximity to the education department or actually inside the education department facilities, which were bursting at that time, so we opted for the former scenario. Since the university library is but one building away from the education department, we were more than fortunate that the library director, Bob Garland, graciously offered half of the third floor of the old library wing for the center. This entailed weeding and moving all the oversized books that were then contained on that floor to some other location. We relied on our circulation department to take over the task of physically moving the books, so while initially mulling over floor plans, I had the advantage of considering our options with an already-emptied half floor, save for the metal shelving units that were kept in reserve for CMC book collections.

Instead of hiring a consultant to advise with plans, I was encouraged in September of that same year by the Dean of the University, Patricia Draves, to make visitations to other, well-established and prominent CMCs in Ohio. Many such institutions came to mind, but I decided to request tours from Kathy Yoder at Bowling Green State University and Mary Cummings from Shawnee State University, whose CMCs were among the best in the state. Though I had already scoured Google Images and consulted leading books on curriculum center design, these searches presented no competition to the personal visitations on which I was able to go, and I realized immediately, upon viewing both Bowling Green and Shawnee State, that other tours might not only consume more valuable time, but might also fail to yield any additional crucial information than that already gleaned from Kathy or Mary, and so I returned to Mount Union bursting with ideas.

Though I had taken many pictures of both centers to which I traveled, I never reviewed them because the interior images of the two CMCs remained quite vivid in my mind. I was able to picture all the shelves, the proportional distance between furniture in the rooms, and the layout of the spaces. I was most interested in these questions:

- What kinds of materials should be collected, and how should they be arranged?

- What kinds of specialized equipment are necessary for optimal functionality?
- Which periodical titles should be included in the collection, and how should they be made available?
- What types of circulation policies should be established?
- How much room would be needed for research in relation to numbers of students and computers available?
- How much room would be required for the graphics area?
- Where should realia be shelved?
- Should teacher strategy books be intershelved with textbooks, and should educational theory books be available elsewhere?
- What types of information does one include on a CMC homepage, and which links are most useful?
- Which databases are most commonly used?
- What type of processing is required for the library materials, and which are retained for reference only?
- What sorts of facilities beyond research, projects, storage, shelving, and classroom should be included?

Nothing can substitute for first-hand viewing when determining the arrangement and services of a center during preconstruction discussions.

I eagerly drew up initial plans and realized that I could create a comfortable, content-rich center without having to purchase any new furniture or shelving and without needing to install any plumbing or large fixtures. I reserved a large adjoining space toward the back and off to one side for a classroom at the request of the education department, and the jurisdiction for this classroom area remains part of the education department's responsibilities, while the main part of the center itself is left to the jurisdiction of the library. Happily, I was able to manage almost the entire center project myself! (See figure 12.1.)

I determined that since the metal shelves already existing on that floor were to hold most of the children's books, teacher strategy guide books, and textbooks, I would not need to purchase any shelving for most fiction and nonfiction. Realia shelving, which is located in the

Figure 12.1. Floor Plan

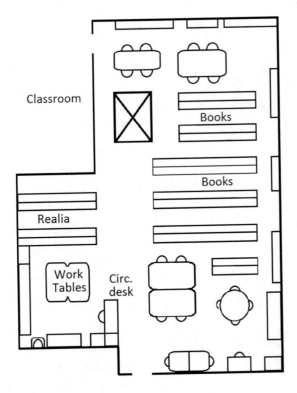

graphics portion of the center, was simply pulled out of storage; I did likewise for the periodical shelves. Short wooden bookcases already lined the walls, whose wraparound windows run the perimeter of the room, and fortunately a small sink was already located in a corner of the front area, which necessarily determined the location of the future graphics area. The center actually comprises one large space that uses the shelving units to divide front and back sections, and there is a large ventilation column located on one side of the center, which further segregates the sections. The layout consists of a front research area with the graphics lab across from it, bookshelves running perpendicularly down the middle, and a horizontal back room that contains long tables for tutoring, small classes, and group study. The classroom opens to the left of the back room and includes a small observation booth, while the right part of the back room holds display items and children's materials such as puppets, bins of toys, play rugs, and costumes, with plenty of room for storytelling. The center is divided from the rest of the old floor by one wall with a windowed door.

In keeping with the "no spend" policy, the library director was very generous in giving furniture and equipment to the center from various parts of the library. The main construction expenses incurred by the library included the erection of the wall dividing the center from the rest of the floor, the inner classroom wall, two doors, carpet squares, vinyl flooring for the graphics portion, paint, and wiring. Since the classroom belongs to the education department and operates somewhat as a separate entity, that department incurred expenses including the Smart Board and audio equipment for the observation room, while the classroom furniture was transferred from another department on campus. The library absorbed the center's equipment expenses, which included three computers, a printer, and a copier, and the supplies expenses, which included art materials, display items, dies, and technical processing materials. The cost to replenish these consumables continues to be undertaken by the library, and the students are not yet charged a laboratory fee at the beginning of each semester to offset some of these expenses. Staffing of the center remains a shared expense between the departments. While students are primarily responsible for circulation desk operations and CMC special projects, their management and training falls to the catalog librarian, and since technical services is largely instrumental in the classification and processing of CMC materials, using the technical services librarian to supervise the center seems to work as an advantage.

At Mount Union, I serve as library liaison to the education faculty and so am already involved in collection development for this department and have also traditionally been responsible for the purchase of children's materials. I had never been involved in the arrangement or classification of the juvenile materials, however, and so just prior to April 2008, I undertook a special technical services project to reclassify the juvenile books, since they seemed difficult to locate. It seemed fortuitous, therefore, that a mere two months prior to discussing the possibility of a CMC on campus with the dean, I had already launched this reclass project of the children's materials, which proved to be just the beginning of a massive rearrangement of the entire juvenile collection.

Arrangement of materials greatly coincides with reclassification, and toward the end of the juvenile reclassification project in September 2009, one month before NCATE's arrival, nearly every book had been reclassed and reshelved. It seemed best that curriculum classification and book collections arrangement be accomplished by someone holding dual roles on the CMC staff and technical services staff, since collaboration of expertise in both areas can yields wonderful results for CMC users. CMC staff are well-versed in both the type of materials education students use and how to go about looking for them, as well as how materials can be used in lessons to fulfill particular standards and indicators. Technical services staff generally lack the acute awareness possessed by CMC staff regarding nuances in teacher education, and so typically assign an LC or Dewey number that is in keeping with traditional classification for the topic. However, the blending of a CMC staff person and library cataloger can serve as an excellent option in meeting of the somewhat unique requirements of education majors. It may be desirable to depart from traditional Dewey classification for particular materials that could belong to a subset collection, such as community items, if one considers it to be advantageous to the patron to shelve those types of materials together.

I have created many such subdivisions and have departed not slightly from the Dewey schedules in the interest of increased browseability and usage. I find that most users in our CMC like to browse or go directly to the section of the library where their items are located instead of consulting the public catalog at length. I have made this type of browsing and searching for children's materials an attractive option by the creation of special locations for popular topics whose material is vast and multifaceted, and especially where including that material in the regular realia shelves would mean overcrowding. Signage that protrudes from the shelves is abundant, increasing browseability.

My flexible stance regarding classification and arrangement of materials has resulted in numerous small subcollections of thematic chunks and usage types, which seems to make finding materials on a desired topic easier once one has become familiar with the physical layout of the room. I have even ventured so far as to shelve some fiction along with nonfiction books of the same topic where doing so would help the students readily find a story on a lesson topic. Ease in locating materials by users is my goal, despite the fact that student workers who reshelve materials may have a longer learning curve. Indeed, subdividing the collection and intershelving some fiction and nonfiction are of great assistance to me in being able to lead someone to exactly what he's looking for, particularly when one considers that many OCLC records for juvenile materials, especially older publications, lack LC subject headings. Unless a librarian has enhanced the OCLC record after exporting it into the library system by entering an authoritative subject heading or two or by including pertinent terms in a 520 MARC tag, it would be almost impossible to locate some of those books that might be quite useful for lessons unless one were to know the content of each title in the collection. I try to further assist the user by typing a one-phrase synopsis of the piece of fiction that's interfiled with the nonfiction so that anyone unfamiliar with the story could immediately understand how that book could be applied to a lesson. *Inch by Inch* and *Counting on Frank* can be easily included in the math section, and *Miss Alaineus* can be appropriately shelved within the literacy aisles. I have adopted a "one-stop shopping" policy in its entirety, so throughout the center one will find numerous specialized collections, some of which contain only books pertaining to the topic as dictated by available space, while others include all the related realia as well. Literacy studies has its own multiple shelving unit, complete with books, DVDs, and realia. One will find no literacy materials anywhere else in the CMC, so users are confident that they are not missing things that could possibly be shelved elsewhere. The Native American studies section occupies a small portion of shelving whose books have their own classification scheme and which also accommodates display items that circulate. All display materials found in the center circulate, and there is a rich, varied collection of artifacts sprinkled around the rooms, giving students ideas of some things they could take to the classrooms to enrich their lessons. I was recently fortunate enough to discover a teepee for sale at a flea market and bought several white sheets to wrap around it. Student teachers fold it up and take it to their classes for the students to paint or draw on, and when the teepee is returned, I simply attach a fresh white sheet.

Some of the subcategories dotting the center are Concept Studies, which includes books and realia on topics such as calendars, time, touch, visual perception, opposites, and the like, and Community Studies, which includes anything available on community helpers, such as pocket charts, wooden traffic signs, books, games, puppets, puzzles, activity books, and costumes—sometimes with classroom sets of accessories so as to avoid the sharing of stethoscopes or masks, for example. Additional subdivisions include Holidays, Multicultural Studies, African American Studies, Hispanic Studies, Folk/Fairy Tales, Children's Literature Studies, and Picture Books. I am continually reviewing books within general categories to determine whether or not they might be more useful elsewhere; I recently culled from the Picture Book collection books that contained numerous compound words so as to be used for literacy lessons on such material. Additionally and most particularly for our CMC, Easy Reader books that contain rhymes, especially repeating rhymes, are in constant demand, and those titles have been segregated from their normal reading level so as to be pulled together in one location.

In a continual effort to keep expenses at a minimum, particularly when first setting up the center, I found it helpful to investigate local stores that were going out of business to see if there were any small fixtures that could be adapted for CMC usage: a chrome hat stand was converted into a puppet stand ($20); a rolling chrome belt and tie rack was turned into a fixture for hanging bags of all sizes ($40); simple garment racks and shower curtain hooks serve quite well for hanging large pocket charts ($10; a used desensitizer found on eBay is used for circulation ($45); large chrome standing signs with inserts were placed outside the center's door with announcements ($20). Indeed, hunting down bargains at discount and thrift stores, eBay, and store liquidators means that I can buy at least three times the materials and supplies as usual by stepping outside the traditional vendor territory. The business office at Mount Union has been quite accommodating in the processing of my unusual receipts, despite the fact that our auditors prefer more customary purchasing arrangements, and if other business offices will likewise entertain such receipts from "Anywhere, U.S.A.," it may be possible to pad your collections and find some out-of-print materials as well. Retired teachers often donate their classroom collections to Goodwill; dollar stores have die-cuts, charts, and word strips for $1 apiece; outlet stores will offer brand-name (Learning Resources) realia for half the publisher's price; and eBay lists a plethora of educational materials, especially dies!

In the spring of 2009, the Office of Advancement at the University of Mount Union was fortunate enough to locate a donor for the center. Thelma Slater is a 1942 Mount Union graduate and retired teacher who has graciously included the center in her financial planning for the next few years. Arrangements are still pending, but with her assistance, I anticipate being able to begin community outreach by "purchasing" Mount Union students to serve as tutors for local schoolchildren. This type of partnership within our community would not be possible for us without her assistance, and our center would continue to be somewhat self-contained. I look forward to extending our services to others in Alliance and the surrounding area; perhaps within the next year or two we can also expand the center so that it occupies more of the floor instead of just its current half. Mount Union's Advancement team, having toured our CMC, decided that someone might be interested in helping to sustain the center and help us create a wider radius of users, but this possibility would not have existed prior to the creation of the center. It is more difficult to locate potential donors when all you have to exhibit is an empty space with concrete floors, or a space that still contains the old collection that's been there for decades. People are much more likely to want to be a part of an already successful operation, and fortunately for us, Mrs. Slater decided that our CMC was a secure enough venture for her to want to partner with us in providing materials beyond our enrolled university students.

My intent was to create a center rich in content, yet high in aesthetics and comfort. I envisioned a center that would explode with exciting materials to spark ideas and a place that would become "home" to students for collaboration and group project purposes. A vibrant, cheerful atmosphere has been inherent in CMC design for decades and seems to have recently become a popular concept for many academic libraries around the nation. CMC personnel have long understood that an inviting environment attracts students and seduces them into wanting to be creative, and a devoted CMC staff person is instrumental in producing such a desirable destination. Whoever takes charge of the center and adopts it as her own will always have the center's best interests in the forefront of her daily thoughts: no personal vacation can be taken without a visit to the local gift or thrift shop that might have some useful treasure for the math section or some musical instrument to be included in the Native American studies bins; no trip to the mall can occur without a quick stop at Goodwill to review the latest children's book titles whose owners have outgrown them or to see if the toys section has a chemistry set or telescope in almost mint condition; no personal perusal of eBay items can be conducted without a quick glance into the toys and games department to see if any TREND Enterprises, Media/Materials, Learning Resources, or AccuCut products have been listed; and no excursion to a liquidation store could fail to include a scouring of the children's aisle for new and inexpensive games, puzzles, and books.

A healthy and vibrant CMC is the result of caring staff members who have adopted it as an extension of themselves, who continually ensure that all aspects are properly taken care of. The year prior to the unveiling of Mount Union's center required that I work a minimum of 80 to over 100 hours weekly, particularly the three months before NCATE's arrival. Interested people asked me why I would do so much work for no extra pay, and I gleefully replied that Mount Union was doing me a favor by leaving the project entirely in my hands. The creation of our CMC has proved to be the most fulfilling work of my life, but has unfortunately demonstrated to me that while also fulfilling, the cataloging arena is not nearly as dynamic nor gratifying as watching prospective teachers leave the room with an armful of materials to be shared in their classrooms. I've not regretted a single moment that the creation of our CMC has demanded of me. I would gladly repeat the entire process if necessary, and it is my hope that anyone who chooses to embark on a similar mission will be fortunate enough to experience the same joy as I.

References

AACTE (American Association of Colleges for Teacher Education). 2010. *Reforming Teacher Preparation: The Critical Clinical Component.* Washington, DC: American Association of Colleges for Teacher Education.

NCATE (National Council for Accreditation of Teacher Education). 2010. *Transforming Teacher Education through Clinical Practice: A National Strategy to Prepare Effective Teachers.* Washington, DC: National Council for Accreditation of Teacher Education.

DATE DUE